Life Without Lottie
How I Coped (or didn't) During my Daughter's Gap Year

Life Without Lottie

*How I Coped (or didn't) During
my Daughter's Gap Year*

Fiona Fridd

First edition
Published in Great Britain
By Mirage Publishing 2008

Text Copyright © Fiona Fridd 2008

First published in paperback 2008

No part of this publication may be reproduced,
stored in a retrieval system or transmitted in any
form or by any means without first seeking
the written authority from the publisher.
The purchase or possession of this book
in any form deems acceptance
of these conditions.

A CIP catalogue record for this book
Is available from the British Library.

ISBN: 978-1-90257-839-2

Mirage Publishing
PO Box 161
Gateshead
NE8 4WW
Great Britain

Printed and bound in Great Britain by

Forward Press
Remus House, Coltsfoot Drive, Woodston, Peterborough, PE2 9JX

Cover © Mirage Publishing
Design by W Alan C Dawson

Papers used in the production of this book are recycled,
thus reducing environmental depletion.

For Lottie, the very best daughter I could have wished for and without whom this book would not be. Lights will guide you home.

Contents

1. Goodbyes — 9
2. Establishing Contact — 23
3. Arriving in Oz — 37
4. Lightning Strikes — 45
5. Massages and Basset Hounds — 53
6. Overland to Adelaide and Melbourne — 65
7. Life Drawing & Sydney — 73
8. Lottie's First Job and Farewell to Harvey — 85
9. Call Centres and Teenagers — 93
10. Majorca — 99
11. Home Again — 111
12. Arrival of the Kittens — 119
13. Rugby and Rats — 129
14. Driving — 139
15. Appledore — 149
16. Christmas and New Year — 161
17. A New Year Begins — 177
18. A Difficult Week — 191
19. Bites — 203
20. Sleep Walking — 213
21. Palma — 223
22. Lottie's Coming Home! — 229
23. Farewell to Oz — 239
24. Bali and Home — 251

Postscript — 263
Other titles

Chapter One

Goodbyes

I'm not ashamed to say that I cried myself to sleep that first night. I thought I'd feel better if I cuddled Snoopy, Lottie's most precious cuddly toy. I thought again that that would be silly of me, but the next moment I found myself slipping out of bed. Five steps later I was standing in front of the large easy chair where Lottie had placed him before she left, in between two very old and much-loved teddies – mine and my husband's. Snoopy had been left in my care whilst Lottie travelled around Australia – for a whole year.

With tears streaming down my face I gently scooped him up into my arms and held him against my neck, bending my head over so my cheek touched what was left of his soft fur.

'Oh Snoopy!' I stammered, 'Lottie's gone!'

He felt so very small and vulnerable. So did I. I could smell Lottie on him. I breathed in deeply; feeling Snoopy so close made Lottie seem not quite so far away, not quite so untouchable. My sobs eased a little and I got back into bed, curling my body up tightly as I nestled my back gratefully against Nick's assuring warmth. Although my face was burning, the rest of my body felt freezing cold.

I pulled the duvet up high around me; I needed to get warm and to feel protected, protected from the harsh truth that I wouldn't see Lottie again for such a long, long time. Not only that, but I wouldn't be there to *protect* her, as a mother does, and to console her during the bad times.

The tears and the sobs increased their intensity once more. I tried my utmost to muffle them – both with an iron will and the help of my now tear-soaked pillow. I curled my body up into an even smaller ball and clutched Snoopy tighter. Why oh why, I thought, are we British brought up to *not* show emotions? Stiff upper lip and all that. Right now I could have done with the Wailing Wall – all to myself.

I kept thinking of the moments of our last tearful hug within the buzzing anonymity of Heathrow airport, only hours ago. I thought of special dates, birthdays and Christmas in particular, and what daily life would be like without her. She deserved my tears, every one of them. And I was proud. Proud to be her mother, proud to feel such emotion, and proud to let it show – to myself and to Nick, lying next to me, stroking me gently and telling me not to worry. I wasn't worried, I just missed her, missed her so desperately that the pain was unbearable.

The last scene I pictured before I finally went to sleep was the familiar one of Lottie returning home from college, bursting through the back door and saying 'Hi Mum!' as she approached me with a lovely smile on her face and her arms outstretched, ready for a hug. Nick told me he cried as he drove to work the next morning. I'm only sorry I wasn't there to help console him, as he had me.

It was Nick's sister, Auntie Pet, who had given Snoopy to Charlotte (as Lottie was then known) when she was born. When she changed junior schools, there was already a 'Charlotte' in her class. That was when she decided to call herself Lottie. Snoopy was almost as big as her as she was a small baby, weighing in at 6lbs 6ozs on 11 January 1988 at 2.29pm with the sun streaming through the delivery room windows.

Now, over eighteen later, it is Snoopy who is small. With super soft fur, bright turquoise and white, he became Lottie's absolute favourite in no time. He went everywhere with her and shared all those important occasions – her first visit to see Father Christmas, inoculations at the doctor, her first day at nursery school, discovering the Tooth Fairy, etc.

When she was one, Snoopy lost his nose. Her first words were *'no nose'* as she held Snoopy up for us to see his injury – which was swiftly repaired with cotton and needle. Later, when she broke her wrist, he accompanied her to the operating theatre. She ended up with plaster of paris from palm to armpit, poor child. So did Snoopy – he emerged with his left paw plastered! After what seemed an enormously long wait, I rejoined them both in the Recovery Room and when Lottie first saw Snoopy's plaster it made her smile; that sweet adorable smile that appeared before she had even reached a few weeks old, and which will remain with her and in my memory forever.

Snoopy also accompanied her on every holiday. Well, nearly every one. He was mistakenly left behind on one of our regular family holidays to Lundy Island. Disaster. How the hell does one console an utterly distraught little girl of only three years of age when her very favourite toy inadvertently gets left at home? Nick and I tried everything - extra cuddles, treats, new stories and games, lending her a special toy of John's, her younger brother, all the while uttering assuring words: that Snoopy would be looking after her toys at home and getting up to lots of mischief whilst we were away - you know the kind of thing.

Eventually, Blue Bunny came to the rescue. Blue Bunny – who was exactly that – was her second favourite toy, who had mercifully got packed at the last minute. And so Blue Bunny stepped in for Snoopy that holiday. She never let him out of her sight. However, throughout the journey home, Lottie chattered incessantly about seeing Snoopy again – he was almost within her grasp - and when they were finally reunited, that special smile appeared on her little face again and stayed for days.

David, Lottie's boyfriend, was travelling with her. They met at the infamous Glastonbury festival amidst the mayhem of half collapsed tents, bodies and litter. It took David quite a while to gain her agreement to go out with him. I am so glad he persisted! He was living in Dorset at the time with his mother Jill and his younger sister Kim, but a few months later moved up to Somerset. They are both very blonde and not very tall and have now been dating for just over 3 years. They make a wonderful couple, full of life, energy and fun.

David and John have become great mates. They have had their ups and downs but are now very close and have spent many happy hours together, particularly when watching rugby on TV. Accompanied by quantities of beer, their exuberant shouts when 'their team' scores a try, or seriously bad swearing when a conversion is missed, can be heard all round the house.

Lottie and David started talking about taking a year off to explore Australia and New Zealand about a year ago. Nick and I secretly hoped their plans would not materialise. We have learnt not to underestimate the dogged determination of youth - or how quickly their quietly made plans can come to fruition! For Lottie, the adventure would be an unofficial Gap year following her completion of two years of A' level study. I have never seen anyone work harder and for such long hours as Lottie. She got the results she so deserved, one being an A grade for IT, which she fast-tracked in a year. It was a proud day for all of us when her results came through!

For David, a talented carpenter, he wanted to go before he, as he put it, became 'too old to escape'. He was born in Perth and so that was decided to be their first port of call. He was too young to remember it when he and his family left for the UK, but it was as good a reason as any for choosing to go there first. They would spend three days in Hong Kong, en route.

I had organised what I hoped would be a special 'send off' in London, the day before their flight. We piled into the old Range Rover, Lottie hesitating as she gave the dogs another hug, and took a last look around before joining David and John on the back seat. I knew she was fighting back the tears but I pretended not to notice.

It was an easy journey, traffic-wise, but a difficult one emotionally. For the first few miles little was said. Lottie focused her attention gazing out of the windows. She seemed to be trying to firmly imprint the familiar Somerset landscape on her memory. More than once she muttered 'I can't believe we're really going'.

Slowly battling through the traffic jams of London, we finally arrived at our hotel. I had selected the *Kensington Close* as it was central and just off Kensington High Street, an area I thought the kids would like. Also, because Nick used to live close by, we knew it well. Absolutely dreading the final 'goodbye' at Heathrow the next day, anything familiar would be a great help.

We left the car in the hotel's underground car park, carried luggage into reception, checked in and then joined David's mother, Jill, his younger sister Kim and my dear friend Hils, in the bar where we had agreed to meet. They were also booked in for the night and coming to the airport with us tomorrow. After more than a few drinks we took two taxis to Covent Garden.

We had an excellent supper at 'The Crusting Pipe', although I couldn't eat much, and then made our way to theatreland for a show – a tribute to Freddie Mercury. I thought it would help to include a bit of organised entertainment to ease the strain we all felt. The show was great but the music was incredibly loud and so, during the interval, Nick and I slipped away. We taxied back to Kensington and to one of our favourite pubs from our old courting days.

Nobody minded us going. Hils, bless her, had ordered vast quantities of double gins from the theatre bar and we left them all laughing, each clutching several glasses. She is a true friend and an exceptional one. Many a time whilst we were in London she always managed to say the right thing to make us feel better. Her being there was an enormous support.

It was wonderful for Nick and I to escape. We sat outside in the pub's pretty garden, overflowing with noisy Friday night revellers. The noise was welcome. It was familiar and we were in a familiar place. Whilst Nick queued for a bottle of wine, I glanced at the youngsters around me, many of them Lottie's age, so happy and jolly. I wondered if any of them were enjoying a year off to travel - like Lottie was about to do. A girl across the other side of the garden smiled at me. I smiled back. Had she noticed I looked rather down?

We sipped our wine and talked for a good hour about how we were going to cope tomorrow, all the while holding hands, oblivious to the surrounding noise. Last orders were called but nobody took any notice – not until the third call that is, when the outside lights were turned off. We returned to the hotel and met up with the others in the bar. It was packed out and with a lively atmosphere, complete with The Rolling Stones hit 'I can't get no satisfaction!' pumping out of several cleverly hidden speakers.

We managed to all squeeze around a small table – the only remaining one – in the corner, and John and David nabbed sufficient spare chairs and stools so we could all sit down. It was fun hearing about the second half of the show, which was better than the first. It helped having this to concentrate on. It served as a welcome distraction from what lay ahead tomorrow, now drawing increasingly close.

After much alcohol all round, Kim and Jill went to bed. The rest of us followed not long after. When I kissed Lottie goodnight, I hugged her for longer than usual. It wasn't until the hug commenced that it dawned on me this would be my last chance to wish her goodnight for a very long time. I fought back the tears as I whispered 'Sleep well, darling.' Lottie clung to me too.

The day arrived. Thursday, the 31st of August, 2006. I woke up early with my heart racing and couldn't decide whether I felt sick from emotion or from the many cocktails the night before. I was already a nervous wreck. When I drew our bedroom curtains back, intense sunlight streamed through the window making me blink. It was going to be a lovely day, weather wise.

I put the kettle on and Nick started to stretch and groan – as he always does each morning. Only this time, I appreciated the groans of life more than usual, and smiled. They were familiar and comforting to hear.

We showered and dressed. Neither of us wanted any breakfast; it wouldn't be served for another fifteen minutes anyway. The hotel was stifling and we needed some air, even the kind London could offer. How I missed the clear Mendip air back home! I grabbed my handbag and sunglasses and we took the stairs down. I didn't let on to Nick that my legs felt very wobbly.

We walked through the huge entrance doors. It was wonderful to escape the oppressive heat of the hotel! We sauntered arm in arm up to Kensington High Street in search of serious coffee. We found a smart little café on the corner and sat outside, the hustle and bustle of a typical weekday morning in central London all around us. It felt good to be in such a busy place, and the espresso was super strong and delicious. My sickness eased, although my heart still raced. The espresso probably was not helping.

I sent John a quick text so he knew where we were. I didn't want to disturb Lottie and David in case they were still asleep. Nick ordered more coffees. We knew that today was going to be extraordinarily difficult but told each other that 'everything will be fine'. We chain-smoked as we sipped our espressos in the bright sunshine, my eyes gratefully hidden behind the darkness of sunglasses.

We returned to the hotel to pack and, by making use of mobile phones, we all met up in the lobby to settle our respective bills. Only Jill and Kim had actually made it to breakfast. I glanced at Lottie and David's rucksacks and hand luggage stacked up in the corner on its own, then at the huge clock behind the reception desk. Only five hours to go. I felt terribly sick. I rummaged inside my bag to find the Rescue Remedy, turning my back on everyone for the few seconds it took me to squirt a couple of sprays onto my tongue. It helped, a bit.

Bills paid, the boys carried luggage down to the car. Then we all taxied to Harrods where we spent the rest of the morning, apart from Nick, who went in search of a secondhand bookshop he remembered in Beauchamp Place, just around the corner.

Lottie and I spent a while admiring the fantastic range of designer handbags – she picked out one by Chloe. It was utterly stunning and with a price tag to match at over £900! Then we browsed the Perfumery, laughing as us girls sprayed ourselves with many expensive bottles, making David and John screw up their faces as the wafts of exotic scent hit their noses.

We then decided to split up. Jill and the kids took the escalator up to the Toy Department; Hils and I headed for the Food Hall. Ever in awe of their fabulous displays, we were certainly not let down during this visit. I bought a pot of rabbit terrine, a large wedge of Gouda with cumin and a tiny jar of caviar, which the assistant packed up most beautifully (I still have the box), all of which I intended to serve up when we got home later. I thought the delicacies would cheer us up.

Whilst I wondered which department to head for next, Hils said 'Fancy a martini?' Without hesitation I replied, 'Not half!'

We took the escalator upstairs and stopped off at the Toy Department en route. The others must have moved on, which was just as well as I wanted to buy a miniature Snoopy for Lottie to take with her. Disappointingly they didn't have one, despite every available assistant conducting a thorough search of the displays and the stock room. They were marvellous, especially when I filled them in with the reason why it was so important.

I did, however, manage to track down a tiny white fluffy baby seal on a key ring. His face looked remarkably like that of 'Sammy Seal' – one of Lottie's favourite big cuddly toys which I had given to her on her first Christmas. I bought it. We made our way to the Terrace Bar. The martinis were enormous! Having had nothing to eat, I couldn't quite finish mine. Hils finished it for me.

We had all agreed to meet at midday outside the main entrance to Harrods and, surprisingly, everyone was on time. One of the window displays was a special arrangement marking the ninth anniversary of Princess Diana and Dodi's deaths, which just happened to be today. Several bunches of flowers had been left on the pavement outside the window. Jill took some photos.

Nick said he'd had a lovely time in the bookshop, but the prices were ridiculously inflated so he hadn't actually bought anything. Lottie was thrilled with the miniature Sammy Seal and gave me a hug. I told her to put him in her pocket and he would keep her safe whilst she was away. She did so without any hesitation and gave me one of her wonderful smiles.

During the weeks leading up to her departure there were so many occasions when I felt tears welling up. When I gave Lottie her key-ring, it was one of the last of them.

We had a happy and very long lunch at 'Bistro Benito's' in Earls Court. Nick has been going there for almost 30 years! It is a wonderful Italian restaurant run by an exceptionally nice family, headed by Benito. He was thrilled to see Nick again and to meet us all and made us feel so relaxed and welcome. It was the perfect choice. Nick stuck to water as he was driving to the airport, but the rest of us downed copious amounts of excellent and beautifully chilled Pinot Grigio, and the lads a fair few bottles of beer. The alcohol helped.

Finally it was time to return to the hotel, collect the Range Rover and make our way to Heathrow. Not everyone could fit in the car so Hils, Jill and Kim took the underground from Earls Court. By now my stomach was churning uncontrollably and I felt desperately sick, but I made a real effort to keep cheerful as it was obvious that Lottie and David were suffering considerably too.

We pulled into the short stay car park at Terminal One just after 4pm; it was earlier than originally planned but somehow you never get it quite right. John put Lottie and David's luggage on to a trolley and wheeled it towards the terminal building. The rest of us followed closely behind.

I held Nick's hand tightly. We were all fighting back the tears, and Lottie looked so frightened as she wiped her eyes with her sleeve. The poor girl had a bit of a cold which didn't help. She was visibly shaking and clung onto David for dear life. Nick and I stopped a couple of times to give her arm a gentle squeeze and softly uttered reassuring words like 'Don't worry, darling, it's going to be fine' and 'you're going to have the trip of a lifetime'.

I thought we'd never reach the terminal building; the walk seemed to go on forever. It was good to be reunited with Hils, Jill and Kim.

Due to recently uncovered terrorist plans to blow up planes in flight, security had been stepped up dramatically. Check-in was required four hours in advance of departure rather than the usual three. Lottie and David's departure time was 9.15pm, but when they reported to the BA desk they were told that check-in would not open until 6pm. The kids were mortified. Now that they were at the airport, they were understandably keen to 'get started' on their journey, and not being able to check-in their rucksacks just added more unwanted stress. Emotions dangerously close to breaking point, Nick, John and I made the decision not to prolong the agony any more and to say our goodbyes there and then, and leave for home.

I cannot possibly put into words how hard it was. We hugged and kissed each other in turn – somehow or another – not knowing who to hug or kiss first. It was all rather clumsy. Final words of love and affection tumbled out in a very mixed up way, tears were fought back and my eyes burned so hot I thought they would catch fire at any second.

It hurt. I don't really remember exactly what was said, apart from one tiny sentence Lottie said to me as we hugged each other for the last time: 'I love you so much Mum!' I knew that, but I needed to hear it. I gently wiped the tears from her eyes first, then mine.

Nick handed her a good luck card for them both (which we had secretly written the day before) with instructions not to open the envelope until they were on the plane. It contained a poem Nick had composed and a note from me to Lottie on a scruffy piece of paper. I had written it on the spur of the moment, just in case I didn't say all of the things I wanted to say to her during our goodbyes. I told her how much I loved her, that she was the most perfect and precious daughter I could possibly have and how proud I was of her. I am so pleased I wrote that note, as I don't think I managed to get out more than half of the words I meant to. This was Nick's poem:

Go...

Go, go wherever you want to go,
Enjoy wherever you are,
Meet whoever you want to meet,
And shine.

You know that we love you.

Share your love
With the people you meet.
And let their love reflect on you,
And shine.

We know that you love us.

Because we know
That wherever you are,
And whoever you're with,
We shall see you shining.

And know that we shall always love you.

* * *

Life Without Lottie: How I Coped (or didn't) During my Daughter's Gap Year

I was totally oblivious to the throngs of strangers at the airport when it came to the crunch to finally let go, turn around and make our way back to the car park. It was dreadfully hard turning away from Lottie. I felt I was abandoning her, literally 'turning my back' on her.

I don't remember walking out of the terminal, but I do remember the strange feeling of relief which swept over me when I hit daylight. I was now out of Lottie's sight and my bravery could be abandoned. Within an instant, tears streamed down my face and I leant gratefully against the building for support. Nick and John were similarly affected.

The three of us sat on a rail for a few moments, needing a little time to just 'let it out' before returning to the car. I could hardly wait to sit down; my legs felt as if they were about to collapse under me. We held onto each other during the walk, but had to stop more than once as one of us broke down again, face in hands.

Nick told me later that night that driving home helped, as he had something to concentrate on. I just sat in the front beside him, stunned, and gratefully hiding behind my sunglasses. We all shared a few words now and then – how much longer the kids had to wait before their flight took off, hoping they were not sad but excited about their year ahead, the car radio station being crap, the weather being good, the traffic, work duties for tomorrow - nothing heavy.

John went to sleep for a while. I also tried to sleep, desperate for a release from the pain, but couldn't.

We all cheered as we passed the Somerset county sign; we were nearly home! That brief instance of joy was quickly followed by an unexpected emotion – the stark realisation that Lottie and David would not be there when we got back.

The remainder of our journey was spent in silence. It was a great relief when Nick eventually swung the car into the drive. It helped to be busy with unpacking and making a fuss of our two bassets, Morse and Einstein, who gave us a wonderful welcome, though I swear they kept looking around for Lottie and David.

Ian, one of our friends, had done a brilliant job in housesitting for us. We shared a drink with him in the garden before he left us on our own.

Back to reality. I checked for messages on the kitchen phone and my indispensable daily diary – a font of knowledge and full of endless lists of things to do. I automatically turned the page to see what tomorrow held and was so touched to see that Lottie had written me a little note: '*Lottie's laptop to go in coat roof. PS: Missing you xxx*'.

Without hesitation I wrote down a short reply: '*And you too darling Lot!!!*' I drew three hearts next to it. The queen of abbreviation, Lottie wanted her laptop to be stored in the roof space above where our coats hang in the kitchen passageway leading towards the old dairy. I knew exactly what she meant. After eighteen years of being her mother, I knew.

Lottie had left me another note which she had given to me two days ago. This one was for Diesel, our much-loved white Boxer, our first family dog, who tragically had to be put to sleep only last week after a wonderfully full life of twelve years. We had him cremated privately and were waiting for his ashes so we could bury them in the garden, together with his red collar - and Lottie's special note. It was sealed up in a small brown envelope marked 'Dweeby', her special nickname for Diesel.

I lit two candles on the garden table and we shared a light supper, all enjoying the treats I had purchased from Harrods that morning. Needless to say, Morse and Einstein were handed a few titbits! The caviar was left for another time as no one fancied it. Afterwards, John phoned his great friend, Will, who lives just a few houses away and invited him round. He was good company for John who was clearly struggling to cope and they shared a few beers.

Later that evening, about the time when Lottie and David's flight was due to leave, we let off two Chinese hot-air paper balloons for them. It was a warm, dry and clear night with many stars twinkling above and only a light breeze - perfect conditions for the launch. We placed them side by side in the middle of the lawn. At the same time, Nick lit one for Lottie and John lit the other one for David.

We stood back and watched in silence whilst the heat from the flames gradually filled up the insides of the balloons with air and they took off. Lottie's balloon left the ground first, and then David's a few seconds later. They both quickly headed up high above the trees and into the night sky. We continued to watch as they whizzed away and became all too rapidly smaller and smaller until they were like tiny stars just visible to the naked eye and then, finally, out of sight.

Although we couldn't see the balloons any more, we waved like mad at the night sky and wished Lottie and David a wonderful and happy holiday and to come home safely. It was a lovely little ceremony and helped us to begin the road of coming to terms with their absence. A few weeks later, an elderly lady from our village told Nick she thought she had seen UFO's that night!

Friends and family were incredibly kind and supportive; I lost track of the number of phone calls received that evening and in the following few days. They did so help. Hils called and told me they had moved into the airport bar until the BA check-in opened and had then left Lottie and David in the queue. She said the kids were relieved that at last the waiting and the farewells were almost over. I was glad to hear that.

One friend who called assured me that, when I speak to Lottie over the telephone, it will seem as if she is in the next room, not thousands of miles away. That was a nice thought. And another, Jennie, whose eighteen year old son had spent his Gap year in South Africa, said she completely understood what I was going through. We arranged to meet for lunch the following Tuesday. It was something for me to look forward to.

Chapter Two

Establishing Contact

I tossed and turned all through that night. When I was awake, which seemed most of the time, all I could think about was Lottie. Was she safe? Had she arrived in Hong Kong? I would have given anything to speak to her, but I knew that wasn't an option. I hoped and prayed; it was all I could do. It was a very long night.

When morning eventually came, my eyes felt swollen and sore, which the bathroom mirror confirmed. I looked dreadful and I felt worse. I splashed liberal amounts of cold water on my face and swore as some of it went up my dressing gown sleeves. I grabbed a hand towel off the rail, quickly patted my face dry, and then slipped downstairs, leaving Nick asleep for a while longer before he had to get ready for court. He is a barrister who specialises in defending white collar fraudsters.

I needed a strong coffee and a cigarette to kick start me into life. The bassets were certainly full of it. They jumped out of bed with excitement the moment I entered the kitchen. I stooped down to stroke them and had my face re-washed with much enthusiasm. I welcomed their affection. I needed it. The memory of my final goodbye to Lottie was still raw. Harvey, our old black cat, was on top of the boiler. That's where he sleeps - on one of the original blankets from Lottie's pram! He batted me fondly with his paw as I passed him. He always does that. I stopped and tickled his ears. He purred and rubbed against me before I moved on to unlock the back door and let the dogs out.

It was a strange sort of day. Oh, the weather was lovely which helped my washing dry quickly, but I moved from task to task in a kind of robotic state. After Nick had left for Gloucester I suddenly felt very alone, and I frequently burst into tears. I hadn't seen John yet; he was still in bed. My mind was terribly confused; everything seemed fuzzy and upside down and I found it impossible to concentrate on any task for more than a few moments. I just couldn't get Lottie out of my mind. Not that I wanted to, but I wished I could have felt more positive about her adventure rather than experiencing such a deep feeling of loss.

Letters I had to write and bills which needed to be paid were left untouched. I did manage to get some ironing done though, accompanied by one of David's CD compilations which he calls 'Bangin' Tunes'. They never fail to cheer me up. I turned the volume up high and sang along to the music (very loudly and very badly!) as I pressed and folded. It helped, but my eyes filled with tears as I recalled the last time I had heard the CD – only a couple of days earlier when we were all together. Coldplay's 'Fix You' started to play. When I heard the words *'Lights will guide you home...'* I broke down and had to abandon the rest of the ironing.

I felt exhausted and tried to have a rest, but I couldn't settle. It would have been nice to take the dogs out for a walk but I simply didn't have the energy. I was glad when Nick returned from work. We hugged each other for a long time. As I had nothing organised for supper, we went into town to pick up a Chinese take-away and had a drink at one of the nearby pubs whilst we waited for our order.

When we got home John shared it with us before he went to a party at Will's house. I was glad for him. The last few days had been an emotional roller-coaster ride and he deserved some fun.

The next morning I woke up early. I had slept better but my eyes were still sore. I repeated the cold water treatment, threw on my dressing gown and, with a determination in my step, headed downstairs. I had to email Lottie – right away! I didn't bother to check on the dogs, I went straight into the study and switched on the light. I turned it off immediately. Loud snores came from under a sleeping bag on the sofa! John must have brought one of his mates back after the party. I tiptoed to my desk and turned my computer on and hoped the whirr as it started up wouldn't wake the body on the sofa. It didn't, for the snores continued.

I signed in. 'Click, click' as the anti-virus package did its stuff. Bloody thing seemed to take ages. But at last I was ready.

Life Without Lottie: How I Coped (or didn't) During my Daughter's Gap Year

2 September 2006

Hi Lottie!

Almost 6am here and I'm in the study writing my first email to you – whoopee! Only thing is I'm in the pitch black! There's someone making god-awful noises on the sofa so I didn't like to turn the lights on. I found more bodies in the Snug. All courtesy of your not-so-little brother and the usual fall-out after another party – this time at Will's. There you go - nothing much has changed at Manor Farm!

It was quite awful saying our farewells at the airport so I won't dwell on that, but I think we were all very brave. Do hope you liked the card and my note. We had a decent journey home and I tracked your flight on BA's website. Sorry it was delayed a bit - I noticed a flight to Beirut had been cancelled so maybe that was the reason. We set off two Chinese paper balloons for you both when you were due to fly and watched them float up, up and away. We waved and wished you both a terrific year!

Can't wait to hear what Hong Kong was like! Hope hotel was good and you managed loads of great shopping. Bet David got fed up with you trying to make up your mind what to buy!

All fine here. Dad was in Glos yesterday. We had a quick drink at the Rose & Crown last night and then picked up a take-away from Ho Ho. Probably not a patch on HK food! Einstein & Morse as naughty as ever – they knocked over the kitchen bin yesterday so the floor was a disgusting mess. John's enrolling for A' levels at Strode on Wed.

Well darling, I have 5 early breakfasts this morning so must go and get dressed. Haven't even let the dogs out yet! Nice family in for 2 nights so that's good. They're off to Longleat today for the 'Red Bull' airplane show. Forecast appalling which is a shame. Do hope your flight to Perth was on time and you're not too jet-lagged.

Loads of love and hugs to you both from us all. Missing you <u>so</u> much and wishing you heaps of fun! Will email again as soon as I hear from you.

Mum xxx

=========

The moment I had hit the 'Send' button on Outlook Express, I thought of a million and one other things I had meant to say. Typical. Was Lottie's cold better? Had they managed to sleep on the plane? Did rucksacks arrive intact? Was it terribly hot? Were people friendly? Were they happy? And so on. Still, it taught me a lesson. I decided to get myself a notebook and jot down reminders about what I wanted to say in my next email.

It felt good to think about my first entry and to do something useful rather than dwell on the wrench of Lottie's departure. It was all part of the commencement of my healing process. I knew I mustn't make my emails too long. Whenever I receive long ones, I tend to switch off half way through and I would hate for that to happen with mine. I had to steel myself to be selective in what I would write, to try and report on things both Lottie and David would be interested in, to be amusing because I so wanted to picture them laughing, to describe events at home in such a way that they could really imagine them, to pass on messages from friends and family. Gosh! I was beginning to realise that it was not going to be an easy task. But I knew I would love it.

Fourteen years ago, we moved from a 3-bed semi in central London to our present home, Manor Farm. The house is huge and homely and sits high up in the beauty of the Mendip Hills in Somerset, in a charming little village two miles from the cathedral city of Wells. Manor Farm dates back to the fifteenth century and is filled with superb original features. There are flagstone floors, many exposed beams (both horizontal and vertical), large open fires and the original cider room and bakehouse.

The move was the best thing we ever did. The children took to living in the country (and to their new school) like ducks to water. They shrieked with delight every time they saw a cow, a sheep or a pig - and there were plenty of them to see. Manor Farm ceased to be a working farm a few years before we bought it but we are surrounded by other farms. Nick joined a great set of barristers' chambers in Bristol and I started to decorate in earnest, room by room. Five years later we hit a bad financial patch; Nick didn't receive fees for a big case he'd done (the wretched solicitor kept them for himself), plus we had grossly overspent on the renovations. That was when I decided to start a Bed and Breakfast business – hence the reference to '5 breakfasts' in my email to Lottie.

The house lends itself perfectly to B&B because of its size, layout and charm. Guests love it and many return again and again. It's a great job as I work from home, so am always here for my family.

I let out two rooms: The West Wing, a large family suite with its own staircase, and The South Room, a double bedroom accessed from the main staircase.

I cook breakfast on my 1970s Aga, positioned in the centre of my workhorse of a kitchen. This is next to what has always been called the 'Breakfast room' where, logically, breakfast is served.

B&B is hard work. The constant cleaning, cooking, washing, ironing and having to be welcoming, charming and helpful at any time of the day certainly takes its toll; plus the high level of house maintenance which results, particularly in the summer season - replacing small items like a broken loo handle, to big items such as a carpet, constant touching up of paintwork and redecorating rooms when we are quiet, emergency call outs to get the septic tank unblocked because an unthinking guest (or horrid child) has flushed a nappy down the loo, replacing bed linen, china, glass, pans, cutlery. The tasks are endless but at least they are varied. And I'm good at them.

My working hours are indeed long. Nick and the children are very supportive and help me when they can and Nick fixes many of the necessary repairs. By the end of the summer season we welcome having the house back to ourselves. It is pure joy not to have to constantly tidy and clean and be on our 'best behaviour'!

3 September 2006

Hi mum! Only got a few mins before money runs out, we are in HK airport and waiting for our flight to Perth. Had an amazing time in HK, so hot and humid, sending you a postcard, just have to find a post box. Did lots of shopping and ate lots of great food, much better than the Ho Ho! Thanks for lovely email, glad to hear you are well, and thanks so much for the letter - it really made me smile. Tell John not to let the house turn into a youth hostel! Going for some beers now and then duty-free shopping! Will email you when I get to Perth, missing you lots, lots of love Lotty xox

==========

Hurray, hurray! I couldn't believe it! I had received my first email from Lottie! If I could cartwheel, I would have done so all round the garden! It was the most wonderful and unexpected surprise as I hadn't reckoned on any contact until Lottie reached Perth. This was what we had agreed before she left.

When I checked my 'Inbox', a number of new emails had arrived and so I didn't see it at first. I had to look twice before it registered.

I quickly scanned down it to check everything was fine, then re-read it again and again and savoured every word. I pressed the *Print* button, swore violently as my printer was switched off, turned it on and watched as the paper gradually came through. It seemed to take forever. I grabbed it from the printer tray, beetled through to the kitchen and shouted 'Nick! Nick!', for I knew he was next door in the dairy doing a much-needed tidy up of his DIY tools.

The excitement was too much for me. I left Lottie's email on the kitchen table and had to make a bolt for the loo! Upon my return I found Nick reading it. His face was a picture of joy.

I can't tell you how relieved I was to know that Lottie and David were safe and happy and had loved their time in Hong Kong. I knew the food would be far superior to our take-away! Although I must add that the Ho Ho produces great food and Stanley, on the desk, is always cheerful and welcoming.

I was thrilled that Lottie had mentioned my letter – and even more so that it made her smile. Fantastic! She said she misses me – as I do her – but it now seems so worth it to know that the first leg of their journey had been such a success.

I ran upstairs to show John her message. He was equally thrilled.

I emailed back the following morning, by which time Lottie should have arrived in Perth. A cascade of excitement ran through me as I pressed the 'send' symbol. My new notebook, purchased over the weekend, was on the desk beside me:

4 September 2006

Hi there you two Down Under!

WELCOME TO PERTH!! It was just fabulous to get your email from HK! Such a lovely surprise – many, many thanks Lot! It made us feel SO much better and it was really kind of you to make contact before reaching Perth. Hope you found a post box! So pleased HK was fantastic - can't wait to see pics! What did you buy? We're having liver tonight (I can hear you saying 'yuk'). I only mention it because it comes from New Zealand! Do hope Youth Hostel is comfy and you've met some nice people. How's the jet lag? Perth must seem freezing after HK. Internet says its 17 degrees by day and falls to 4 at night. Brrr! Beautiful day here – 21 and a good forecast ahead - better than Perth! Your dressing gowns are in the washing machine – pity you couldn't have taken them with you. Hope your new sleeping bags are nice & warm.

Talking of washing, we hit your bedroom yesterday. I have never seen so much rubbish to clear out and washing to do!!! But I was surprised at the small number of towels hanging behind the door – thank you David! Dad & John moved most of your furniture into the dining room which now resembles an overflowing bric-a-brac shop. I painted, Dad repaired the 2 plug sockets which took him ages (he felt very guilty about not fixing them for you). He had to use 4 inch screws, massive raw plugs, loads of Gripfill and several glasses of calming wine! Sockets now solid as a rock. Decided against putting up the curtains from eBay (they were far too long) so your room now has the spare Sanderson pair - perfect size and look great. Claire coming in today to help clean and hoover, then John can start moving his stuff in. He's really excited about it but it will always be your room!

Dad & I were in heaven on Saturday evening; we ate the caviar I got in Harrods. It was so delicious I've decided to treat ourselves now and then whilst you are away and today I bought 8oz for £40 from eBay. Absolute bargain considering the 2oz Harrods jar was £70! I'll let you know what it's like. Your surplus Easter eggs are disappearing fast. Attacked by Dad last night and no doubt soon by John – probably next time he opens up the meat safe…

Had a lovely long chat with Jill. She & Kim fine and send lots of love. I'll phone this evening to let them know we've heard from you. Hils also sends love. She's put David's mobile somewhere safe but can't remember where!

Hope you're having just the most wonderful time ever. Missing you lots too and thinking of you so much and sending this with loads of love from us all to you both. So glad my note made you smile. Am off to put on some 'Bangin Tunes' – extra loud!!!

Mum xxx

==========

John's and Lottie's bedrooms are upstairs through a little door at the end of the main corridor. Down three steps, you reach John's first, then along a short passageway to get to Lottie's. When we moved into Manor Farm, we let the children choose their own bedrooms. Lottie opted for the end room which is the bigger of the two and looks over the courtyard, which is now very pretty. At the time it was in a shocking state with broken flagstones covered by towering nettles and brambles. It hadn't been used for years. John was quite happy with the smaller room. They couldn't move into them for a few months as the floors were unsafe - thanks to woodworm and death watch beetle infestation! But we had those treated, along with the rest of the house, replaced several floorboards and metal-strapped some of the joists in the process. In the meantime, they shared The South Room, which was then a twin. It is now a double for B&B guests.

When Lottie confirmed her travel plans we decided to move John into her room once she had left. He would have more space which, hopefully, he would find more conducive to study. He can be rather lazy in that department! John's present bedroom would be redecorated and furnished ready for Lottie's return. In the meantime I would let it out, during busy periods, as an extra B&B room.

Curtains and caviar are not the only items I have purchased from eBay. I must confess that I'm a bit of an addict! I mostly buy rather than sell, but have had the occasional clear out and offered up items for sale. Many of our curtains are courtesy of eBay, as are some of the children's clothes, particularly Abercrombie jeans, rugby shirts and sports equipment for John, plus Diesel and Barbour jeans for myself. The savings are huge! I also use eBay to top up my Portmeirion breakfast pottery; breakages are not infrequent!

Yes, we have a meat safe but it is not used for meat. It is mounted on the wall next to the kitchen table. A strange mixture of items are kept in it which range from mobile phone chargers, dog treats and pasta, to old videos, a large torch and now, thanks to Lottie, her leftover Easter eggs.

5 September 2006

Hi Lot!

This attachment came through for you from Anita – she thought you'd enjoy it. They all send lots of love.

I'm sure you can manage 11! Avoid 13 & 14, ignore 19 – stick with Marmite (!), go for 29, seek out a great 32 – must have happy hours, 33 & 34 rule OK. And 'barbie' on! Oh, and what the hell's a Tim Tam? (20)!!!

Mum xxx

'BEING STRAYLYAN'

At last, a yardstick by which you can measure an 'Australian'. For those of you who haven't met an Australian and are not sure what one is REALLY like!

You're not Australian until...

1) You've mimicked Alf Stewart from the TV show Home and Away's broad, Australian accent, eg. 'push off, ya flamin' drongo!'
2) You've had an argument with your mate over whether Ford or Holden makes the better car! (FORD of course!).
3) You've done the 'hot sand' dance at the beach while running from the ocean back to your towel.
4) You know who Ray Martin is.
5) You start using words like 'reckon' and 'root' and call people 'mate'.
6) You stop greeting people with 'hello' and go straight to the 'how ya doin'?'
7) You've seriously considered running down the shop in a pair of Ugg boots.

8) You own a pair of ugg boots.
9) You've been to a day-nighter cricket match and screamed out incomprehensibly until your throat went raw.
10) You kind of know the first verse to the national anthem, but don't know what 'girt' means.
11) You have a story that somehow revolves around excess consumption of alcohol and a mate named 'Dave'.
12) You've risked attending an outdoor music festival on the hottest day of the year.
13) You've tried to hang off a clothesline while pretending you can fly.
14) You've had a visit to the emergency room after hanging off the clothesline pretending you can fly.
15) You own a pair of thongs for everyday use, and another pair of dress thongs for special occasions.
16) You don't know what's in a meat pie, and you don't care.
17) You pronounce Australia as 'Stralya'.
18) You call soccer 'soccer', not football.
19) You've squeezed Vegemite through vita wheat to make little Vegemite worms.
20) You suck your coffee through a Tim Tam.
21) You realise that lifeguards are the only people who can get away with wearing Speedos.
22) You pledge allegiance to Vegemite over Promite (DEFINITELY).
23) You understand the value of public holidays.
24) Your weekends are spent barracking for your favourite sports team.
25) You have a toilet dolly.
26) Your Mum or Nan made it.
27) You've played beach cricket with a tennis ball and a bat fashioned out of a fence post.
28) You firmly believe that in the end, everything will be ok, and have told a mate in tough times that 'She'll be right, mate'.
29) You use the phrase 'no worries' at least once a day.
30) You've been on a beach holiday and have probably stayed in a caravan.
31) You constantly shorten words to 'brekkie', 'arvo' and 'barbie'.
32) You've adopted a local bar as your own.
33) You know the oath of mateship can never be limited by geographical distance.

Life Without Lottie: How I Coped (or didn't) During my Daughter's Gap Year

34) *You measure a journey in beer, not kilometres or time. (That's a 3 beer trip, mate).*
   'ave a nice day, mate...
=========

One evening, Harvey, our elderly cat, had another seizure. He is the only family pet who still survived our move from London. Lottie's hamster did but only for a few days. He was definitely past his prime and I think the cold got to him. We brought another cat with us, Paris. She was run over five years ago by a speeding police car. We have loved and lost three 'Somerset' cats due to idiotic motorists, and more hamsters than I can remember. Unknown to us, one particular hamster was bought heavily pregnant. The children called her 'Beer'. She produced her litter during her first night at Manor Farm. The following morning, Lottie and John were thrilled to bits to discover four tiny babies. Unfortunately, Beer proceeded to eat them all whilst the children were at school. That particular hamster was not loved quite as much as the others! Manor Farm has also loved and lost three dogs, two guinea pigs, two rabbits, a number of goldfish and oodles of stick insects.

This time, Harvey's seizure was a bad one. Nick and I were in the kitchen watching the BBC 10 o'clock news. Our elbows rested on the old pine table, stained and pitted from years of use and sporting the remains of our supper. I suddenly caught a movement out of the corner of my eye. Harvey was on the outside window sill where he loves to sit and watch for birds. The window sill is quite high, about four feet above the kitchen floor and the table sits underneath it, opposite the Aga. Harvey's back end started to twitch.

'Mind your wine!' I warned Nick.

We both knew only too well what was about to happen and watched, helpless. Harvey twitched slowly at first but within seconds the poor cat raced round and round in a frenzied ball. All of a sudden his battle stopped, he lost his balance, fell off the sill and headed straight for the table. Nick tried to catch him and knocked over his glass in the process. Harvey twisted in the air and continued his fall. He landed on the flagstone floor below. We both got down on our hands and knees to check he was alright. He stared ahead vacantly. We said his name but he didn't react. A few seconds later he stood up, sauntered over to the table where his food was kept, jumped up and scoffed the remainder of his Whiskas! He was back to normal again – phew!

Harvey's seizures resulted from a horrific injury he suffered about ten years ago. He disappeared for two weeks. We asked around the village and put his photo up on the notice board with the usual 'Have you seen...?' message. Neighbours were incredibly kind and helped us search for him, but to no avail.

Much to everyone's delight, particularly the children's, Harvey eventually came home on Christmas Eve but with one of his back legs hanging off. He had been caught in a trap and somehow had pulled himself free. Miraculously, our vet managed to save his leg (with the help of several metal pins). Harvey recovered and soon became accustomed to three good legs; his jumping up and down was unaffected. I marvelled at how adjustable cats are!

Now, poor thing, a nerve has become trapped somewhere along one of the pins which causes his seizures. They started a few weeks ago but he now has two per day (that we are aware of) and each time they are worse. Unfortunately, sooner rather than later, we would have to make that awful decision, as we had done so for Diesel, less than two weeks ago. Life's a shit sometimes.

I switched off the TV and went through to the study to check my emails. 'Bugger, bugger,' I muttered, for Outlook Express was down and gave me that oh-so-annoying problem message about 'protocol' and 'servers' and 'connection failure'. I tried again, several times, but without success. I was not to be beaten. Within a couple of minutes I had accessed my emails through the internet.

There was nothing of any interest in my Inbox, but over 1,000 messages in my Spam folder. I usually ignored this folder but tonight, for some reason, I opened it, scrolled down the first tranche and there, just over half way down, was a message from 'Lottie'. Wow! Silly me, I hadn't yet inserted my list of 'accepted' email addresses on to the system, hence her message was taken as spam. Bloody cheek! It was fantastic news - the kids had arrived safely in Perth. I printed her email out and grinned broadly as I took it through to the kitchen to show Nick. I smiled my way through the rest of the evening and all of the following day.

Chapter Three

Arriving in Oz

4 September, 2006

Hi everyone!

    Arrived in Perth this morning and it was raining. Obviously followed us from Somerset! Had an *amazing* time in Hong Kong. The hotel was OK - we got a room upgrade because they had double-booked. We were on the 20th floor with great views over the harbour - if you looked out the corner and around the skyscrapers!

    Went to a few markets but didn't buy anything as all they seemed to sell were tiny, tiny clothes. Apparently I'm an XXL! And those funny things that dangle off your mobile phone that all Asians have!

    Went to the botanical gardens and a walk-through aviary with loads of parrots, pelicans and toucans! We will send the pics on! There was also a jaguar enclosure and loads of monkeys, turtles and snakes.

    We went up the Peak Tower, the highest point in the city with a massive mall at the top. Didn't do much shopping as our hotel was in the Interior Design shopping district and didn't have time to get out to the bargain markets closer to the edge of the city.

    Everything was actually quite expensive, particularly clothes. Fendi, Gucci etc is pretty much all they sell with only about 10% discount.

    Spent some of the money you gave us for supper in an authentic Chinese restaurant and the food was fab. We stuck to the chicken dishes but they served everything from fish heads and softened pork bones to shark balls! We also ate from a Chinese street café and had chow mein which was yummy but tasted strangely fishy. It cost less than £1 for both of us!

Now in the hostel in Perth. It's quite nice but I think we'll move on after our two days are up and get a bit closer to the centre - we're in the Chinese and Asian district about 2km walk away. The city is so clean and the centre looks really European. We're going out to Northbridge later (where all the bars and restaurants are) to get something to eat. We've sorted out our bank accounts and our cards will be sent to the local post office next week. We have also looked into mobiles and can get them for $70 so you can ring me soon!

Apart from that David and I are great, could you please pass this on to Jill. Did you know Steve Irwin died today?! He's the crocodile hunter and got stung in the heart by a stingray in the Great Barrier Reef. Will remember to look out for them!

Missing you lots and lots and hope everything is OK at home (AKA John's youth hostel) He! he! Lots and lots and lots of love to everyone! Lotty xoxx

==========

John was in Wells so I called his mobile and gave him Lottie's news. He was thrilled to bits and said he'd heard from some friends at school that the pelican park was fantastic. I told him not to miss the last bus home.

'Don't worry, Mum!' he said. 'Will's got a torch so we can walk home if we have to!'

'Hmm. OK then, but do try and make the bus. Don't be too late!' I replied.

Lottie is definitely NOT an XXL! She is a beautifully slim UK size 8! What a pity she couldn't find any real bargains. We had also learnt about the sad and unfortunate death of Steve Irwin. How ironic that for years he survived supreme acts of bravery with alligators and crocodiles and ended up being killed by a stingray. I'm glad Lottie mentioned she would be careful. I dreaded to think what dangerous and poisonous creatures she would encounter during her travels.

The next morning I went into John's bedroom to wake him up, as he had some important forms to complete for his enrolment at college. Not early, it was 11 o'clock. His bed was empty. I called his mobile. For once he answered it quickly. He sounded jolly tired.

'Hi Mum!'

'Morning, darling!' I replied. 'Where are you? Everything all right?'

'Yeah, yeah, I'm fine. I'm at a mate's house,' he said and let out a long yawn.

'I thought you were coming home!'

'Yeah, well, sorry Mum,' he paused. 'We missed the bus and, well, it got a bit late. Don't worry, I'll be back this afternoon.'

'OK, but please don't be long…you've got to finish those forms!'

Instead, when he eventually turned up, he spent the rest of the day moving his stuff into Lottie's room. Teenagers!

5 September, 2006

Hello!

Went out for a Chinese last night. Was very, very, very cold - we were dressed in all our layers and coats, its so, so windy here and it feels like the arctic at night with ice cold winds! All the locals say it should heat up in about a month but I think we'll move on before then. Changing hostels tomorrow, the one we're in doesn't have a printer or let you open internet attachments so I can't open Anita's attachment. The new hostel is a bit more expensive but a lot bigger and it's got a pool, games room, free DVD rental and full English brekkie included + its closer to nightlife! Went out to a couple of pubs last night… it was $8 for a pint of beer, which is about £4/5!!!

We've been thinking about what to do next and I think we're going to book a tour up the west coast to the Nigaloo reef and Monkey Mia. At the reef we can swim with giant manta rays (not dangerous like stingrays) and giant turtles, and in Monkey Mia they have wild dolphins that come to the beach and let you feed and play with them.

We also get to go sand boarding and try sheep ranching! The only thing is its a little bit expensive! We spoke to a really helpful guy today about trips and travelling and I think we'll mainly fly around Australia as you can get cheap flights last minute. He also said there is no work in Perth because it's so cold and no one is around so we'll start work once we hit Sydney. Trying to plan a trip to go humpback whale watching tomorrow which should be fun - there's hundreds of them migrating up the west coast.

Photo-wise, the computers here don't accept USB devices - they're worried about viruses so we can't send any photos yet, hopefully we'll be able to at the new hostel but if not there's hundreds of cafés with internet access. Also had another look into phones - going to cost more around $100; they didn't tell us there were hidden added charges.

Tried to sort out our Medicare and tax reference numbers today, managed not to get any of that done and went shopping! Found the most amazing girls surf shop which was massive and over two floors. I could have literally spent all my money there but David restricted me, luckily!!! I bought a little handbag, a new bikini and some flip flops. Makes like Quicksilver etc are even more expensive here!

I just realised I've been writing this message for half an hour and my money is about to run out! It's great to hear all about what's happening at home. Is John going for his induction day tomorrow? Wish him good luck from me, he'll really enjoy it.

Strode's full of lots of team building games and you make loads of friends. You must be going to Cedar Falls soon? I'd better finish now, so so so nice to hear from you and I miss you lots and lots! I don't know if the postcard will get to you; everyone is terribly vague on what stamps are needed for the UK - very helpful! Lots and lots and love to everyone and speak to you very soon!! Lotty xox

==========

God, I felt awful as I imagined the children so cold! But thank goodness they've decided to leave Perth and head for the sun. How fantastic to be free of responsibility and able to move on whenever they felt like it. I couldn't wait to hear where they planned to go and what they experienced.

Five days since their departure, my emotions had just started to settle down. I still constantly thought about Lottie and missed her terribly, but it did gradually become easier as each day passed. And the fact that we were now in contact helped enormously.

Life Without Lottie: How I Coped (or didn't) During my Daughter's Gap Year

My notebook for email jottings proved invaluable. I kept it in the kitchen next to my diary. Only trouble was, I needed four or five! Each time I thought of something to tell Lottie, I was seldom in the kitchen. I managed with scraps of paper and a small pencil in my pocket and made notes as they sprung to mind and then popped them into my notebook. The system was not perfected yet, as I omitted to tell Lottie in my next email how sorry we all were too about Steve Irwin's demise. Practice makes perfect and I would have plenty of that before the year is out.

6 September, 2006

Hi Lottie!

Meant to email earlier this morning so you'd hopefully get this before bedtime. Alas, things don't always work out the way you want! Fantastic to get your lovely long email. SO sorry weather crap. Hate to think of you being cold. You need an Aga! Great idea to move on from Perth - you can always return when it's warmer, particularly as flights are cheap - wonderful news! All fine here. Dogs miss you – they keep looking for you both! Pity you can't open attachments. Don't worry - let me know when you can. John enrolled at Strode today. He was *so* pleased you wished him luck and said 'I miss her loads!'

He had a nightmare getting there. I drove him into Wells and he got on the wrong bus! He jumped off it halfway down the road, raced back to station, got on right bus, then realised he'd left his wallet on wrong bus. Jumped off right bus, raced after wrong bus waving like mad at the driver but was ignored. Raced back to right bus, just made it. What a start! Boys! Luckily someone found the wallet and phoned his bank who then phoned me. John's meeting the man at Temple Cloud this evening to collect it. No, I won't drive him there - he can catch the bus! Anyway, he's just phoned me, delighted wallet found and enrolment went fine.

Hope new hostel better - certainly sounds it and glad closer to night life. Try out your new bikini in the pool and make use of full English brekkie! It will set you up for the day and save some money for the odd drink or two. Totally shocked by the price of a pint.

Switch to wine! The girlie shop sounded fab. I had no idea Quicksilver would cost even more in Oz than here.

A tour up the west coast – fantastic - so many exciting new things to see and do. Please stroke a dolphin for me! Reinforce your pants if you go sheep ranching on horseback... could be a bumpy ride! Humpy whale watching - wow - how amazing. Have you seen any Skippys yet?

Dustbin day today so Dad did his jumping bit last night. I put David's old work shoes out for recycling!!! Dad in Bath tonight for his first autumn tutorial (changed from Monday just for this week) which he's looking forward to. I start pottery and life drawing classes a week on Tuesday. John's spent his first night in your room and loved it. It's not finished, although the sound system is set up... I'll send pics when completed. His old room is an utter tip so will hit that later today when he's back. He confessed he punched a hole in the wall next to his bed the day Diesel was put to sleep. I couldn't be cross. Collected his ashes yesterday.

I called Jill last night and passed on all your latest news. Kim did OK at first day of big school though was boiling hot (temp 24) and not allowed to take her jumper off. School rules and all that but Jill is pleased they are strict. She's a bit upset that David hasn't made contact direct so could you plse get him to email asap!

7 guests arriving tonight, beds etc ready. Another lovely day, washing out, dogs playing in garden. They pinched Variety cereal pack again... Ian did sterling work yesterday so apart from chewed up little boxes all over the lawn, the garden looks great. Off to Hunt Ball with Jane & Ken on Friday. John coming too. Dad's bought a new dinner jacket. Hils can't make it as she won't be back from London in time. Yes - I'm off to Cedar Falls with Chris on Monday. Can't wait! I am now worried about the state of my feet as I have a pedicure booked but I'm sure they've seen worse! Will email you when I get back and get Dad/John to let me know if they hear from you whilst I'm away.

Keep the emails coming! It's fantastic to hear from you and I can picture you doing things which is lovely. All the McNeil's send love. Max loving Uni - has best room on campus with a balcony, sharing with 2 guys, one a rich Egyptian. They missed last bus after a freshers' Thames cruise so checked in to the rich guy's Dads hotel for free, including room service. I ask you!

HUGE amounts of love and cuddles from us all and Snoopy too and we continue to miss you loads and loads. Bung a shrimp or two on the barbie and shop on!

Mum xxxxxxxxxxxx

=========

We have three large green wheelie bins for our rubbish, which are emptied fortnightly. Despite cardboard waste being burnt (we missed David's help with that) and all left over food, cans, bottles and papers recycled separately, the wheelie bins always absolutely heave after *one* week, let alone two. We seem to generate a ridiculously vast amount of rubbish! Mind you, B&B guests contribute greatly, particularly if they are American.

Nick jumps on the bins in order to squash the contents down so we can fit more inside. One day, my guests caught him in the act and doubled up with laughter. I'm glad they didn't think they'd ended up in a mad house! They were a wonderful couple from San Francisco who had come over to see, amongst other things, Stonehenge and Glastonbury.

Their car wasn't back when we went to bed one night. That wasn't unusual but I did worry when it still wasn't back the next morning. I was relieved when they returned just before midday. They had spent the entire night at Stonehenge for the summer solstice. I cooked them a late breakfast, which was wolfed down whilst they enthused about how amazing the experience was, despite some heavy rain during the night when they had to race back to their car for cover. They spent the rest of the day, and that night, in bed!

Chapter Four

Lightning Strikes

Nick bought me a USB stick. It is a similar shape to one of those yellow or green or pink fluorescent highlighter pens but a third of the size. How technology moves on! All I had to do was plug the stick into a special socket on my computer, open up the file I wanted to transfer and 'save' it to the stick. Fantastic! It was so quick and easy! From then on, I downloaded my updates to this book each day. This was of great importance to me, as on Mendip we often suffer from electric storms, some of which are pretty dramatic.

Three years ago, the telegraph pole on the village crossroads was struck by lightning. I don't mind thunder so much – it's lightning which really scares me. I want to bury my head under a pillow or hide under a table. Pathetic! This particular storm was a serious one with frequent cracks of forked lightning. The noise of the lightning coupled with torrential rain woke me up. The rain was so heavy that the gutter outside our bedroom window couldn't cope. I could hear water gushing over the top and cascading down the outside wall of the house. The storm finally reached its crescendo with the most enormously loud 'crack-bang' which made Nick and I both jump up in bed. My head buzzed with the overhead energy. That was a horrid sensation.

I switched on my bedside light which flashed wildly, went out and stayed out. We knew something had been struck but didn't know what - or the extent of the damage. We got torches out of our bedside cabinets and switched them on. Nick headed downstairs and I went to check on the children. Lottie was awake and fine but John was still asleep! I joined Nick in the kitchen. The poor dogs shook with fear and were very pleased to see me. Whilst I stroked them and gave them each a biscuit, Nick donned waterproofs and went outside to have a look around. Thankfully, Manor Farm had survived unscathed, or so we thought. We had a cup of tea and returned to bed.

When daylight came, we soon realised that the damage was extensive. Our next door neighbour's roof sported a six foot hole! All power was off for most of the rest of the day, both in the village and in parts of Wells. As for us, the actual house hadn't been damaged but many of our electrical goods had been destroyed. We lost all our TVs, DVD players, video recorders and telephones, plus the toaster, the microwave and other smaller appliances that had been plugged in at the time of the strike. Even worse, we discovered that our entire computer system had also been zapped and rendered totally useless. Thank goodness for insurance! Luckily, our local computer maintenance shop managed to 'retrieve' most of the data from our computer and transfer it onto a new system, but it was a lengthy and nail-biting process. Nick's gift of a USB stick was of great value to me indeed.

8 September 2006

G'day everyone!

Just a quick message. Still pretty cold here, not much sun! Really enjoying the new hostel. Went with some backpackers to a club just round the corner with a live band and all the beer you could drink for 2hrs - for only 12 dollars! Got rather drunk! Hung around the hostel yesterday taking advantage of midday happy hour to get rid of hangover!

Going whale watching in Fremantle on Sunday. Next Wed. we are off up the west coast to Monkey Mia to see wild dolphins and to sand-board. The trip lasts 4 days so you won't here from me til prob Monday but I'll email before we go. Not up to much at the mo, just trying not to spend all our money!

Everything sounds great at home, good to hear nothing changes - dogs eating things they shouldn't, John getting himself into trouble! Trying to sort out which pictures to keep, taken so many but lots are rubbish. Got some good ones of a 12ft croc we saw at the zoo plus loads of other animals - the wallabies were lying around

Life Without Lottie: How I Coped (or didn't) During my Daughter's Gap Year

in the sun not even in a pen so you could go up and touch them. They didn't look very friendly though!

Will send some pics on next time we're on the computer from internet café in town as internet in hostel v expensive. Lots and lots of love and missing you very very much! Lotty xox

=========

It had been three days since I'd last heard from Lottie so her email was received with much relief. I was delighted to learn that she and David were behaving like true student back-packers! They had certainly got their money's worth at the night club and the next day's hair-of-the-dog session and I was glad they had found cheap beer, especially for David's sake, as he's not much of a wine drinker. Dear Lottie continued to send regular emails despite the cost, bless her. I was saddened that she missed us so much and hoped this would ease soon. I hated to think of her being homesick.

I recognised the sound of my hoover. Claire, my cleaner, had arrived. She helps out once a week. I could also hear the loud 'thump thump' of music coming from John's room upstairs. He must be awake. Manor Farm was not peaceful at the moment! I had finished breakfasts, cleared away, hung two loads of washing out and bunged two more in the machines, cleaned one room, and had one more to do once my guests headed out for the day.

That done, John and I went into Wells as he needed some stationery supplies for college. I dropped him off in the Market Place and went to the bank. I then battled my way through Tesco for my usual big Friday shop. I also picked up a birthday card for Finn, Joe and Anita's youngest, who would be four next week. I had to post it that day for the mail service to Donegal is rather on the slow side! Hils phoned last night and reminded me of that.

Just before she called, Harvey suffered another seizure. Nick tried to break his fall (this time from the boiler) but in the process got his finger badly bitten. I fetched a bottle of iodine and a plaster from our medicine cupboard. Nick was visibly shaken and said he was worried his tetanus jab may be out of date. During the night I woke up and Nick wasn't there. Furthermore, he hadn't been to bed yet. I thought he was probably studying and went back to sleep.

When morning came I asked him why he was so late to bed. He said he was too terrified to go to sleep in case he got lockjaw and died. Men!

8 September 2006

G'day to you!

Super getting your email darling - thanks a million. Sorry weather cold. I hate to say it but beautifully warm here and forecast good. Excellent news you found a club with cheap beer - bet David was mighty glad! Can he remember?!!!

Have a FANTASTIC time whale watching. Wish I could be there. At least you're not seasick like John! Thanks for warning about no emails for a while. Don't worry, we shall be fine and thinking of you loads.

Perth Zoo sounded fascinating – and must have been so different from our visits to London Zoo with Uncle John. Glad you didn't fancy yourselves as Steve Irwin and jump in with the crocs! It was terrible that a stingray of all things got him in the end. Did you see koala bears? I've always wanted to cuddle a real one. How lovely to see wallabies roaming freely.

Funny story for you - Daddy bumped into Mary, the lady who lives in one of the bungalows. She told Daddy that as she was saying goodbye to a friend who'd been round for supper, they spotted two lights heading across the sky. Convinced these were UFO's, her friend was so scared she refused to go home and had to stay the night! Daddy did come clean. She was rather disappointed but said it was a lovely thing for us to do. She sends her best.

Have been into town and done shopping, bank etc. Tesco was a bloody nightmare. Got a card for Finn - he's 4 soon. Nick Hunter popped in earlier. He had a great time in Dublin and sends his best to you both. He said to watch those crocs! I've booked him to redecorate the kitchen in October.

When are you buying mobiles? Take great care and get some good pics of the whales. Don't stand too near the edge of the boat!

Loads of love and cuddles, and more.

Mum xxxxxxxx

PS: Forgot to tell you. Hils says to watch out for those dolphins if you swim with them. Apparently they can get rather randy!!!
==========

Nick Hunter is an excellent local roofer and decorator. He has done much work for us over the years. He is also an exceptional rat-catcher. We suffered an intrusion earlier this year, as did our neighbours. The rats had made their way up the hill from two of the village farms. Nick was wonderful. He set traps and checked and re-baited them regularly and I was relieved when, after three weeks, our unwelcome visitors had gone. I never asked what he did with the bodies.

10 September 2006

Hiya!
Just a very quick message as on hostel computer which eats money and keeps crashing. Someone has also changed the font size and so I'm squinting because it's so small! Left glasses behind! You might have to send them to me because my eyes are sore without them.
Not been up to much. Didn't see a koala which was a disappointment. Went to Cottisloe beach which was beautiful, really clean and clear water, no sharks!!
Say hi to Hils. David says you are welcome to use his mobile when she finds it! Not sure about the monkey mia trip because most people in the hostel say its rubbish and just not worth the money. Might head off to Ayres Rock next week instead or stay in Perth for a while because it's getting warmer and have been told we can both earn lots.
There's loads of carpentry work available and I can get a decent office job. Got to go now as stupid computer has just eaten another $4!! Plus this is the third time I've tried to write this email without it crashing!! Grrr!!!! Missing you lots and lots and will be in contact prob. tomorrow. Xoxoxoxox
==========

11 September 2006

Hi Darling!

Fab getting your message! And thanks so much for persevering despite connection crashing. Damned computers! Haven't seen your specs - any idea where you left them? I can post on to you, no worries! Can you get a cheap pair in the meantime?

Sorry Monkey Mia doesn't sound up to much. As you say, best to ask around and find out what's worth seeing. Ayers Rock - wow! I found Cottisloe beach on Google images. Looks fantastic and I've set a picture of it as my desktop background. I can then imagine you there every time I'm at computer! Thought I'd do this as you travel around. I wonder what my next background will be?!!

Your lovely postcard arrived - from Perth! Thank you so much. Guess you never did find that post box at HK airport! Didn't take long did it? Keep them coming.

The caviar I bought from eBay arrived Sat morning - all the way from Russia. Daddy and I couldn't resist trying it out - just a tiny bit - at 10.30 am! It was absolutely delicious! Hils came up for supper and brought two lobsters with her so with caviar as a starter and lobster to follow we had a feast. Thought of you and 'Larry' - aah! Hils has found David's mobile which is now in the meat safe. Unfortunately I can't use it as it's on a different network but many thanks for the offer.

Grannie & Grandad celebrate their 60th anniversary this Thursday - and Daddy and I our 21st! Ganda & Ann off on another cruise on Tuesday, first stop Stockholm. All send lots of love. Matt & Kim flew to Egypt yesterday for 2 weeks and I'm looking after their tropical fish. They are really beautiful. Will had a party on Saturday. Kieran & Andy stayed afterwards. In the morning, the boys were 'hanging' and went into town for a greasy-spoon breakfast.

I'm off to Cedar Falls today! Chris has given me a new swimming cossie so you won't have to think of me in the old black number. Phew! If I can I'll email you with details of waxing, body wraps etc!!! Am taking Daddy's wine carrier...

Had a huge bonfire last night. David was sorely missed. We can now get through the bakehouse again!

Hope the whale watching jaunt was awesome. So pleased you can get good work in Perth but do try and take time out for a holiday first.

Loads and loads of special love and hugs. Missing you much!

Mum xxxxxxxxx

==========

Lottie was five years old when she named 'Larry'. He was the lobster Nick and I had for lunch one day on Lundy Island. We started to holiday there when the children were just a few months old and continued to do so for the following 12 years.

Lundy is a tiny island in the Bristol Channel, about 20 miles north of Ilfracombe. It was (and still is) the perfect place for young families with no traffic (apart from a couple of tractors and quad bikes), wild and beautiful scenery, lovely walks and many farm animals. It also has no TV, no newspapers and no public telephones and is very much a get-away-from-it-all place and safe for children.

On the Larry occasion, we were in the 'Tavern' (the island's only pub) deciding what to order for lunch. The children chose typical kids food – fish fingers, chips and peas. Nick and I opted for the lobster, that day's 'special'. Five minutes later, a massive platter was put in front of us that contained a huge lobster surrounded by prawns, muscles and clams. It looked absolutely delicious. Just as Nick and I were about to start, Lottie frowned and said with complete sincerity, 'I don't think that lobster likes being dead!' Nick and I didn't know whether to laugh or cry. She added 'I shall call him Larry', and went on to tell us she would never eat one. She hasn't and I am certain she never will. Since that day, any lobsters we come across are always referred to as 'Larry'.

Grannie and Grandad (Beryl and Norman) are Nick's parents. They live near Taunton, about an hour's drive from Manor Farm. They met at ballroom dancing classes in Salisbury during the War and on 14th September 2006 they celebrated their sixtieth wedding anniversary. How wonderful for them and quite a feat! Matt and Kim are our tenants. They live in the Dairy flat – the one that Joe converted for us a few years back. Their fish get so excited when their light is switched on – they know it is feeding time and dart around incredibly fast. I do like them!

Ganda is my father, Keir, who I am devoted to, and Ann is my gorgeous stepmother. Both widowed for some time, they met on a Fred Olsen cruise and, within a year, were married. The name 'Ganda' resulted from Lottie being unable to pronounce 'Grandad' when she was little. Both she and John use it to this day.

Chapter Five

Massages and Basset Hounds

13 September 2006

Hi Mum! Just a quick hello to tell you I'm still alive! Changed our plans again and heading off to Adelaide on the train next Wednesday - journey takes 42hrs! But has bar and lounge so shouldn't be too bad. Just found out that all hostels in Adelaide are full because there is some special student event happening next week so we will prob have to move on straight away to Melbourne where we are going to look for work. Supposed to be going whale watching today but they've changed the timetable - apparently there are no whales on Wednesdays! It appears whales only migrate on Saturdays! Apart from that the weather is picking up so just lazing by the pool. Missing you lots and lots. Lots and lots of love Lotty xox

=========

13 September 2006

Hi Darling!
 Fantastic to get your email! And your super postcard of Perth which has joined the HK one above the Rayburn. Just got home from Cedar Falls - utter bliss! Chris and I had such a laugh. Sorry about lack of whales! You're off to Adelaide - wow! That will be some journey - hope train follows the coast. Dad just got home and sends LOL. Loads from me. Missing you heaps too! Hope we can speak soon. How's the tan coming along? Do remind David to email Jill if he hasn't done so already.
 M xxxxxxxx
=========

Any postcards we receive are kept and displayed on the mantelpiece above the Rayburn stove in the breakfast room. My guests sometimes browse through them, for our collection is an interesting one with cards from all over the world. Lottie's postcards have pride of place at the front.

My visit to Cedar Falls Health Farm was quite wonderful. When Chris and I arrived our rooms were not quite ready so we were served coffee in the rose garden. The grounds were beautiful. As we relished in our escape from everyday life and began to unwind, my mobile phone beeped - I had a new text message. It was from Lottie!

She said she had bought a mobile and gave me her number. At last I could actually speak to her! I sent a quick text back to say how thrilled I was and would phone her later. I needed to collect my thoughts together beforehand – make a list of things to ask and tell her. I didn't want to forget anything. As it turned out, I didn't speak to her until I returned home, but we communicated by text many times. Mobiles were not encouraged either in the house or in the grounds and for some unknown reason it just didn't feel right to phone her away from home.

My first treatment was a half leg wax. I was rather nervous as the last one I had had, many years ago, was sheer agony. Not this time. Thanks to new techniques and a skilful beautician, the whole process was *almost* pain free and I proudly emerged with silky smooth legs.

Then I had a 'fast tan' session. I was shown into a tall round tube, told to stand in the middle and hold onto handles about a foot above my head. I felt like a monkey. The door closed behind me and with a whirr the entire inside lit up with UV bulbs. I gradually got hotter and hotter despite the floor fans, which jetted up cool air. By the time the session was over, all six minutes of it, my arms ached and I was horribly sweaty. I did, however, return for two more. What we girls do for vanity!

Afterwards I met up with Chris for a swim. She'd just had an 'aqua jet' session which she said was fabulous. She had to lie down on a water bed which had a thick rubber top. When she switched the machine on, she was pummelled from underneath with jets of water which gradually moved up and down her body. She could regulate the pummelling from very strong down to very light. I had that treat still to come. We joined two other ladies in the Jacuzzi. Bliss!

After a few moments, I noticed a lady dressed in one of the health farm's ubiquitous white towelling robes – standard day wear. She stood and faced the wall, about 15 feet away. I wondered what she was doing and asked Chris.

'She's drying her swimming costume,' Chris told me. I couldn't see how and frowned.

Chris pointed towards the lady and continued '…that's a hot air machine.' Ah! I thought, it must be under the floor and the lady is standing over it. Well, when I told Chris this she let out a shriek of laughter and it was a while before she could compose herself to speak. She was in hysterics!

'No, no,' she cried, as tears rolled down her face. 'The machine's on the wall in front of her…you put your cossie inside, press a button and it spin dries it!'

Now I too was hysterical. What the other two ladies in the Jacuzzi thought of us I don't know, but we did get some rather disdainful looks!

My bedroom was large and had a balcony - great for the odd ciggie. A bowl of fruit was on the dressing table with a note which said 'Welcome back'. I hoped I hadn't been given Chris' fruit by mistake; she'd been before, not me! I later found out that she had one too.

Once, when I was on the balcony, I heard a familiar 'Whoo! Whoo!' Through the trees I could see a steam train. It made me think so fondly of the children. When they were younger they adored the Thomas the Tank Engine stories, and many a time Nick and I had taken them on the West Somerset railway. They would hang their heads out of the corridor window and proudly collect engine 'smuts' on their faces. They loved it!

The food was superb. Naturally, it was exceedingly healthy and beautifully presented. We devoured three courses at both lunch and dinner; all that beauty therapy made us ravenous! My treatments continued, although I wouldn't have the professional sports massage again – a bit on the hefty side for me. I'm sure it did me a lot of good but, at times, it was jolly sore. At the end of our stay, Chris and I vowed to return as soon as our bank balances would allow.

I called Lottie the following morning. I was as nervous as hell. After two weeks without her, the initial sharp pain of our separation had at last dulled down to a manageable level. Would a phone call bring it all back to me? I had a list in front of me of things to tell her but what should I say first?

When I dialled her number it was a huge disappointment, for I only got her ansafone. A strange Aussie voice, pre recorded, asked me to leave a message. I did so and said I hoped she was okay and I'd try later. I dialled again. Same result. I left another message. Then I sent a text. 'Beep beep' – shortly afterwards she sent one back to me! She was returning from the beach and hadn't heard her mobile. Third time lucky – she answered – but as soon as I heard her voice my insides flipped and my eyes filled with tears.

Once I had established that everything was fine with Lottie (and vice versa) it was fabulous to hear all her news. Lottie told me she'd been body boarding which was fun, even though she wasn't much good at it. But what frightened me was her report of the height of the waves – over six feet and incredibly powerful - and she had been in the sea up to shoulder level. Blimey, I thought, and told her to swim nearer the shore. She said she would but, from the tone of her voice, I didn't believe her.

We spoke for over half an hour during which time the youth hostel tannoy repeatedly blared out 'happy hour' venues and barbeque times. That annoyed us both, particularly Lottie, for we couldn't hear one other and each time had to wait until the announcement finished. As for the shower rooms, she told me they were quite filthy, particularly after parties when many residents were sick in them. Furthermore, the actual showers had no doors, only totally-see-through plastic curtains. Poor Lottie! I told her to get David to stand guard in front.

She said their room was okay – bunk beds with a small double on the bottom and single on the top – where they dump all their stuff. I found it crazy that Fosters lager was not available. So much for the UK TV ads…

Neither of us wanted to say goodbye. We delayed it for as long as possible and I tried my utmost to sound cheerful when it had to be said. Although the line was clear, she sounded so little and vulnerable. Afterwards, the memory of Heathrow was crystal clear to me. I felt completely at a loss and desperately wanted to phone her again, but I knew that would be silly and certainly not good for Lottie. It took me a long time to compose myself enough to continue my daily chores.

16 September 2006

Hi Lottie!

Wow! It was so amazing to speak to you after such a long time! And the connection was excellent - it seemed as if you were not very far away at all! Lord knows what the call cost but I don't care! It was hard to put the phone down. Anyway, will call again v. soon.

Life here continues as ever. At last I have the dogs booked in for a shampoo - 9am this morning. Dad's taking them but has to go to the Tip first. We spent yesterday afternoon clearing out the Dairy. You should see the rubbish piled into his car - it is overflowing! I had no idea we had so many broken TVs!

I tidied David's tools and boxed up your remote control cars, the latter which have been stored in the Bakehouse. So pleased you found your specs. Cedar Falls was fantastic - I shall take you there for some serious pampering when you get home! You would love the mud wrap. After being plastered from neck to toe in the stuff I was wrapped up in silver foil! It leaves your skin so smooth. I left some notes for Dad & John - you know - things to do whilst I was away - needless to say very few got done.

The crab apple crop is huge this year! We picked loads yesterday so I shall be busy making jelly over the weekend. Also found a new marmalade recipe so will try that out soon.

John's loving Strode, says the facilities are 'awesome' and has made loads of new friends - the 'right type' he tells me! Spoke to Jill last night. She and Kim are fine and delighted with email and postcard from David and will phone him soon. She suggested you may like to stay with her family in Adelaide for a while.

Hostel showers sounded absolutely disgusting - poor you. Glad the ones up a floor are a bit cleaner. Super you've met nice fellow travellers - must be fun all going out together.

Well, had better get dressed (4 for brekkie) and generally get cracking. No, Dad didn't do any washing whilst I was away - amazing what 2 men can produce in just 2 days!

Thousands of leaves falling off the trees - autumn is here. Lovely colours though.

Will call again soon! And text you. Glad to hear that David can watch 'The Simpsons'!

Snoopy and Co are all thriving, missing you but thrilled you're having such a good time!

Loads and loads and loads of love and big hugs from us all and keep happy!

Mum xxxxxxxxxxxxxx

=========

The next morning, whilst I waited for my emails to come through, I added Lottie's new mobile number to my 'often used' phone list in the study. Whoopee! She'd sent me another one!

17 September 2006

Hi again from Oz! Had an amazing couple of days on the beach as the weather has really picked up. Looking forward to moving on to Melbourne - running out of things to see and do in Perth. Going to Fremantle for the Sunday markets which are in big boat sheds and to the 'Sunday sessions' where everyone spends all day drinking in the pub! Only a quick message as on hostel computer again which eats my money and won't let you send pictures. Will try and get to the good internet café in town before we leave but our days are pretty packed, if not I'll text you. Not going whale watching anymore as been told that there are no whales, might go to a kangaroo park tomorrow. Glad everything good at home and lots and lots of love to everyone, missing you! Give Snoopy a big cuddle from me! Lotty xox

=========

17 September 2006

Hi Lot!

Great to get your email! Thrilled weather better. Sorry no whales but kangaroo park should be fun. Good thing you bought a new camera before you left. Enjoy the 'Sunday sessions'!!!

Yesterday was really busy. Julie shampooed the dogs and they both returned with coats gleaming and very proud of themselves! I started the crab apple jelly so the old stool is upturned in the kitchen with juice dripping through into a bowl. Made some more lemon marmalade as stocks getting low. Did big Tesco shop - not fun on a Saturday - and finished ironing (well, almost).

Dad extended the electric fence as dogs have rampaged all over my new plants! And he's made great progress in the Bakehouse. Wow! David would be proud! Another Tip visit today and a bonfire tonight.

John's got a job! Saturdays 10-2 at Café Piano. £4 per hour. He's their 'Ad man' - has to wander around town with a big board on his front and back!!! He's thrilled to bits. He watched WCS 1st team rugby match (they lost). It was Will's debut and John said he played really well though got concussed 10 mins before the end. Such bad luck but he's okay.

Next time we speak do have your Oz bank details to hand so I can make a note of them. When I am feeling flush (!!!) I shall transfer a little something to go towards a special trip.

Have a super time - don't spend any more money on hostel internet – I'll wait til you get to a decent internet café. Will be such fun to receive pics! I can choose one for my new background.

Huge love and hugs! Missing you lots too! Home is just not the same without you!

M xxxxxxxxxxx

==========

Einstein and Morse are our two basset hounds. Before them, we had a basset called Portia. The children named her after one of the pet pigs on Lundy Island they fed leftovers to – particularly sausages! Portia was an incredible dog – intelligent, affectionate, enormous fun and a great companion. Tragically, she died suddenly at the young age of six.

Portia was naughty as a puppy but Morse excelled himself in this regard. He certainly kept us all busy when he first arrived, which helped us to recover from Portia's death. Despite an array of toys and bones from our local pet shop and a couple of the children's old smelly trainers (which he adored), he chewed everything he shouldn't. Shoes, socks and dirty washing left on the floor in the laundry room would disappear only to be found later in bits. He also pulled newspapers, magazines and books off the coffee table and would race out into the garden and shred them. The lawn was constantly littered with what he deemed as his gains, not our losses.

That wasn't all. He reduced the round wooden handles on the pine kitchen dresser to pathetic thin spikes. He also had several goes at table legs. He dug up plants willy nilly. I gave up sowing carrot seeds after my third attempt was ruined. We only managed to grow potatoes that year! One time he even dug up and ate cat poo (together with much earth) which warranted a trip to the vet due to a badly upset tummy.

I was warned that we had a 'scavenger' on our hands. Indeed we did! However, to our peril we soon learnt that our coats and jackets were his absolute favourite. They hang on a long rail in a passageway off the end of the kitchen toward the dairy. One day, when I returned home after a brief shop in Wells, to my utter dismay I found that he had pulled down several coats and jackets and ripped them to shreds. A melee of remnants was strewn all over the kitchen floor. Amongst other items, my treasured black velvet 'Goth' coat was ruined, as was David's red jacket and John's new fleece. Beyond repair, there was nothing for it but to put them straight into the bin.

I scolded Morse each time he was naughty but it made not the slightest bit of difference. He repeated his antics again and again and we revisited the vet for more upset tummies. At least coats were safe once Nick had installed a baby gate across the passageway.

It was clear that Morse needed young company. We couldn't afford another puppy, so I called his breeder and asked her if she knew of a young basset who needed a 'good home'. She said she would give this some thought and, two weeks' later, she phoned me back. She told me that she knew of a thirteen month old dog that could be our answer. He was one of her own puppies which she had sold to a woman who planned to show and breed from him as he had all the right attributes for a future champion. However, when he developed, his jaw was slightly undershot and thus no money could be made from him.

That night we had a house conference. It didn't last long and a week later Nick and the children drove down to Dorset to collect him, on a week's trial. I had guests in and so had to stay at home.

When I first saw the dog, I was astonished by his size. He was huge! Nick and David had to pick him up out of the car together. He weighed just over 35 kilos and had the most massive feet and ears I had ever seen! He was beautifully marked - a dark tricolour with a streak of white in the middle of his back and a dappled chest. I showed him into the garden. He sat down beside me and didn't move.

Morse and Diesel were in the kitchen. John let them out. I was concerned how they would react to a strange dog and vice versa, but I need not have worried. Diesel did a quick sniff round him, wagged his tail and returned to bed. He seemed happy enough. Morse took to him straight away and very proudly proceeded to show his new pal around the garden. At one point all I could see were the white tips of two basset tails just above the shrubs at the top of the garden. So far, so good. Nick told me that the house they had collected him from was tiny. When they arrived, the owner had taken them out into a small back yard where they found the dog in a metal cage which rested on concrete. When he was let out, he made a beeline for Nick and deposited himself firmly on top of his feet!

On closer inspection, I discovered with horror that the poor dog was in a sorry state of neglect. His fur was dull and dirty and very coarse to the touch. His neck and undercarriage (particularly around his back legs) were very red and smelly and he had several nasty sores which clearly needed urgent veterinary attention. He was also terribly nervous. Any sudden noise or movement immediately made him cower and run away. That did it. There was no week's trial. Manor Farm was his new home.

We decided to re-name him and, after several more house conferences, he became 'Einstein', named after a St Bernard dog owned by the helicopter pilot who flew us across to Lundy Island. Like Portia, once again our family holiday haunt had helped us out with the name for a new pet. Less than two weeks later, Einstein knew his name, the vet had successfully treated his sores, his coat began to soften and shine and his confidence had begun to improve. Diesel was happier to be left alone whilst Morse and his new pal played together and quickly became devoted to one another.

But all was not well. Morse developed a bad limp and was obviously in pain. Back to the vet. The good news was, the limp could be treated. The bad news was, he would have to undergo a big operation by a specialist veterinary surgeon in Bristol; our vet couldn't help.

Morse's right front leg was deformed due to a congenital disorder - his elbow was pulling apart and his leg could break at any time. We took the vet's advice and, at the tender age of seven and a half months, Morse was operated on. The operation was a success, but what was to follow turned out to be an utter nightmare recovery period for all parties.

Morse had to be caged for six weeks and only allowed five minute walks on a short lead every two hours. He absolutely hated that cage and his howls could be heard during the day and long into the night. One evening I climbed in and cuddled him until he eventually went to sleep. The first couple of days in the cage did not pose a problem as he was heavily sedated. Thank goodness that David had a few days off work, as Morse needed to be carried outside to do his business and I couldn't have managed that on my own.

On the third day, some of Morse's sparkle returned. He chewed his bandage off! Back to the vet again where a very thick and very sticky bandage was applied. Thankfully, his attempts at chewing that one off failed. Einstein and Diesel were wonderfully gentle with him, although I did have to keep a close eye on Einstein due to his weight. It was as if they knew what Morse had to endure. When he finally recovered, his naughtiness returned full pelt which initially was a delight.

But two young bassets was an utter disaster in the garden. Action was taken the following spring. Nick installed a low electric fence around the vegetable patch before I commenced my seed-planting. It was the only sure way to keep the dogs out, although Morse did manage to get through, just the once. I hadn't seen him for a while and Nick went to look for him. He found him in the middle of the veggie patch, howling. He was too scared to come back through the fence in case he got re-zapped. Poor puppy, he was mighty grateful for being rescued. Neither dog has been near the fence since, and I am pleased to say we had a bumper crop of vegetables that summer, including carrots!

Undaunted, the dogs found a new game. They pinched cereal packets from the trolley in the Breakfast room, took them into the garden, ripped them up and devoured the contents. All that was left were hundreds of pieces of shredded cardboard and inner packaging - strewn across the lawn. Several times they have eaten a whole box of Shreddies (aptly named!) or a complete Variety pack. The latter is much preferred.

19 September, 2006

Hey! Another quick message from the rubbish internet in the hostel! Not going to be able to email you for about 4/5 days but you can contact me on the mobile and we can text. Have seen the train that will take us to Adelaide - the 'Indian Pacific'. It's colossal! Got early start tomorrow (8am!).

Weather better. David has been in the pool a few times but too cold for me! Went to a backpackers bar down the road last night which was great. It was packed out and had a good live band and cheap drinks etc! Also did the kangaroo reserve yesterday - no kangaroos and we got caught in a hail storm! So, went to the museum which was a bit dull apart from David almost knocking over a giant dinosaur skeleton! Typical!

John's job sounds great! You'll have to send me pictures of him with his board on. Next time I email I'll be the other side of Australia! Wow! Really looking forward to the journey but not the length of it. We've made lots of sarnies and taking a box of wine!

Missing you lots and lots and all my love to everyone, will send pics once we get to Melbourne.
Lots of love Lotty xox
=========

How sweet of Lottie to have emailed me before she left for Melbourne. They hadn't had much luck with animal viewings – first no whales, then no kangaroos but a hail storm instead. I imagined them both creased up with laughter when David almost knocked the dinosaur over! He is rather accident prone. I looked up The Indian Pacific train on the internet; it is 'absolutely colossal!' I was pleased to find pictures of the interior too, which looked spacious and comfortable. It will be an exciting journey, albeit very long and tiring. Maybe they'll see some kangaroos en route! I chose a most impressive picture of the train, set it as my new background and sent Lottie a text:

Thx so much for email. Enjoy last day in Perth. Seen pics of train – its vast! Don't miss it! Safe journey. LOL Mxxx'

There is only so much you can say in a text message. I shall be mighty glad when we can email each other again. I had a bad cold and didn't want her to know, so I put off phoning her for a couple of days.

Chapter Six

Overland to Adelaide and Melbourne

Lottie texted me from the train:

'Train OK – bit like a plane but with more room. Haven't got beds cos sleeper car was extra £500! Stopped in Kalgoorlie for re-fuel and quick bus tour of boulder. Night time tho so didn't see much! Will contact u when in Melbourne as no signal from now on – in middle of desert. Wish Daddy a really happy birthday and hope my card arrived. Xxx'

What a long journey without a bed! I hoped they managed to 'bag' a few seats so they could stretch out. I tried to text but it was refused. 'Error sending message' popped up on my mobile. Damn! I had hoped to get through before the train entered the desert. I would just have to wait until I heard from Lottie again.

The zero contact was hard. I kept my mobile with me day and night for I wanted to read Lottie's next text as soon as it arrived.

The following day was Nick's birthday. He had a hell of a schedule - several cases in Gloucester in the morning which meant a very early start, then two conferences in chambers so he wouldn't be home until 7.30pm at the earliest. No time for cards and presents before he left, he had to wait until he got back. We normally go out for supper on birthdays, but Nick would be tired so we decided to stay in and book a restaurant for one evening next week.

Three days later, contact from Lottie was resumed:

'Hello from Adelaide! Glad 2 get off train and stretch legs. Got until 8.30pm (we're 8 ½ hrs ahead of gmt) so having a look around city before we get bus to Melbourne which takes 9hrs. Phone prob won't work when on bus. LOL x x x'

Fantastic! They'd arrived safely in Adelaide! I couldn't reply for the error message popped up on my mobile again. Bugger! Despite that, I kept trying and twenty four hours later I got one through. Within ten minutes a reply came back. Hooray!

'Melbourne + YH gd. Went 2 sea life centre 2day, lots of sharks! + casino – had go on slot machines. Zoo 2moz, will try 2 find internet café + email. Lolxxx'

My relief was huge. I replied to say how happy I was that all was well and I'd email her with all news later. I changed my background picture to one of the sea life centre, minus the sharks, and grinned my way through the rest of the day.

23 *September 2006*

Hi Darlings!

Wonderful, you've arrived safely in Melbourne and youth hostel okay. You haven't wasted any time in sight-seeing! Bet sharks were awesome - there was a TV prog. on last night about the great white. Got a bit nasty so we switched it off! Enjoy the zoo tomorrow. All well here. Daddy gone to Kingsley's 100th birthday party. Just spoke to John who is carrying his ad. board around Wells - he says it's 'cool' and meeting up with mates later. Hugo & Gus are down for w/end.

Daddy had super birthday supper - he was home late so we all had fillet steak here followed by choc birthday cake with 3 candles (for 53!). Took pics of us all so will send on. Daddy *loved* his card of Perth! I gave him Leonard Cohen's latest book of poems which he was really pleased with.

Do hope your legs have recovered from being stuck on a train/bus for so long. How was tour of boulder? Any skippys spotted yet?! Hope trip round Adelaide was fun. Is Melbourne very different from Perth? Questions, questions!!!!

Ganda & Ann sail home Monday. They had complimentary 'Woo woo' cocktails last night - not up to much so they switched back to whisky! They send much love. Will is coming to Majorca with us which is great. John still enjoying Strode and working hard. Dogs fine but continue to be very bad. Morse chewed up a book which someone had lent us... Made damson jam yesterday (fruit from Norman & Marianne's tree) which turned out well. Sad news about Top Gear's Richard Hammond's accident - at 300mph! But he's out of ICU and getting better.

Life Without Lottie: How I Coped (or didn't) During my Daughter's Gap Year

Altho weather lovely, autumn definitely here. The virginia creeper outside your bedroom window is beautifully red. Have planted lots of new spring bulbs.

Ezetie returned your CD of 'V' pictures - she said they'd be great when she starts Uni to help with home sickness and asked you to keep in touch.

That's it for now guys - have incredible time in Melb! Missing you both loads and sending oodles of love and hugs.

Mum xxxxxxxxxxx

==========

24 September 2006

Hi everyone,

Having a good time in not so sunny Melbourne! Surprise, surprise it's raining! I think we're going to move to Sydney pretty quickly as mid 30's there! Too wet to visit zoo today. Going on a day trip up the Great Ocean Road on Monday. We get to see some amazing scenery like the 12 apostles and the lighthouse where the Ozzy children's TV program 'Going round the twist' was filmed - John will remember it! Plus we see seals and koalas etc. Also going to the 'Neighbours' set! Internet here is super pricey plus can't upload pictures.

The train journey was long but saw some great scenery - it was so diverse - went from green forests with waterfalls to miles of arid desert. Stopped in a small town called Kalgoorlie on the way - very, very local and everyone appeared to be related. Prostitution is legal and all the bars had topless bar maids! Very strange! Also stopped in Cook, a ghost town in the middle of the Nullabor desert which once had a big population but now only 4 people live there. When the train service was privatised, trains no longer stopped there and everyone left.

Nearly run out of time but will contact you again soon, prob by text. Hope everything is going well at home. Missing you lots and lots. May move to Sydney thurs or fri.

Lots of love Lotty xox

==========

Good grief! I was amazed at the speed they had so far travelled across Australia! My background had never been changed so frequently! Were they unsettled, unsure of what to do next or where to go, did the sheer size of Australia daunt them? Or were they really moving on to Sydney just for the sunshine? Would they stop over in Canberra en route? Would they fly this time? I sent a text to thank her for the email and also said '...*follow the sun! Hope you make ocean road trip...*'

David had often spoken about how much he wanted to see the twelve apostles. It was such a pity that internet usage was expensive – poor Lottie. I became increasingly appreciative of her supreme efforts to email me. After a five day gap, her latest email was so welcomed. Kalgoorlie – topless barmaids - sounded a den of iniquity! Quite an experience for them. I received a text to say she hadn't received my last email so I sent it again with an extra note:

24 September 2006

Hi Lot!

SO sorry you didn't get this email. Here it is again. Daddy & I picked enough sloes to make 3 gallons of sloe gin! Had drinks afterwards with Norman & Marianne at golf club. Sat on balcony - boiling hot sunshine! (sorry). They send their love to you both. Empty tonite and tomorrow - phew!

Roast beef & spuds in oven, yorkie puds made (10/12 remaining!), having with beetroot, leeks & carrots – all from the veggie garden, wonderful!

Will keep in touch by text and speak to you soon! Loads of love, missing you hugely, keep safe!

Mum xxxxxxxxx

=========

Norman and Marianne live just down the road from us. Marianne and I were at boarding school together but didn't actually meet until some four years ago when she spotted my details in the old girls' magazine and gave me a call. How extraordinary that we should live so close! Marianne told us where to pick sloes. I'd exchanged texts with Lottie whilst we picked them as I thought she would like to know how well we had done.

Thanks to my Aga, I can make Yorkshire puddings in advance and heat them up when needed. The only snag I always hit is to 'lose' a few to certain household members (i.e. Nick and the kids) so I thought the story would amuse Lottie. With her and David away, I didn't lose nearly so many. That was another hurtful reminder of her absence.

Over the next couple of days we kept in touch by text - when we could get a signal. The frustration of receiving a text and not being able to send one in reply drove me mad. My delight when I got her next email was absolute although I doubted that she had received my previous one.

27 September 2006

Hi! Having good time in Melbourne, weather still rubbish so heading to Sydney on Thurs. The tour of the Great Ocean Road was amazing! We saw koalas (apparently really rare to see in the wild) and seals and some amazing coastline and sea views. The best bit was the helicopter ride over the 12 apostles (sorry 4 charging to your card!!). Sent the cd of pictures off yesterday so should arrive soon. Pics mainly of the animals we've seen as not been able to take any with us in it unless 1 person holds the camera - bought a mini tripod yesterday so will be easier to get us in the pictures 2!

Going to do the 'Neighbours' tour tomorrow - you can walk around Ramsey Street. Dragging David along - he doesn't want to go!

Once in Sydney will try and get work. We're booked into the Sydney central backpackers and have a TV and fridge in our room as standard which will be cool!

Not doing much today - weather a little better so going to take some pictures of Melbourne and have a bit of a walk around. Melbourne isn't as great as people say - there's not really much to do. Will have lots more to write once in Sydney! Hope everyone is well and lots of big cyber hugs and kisses! Love Lotty xox

=========

The helicopter flight must have been fantastic and very good value for £60. Lottie charged it to our shared Barclaycard (taken out just before she left and to be used for emergencies only). Her text told me that credit cards only were accepted and David had left his in the youth hostel safe. No problem! I could hardly wait for their photos to arrive. Surely they could ask someone to take photos of the two of them together? Ah well, the tripod was a good idea. I wished that I could see the 'Neighbours' set too. Lottie and I are avid watchers. Poor David!

I found it hard to believe that there was *'not really much to do'* in Melbourne. I hoped that Sydney would keep them occupied and they found decent work. TV and fridge in their room? Going a bit up market now! I looked up the Central Backpackers on Google and found out that it is 'ideally placed' in Kings Cross, one of Sydney's 'most vibrant neighbourhoods' and just a short stroll from the Opera House. Breakfast is free, as is internet usage – fantastic! And it has a tropical roof top garden where barbecues are held each Friday, pub crawls organised each Saturday, free drinks on Wednesday at O'Malleys bar, and so on. Well chosen kids!

27 September 2006

Hi Lot!

So good to get email from you! Fantastic you did the heli flight - I am thrilled for you! Don't worry about charging card. My treat. Mini Sammy must have loved it!

All fine at home. Not much news really. Got v frustrated not being able to text you back cos of signal problem. Went to pottery class last night. Dreadful so not going again. Life drawing tonight which I'm looking forward to.

Daddy off to God camp on Friday for weekend. Hils and I having supper out on Sat. which will be fun. Probably going to Waggon & Horses (margueritas!!!). John's also out – at Horrington 1st's cricket dinner. His Monday timetable is awful - only has first and last lessons. Still, he stays at college in between and does all homework which is good. Once you're in Sydney and I hear from you I'll phone.

Life Without Lottie: How I Coped (or didn't) During my Daughter's Gap Year

Huge love and hugs from us all. Enjoy last day in Melbourne - and the Neighbours tour. Maybe you'll meet some of the stars?!

M xxxooxxx

=========

In his spare time, Nick is training to be a vicar and 'God camp' is Lottie's nickname for the theological college in Salisbury! He's now a year into the three year course. He didn't wake up one day and decide to do it; it was more of a gradual desire that built up over the years. His workload is enormous. As well as mountains of reading to do and regular essays to write, plus weekly evening tutorials in Bath, he has to attend several residential weekends at God camp. Before he was accepted, God camp put him (and many other poor souls) through the most ghastly selection process. I don't know exactly what happened, but when he came home he was like a broken man. Christians behave strangely at times. I don't do church. I simply can't bear organised services. I much prefer to occasionally pop into a church for a few minutes when the feeling grabs me. This is probably as a result of my boarding school years and having to walk a mile to church and back each Sunday, come rain or shine! Nick will continue to work as a barrister; his training is paid for but he will not receive any salary when he is ordained. I'll just be glad when it's all over and we can spend more time together.

I couldn't wait until Lottie contacted me from Sydney and so I sent her the odd text or five! Early evening – and no word from her. Not even a text. Had they arrived safely? Come on Fiona, I told myself, no news is good news. I called Jill. Maybe she had heard something. She had, but only a quick phone call from David a few days ago when they were still in Melbourne. He said all was well and they couldn't wait to get to Sydney and the sunshine. With all my heart, I hoped they were there, and safe and well.

Chapter Seven

Life Drawing & Sydney

Yesterday evening I went to my life drawing class. It was a scream! I hadn't been near a life class for four years and had previously only worked from female models. I found that the fatter they were, the easier it was to draw them. I produced a few great pieces, two of which I sold.

Alas, when I arrived at my new class, a male model welcomed me. His name was Dave and he was as skinny as hell. Bugger! However, he was terribly friendly and told me he wanted to be an actor. He had already played small parts in 'Casualty' (as a casualty!) and other similar TV series and was delighted to tell me that both Yul Brynner and Robert Mitchum had started out as life models! I asked him if he was there just for this session. 'Oh no!' he replied. 'I'm your model for the whole term.' I tried to look enthusiastic as I groaned within.

My eyes scanned the room. There were six fellow 'artists' all of whom looked mighty serious. None of them spoke to me, although one woman gave me a quick nod. Things did not look good. Dave didn't even have long hair which would have helped to hide his shoulder blades – always difficult to draw. Still, I was determined to 'give it a go' and chose a spot, sat down and arranged my materials (a large pad, two soft pencils and an all important rubber) on the desk in front of me. The woman opposite started to tap a pencil on her desk whilst she glanced scornfully at her watch. The session should have commenced ten minutes ago. We had a model but as yet no tutor.

Five minutes later our tutor rushed in. He looked dishevelled and sweaty, apologised for being late and muttered something about an urgent phone call he had to attend to. The pencil woman raised her eyebrows and tutted loudly. Our tutor didn't seem to notice this and introduced himself as Andrew, shook hands with us all and asked Dave to make a start. Without further ado, Dave stripped off, all apart from a pair of heavy black boots bedecked with steel chains and buckles. The pencil woman suggested rather sarcastically that he leave them on. That broke the ice and everyone smiled. I giggled.

Dave removed his boots and got himself into an incredibly complicated pose on all fours with his right leg and arm extended out as wide as he could. His back faced me and his balls dangled down between his legs like oversized prunes. I tried my hardest not to look at them. Inside, I chuckled with laughter and had to stifle a snort.

The tutor announced that we had three minutes for the sketch. Three minutes! How the hell was I supposed to size up arms, legs, torso, head, hands, feet etc (not forgetting the prunes) in less than three minutes and then actually make some sensible pencil marks on the paper?! I scrapped the sizing up bit and went straight in for the kill. Disaster. I produced a one-armed, hunchbacked pygmy with absolutely no chance whatsoever of keeping his balance, pruneless.

Dave changed position. We had to do two further three minute sketches and then moved on to five minutes. Those extra two minutes were invaluable! When we were allowed ten minutes, my drawing was half decent. At last! But my encouragement was short-lived. Our next task was to draw with our opposite hand. Well, what I managed could only be called a 'naïve' piece of art. The strange thing was, when I changed back to my normal hand, my work greatly improved. This tutor was good, I thought.

The poses got longer and Dave's ability to contort himself continued to amaze me. The two hour session quickly came to a close. I felt utterly exhausted; the concentration required for life drawing is intense. Horrified when Andrew asked us all to show our work to Dave before we left, I shuffled my best effort to the top. His reaction was positive, as was Andrew's. I would be back next week.

Two days later, although it seemed much longer, I still hadn't heard from Lottie and I couldn't get a signal to text her. Where was she? My worries were temporarily put to one side when her first batch of photos arrived. Fantastic! I rushed into the study, popped the CD into the tower and opened the file. There were 395 pictures! It was fabulous to see photos of them both and to share some of the amazing sights they had seen.

I felt dizzy when I saw views of Hong Kong taken from the highest point of the city. They made me shiver! The pictures of Perth zoo were great although I didn't recognise half of the animals. The colours of the birds were radiant blues, oranges, reds and yellows. So pretty! I wondered if their songs were pretty too. Lottie knows that I adore otters and, bless her, she had taken several shots of them as they rollicked around on the grass. There weren't many photos of the kids but I loved every one, even the shots of them after their train journey when they looked tired out. I could feel their tiredness. I viewed them again and again.

29 September 2006

Hi Lot!

Welcome to Sydney! Well, I think you are there - haven't heard and can't get texts through which is awful! Hope the youth hostel OK and your fridge is full of tinnies by now!!

Great news! Your first batch of photos arrived today! Only took 3 days - puts our postal service to shame. They are wonderful! Hong Kong looked packed out and the views were terrifying! Fascinating shots of train journey and strange looking creatures at the zoo (thanks for taking some of the otters) and the sharks at aquarium were awesome. Lovely to see happy (and some grumpy!) pics of you and David. I'll get John to send copies to Jill.

All well at home. Daddy wasn't thrilled to leave for God camp. Some sort of racial discrimination theme this time... He's taken his wine carrier with him. Well, just a quick email to let you know photos arrived safely. Do get in touch when you can.

Lots and lots of love to you both. Missing you heaps!

Mum xxxxxxxxxx

=========

John set my background to a photo of a parrot perched amidst a sea of greenery. It was far nicer and more personal to use a photo that Lottie or David had taken rather than one I had downloaded from Google Images.

The next morning, my mobile beeped. I grabbed it out of my pinny pocket, flipped it open and willed it to be a text from Lottie. It was! She was fine, she said. Her phone had played up hence no contact for a while, for which she was sorry. Sydney was great, the weather was wonderful and they'd seen the opera house and bridge. Hostel was not so great (and had no internet) so they will move to a better one next week. I heaved a sigh of relief. I couldn't get a signal to text her back until 24 hours later, by which time Lottie had sent another text, worried that I hadn't replied to her first one. Don't listen to mobile advertisements which tell you how easy it is to connect long distance. I changed my background to a picture of the opera house.

2 October 2006

Hi mum - just a quick message from new hostel but not checked in yet. In the Billabong Backpackers in a suburb called Newtown just outside Sydney, about 10 mins on the train or 25 mins walk from the opera hse. Moved away from city central backpackers pretty quickly - was in Kings Cross which is full of heroin addicts, prostitutes and weirdoes. Newtown is much nicer and has loads of pubs and cafés. We're going 2 try and find work here and will prob book in for Xmas & NY. Anyway, as I said a very quick email - the internet here is free but they have a strict policy on time limits if other people are waiting and they are! Will come down again when it's quieter and hopefully send u some pictures of us in the helicopter!

Missing u lots and lots, thank john 4 his email - I'll reply when I have more time. Lots and lots of love xoxox Lotty xoxox

==========

2 October 2006

Hi Darling!

Life Without Lottie: How I Coped (or didn't) During my Daughter's Gap Year

I can't thank you enough for emailing before you had even checked in! I wish I could give you a huge hug. Thrilled you love Sydney and will stay for a while. You always said you planned to be there over Christmas - and the beach BBQ!

First hostel must have been dreadful - shocking how misleading their internet site is. But the new one sounds loads better. Their internet site shows a wonderful picture of the pool lit up at night - looks 'awesome' as John would say!

All well here. Dad enjoyed God camp after all and John had great time at his cricket dinner. Only 3 weeks to go and we shall be in Majorca! I'll find an internet café and email you from there. Must ensure my mobile is on international. When would be a good time to phone? Can't wait to speak.

Missing you so much too! But am a lot happier now you've found a decent hostel. Good luck with the job hunting - do hope you both find great ones.

Loads and loads of love, hugs and cuddles!

Mum xxxxooooooooo

=========

We maintained contact by text and I learnt that they had been to Bondi beach, which Lottie described as *'wow,'* and body boarded - not so wow! The new hostel was an improvement but *'a bit boring'* as everyone else went to bed at 9pm! So they were on the move again – to Manly, where Lottie had been offered a job in a beach sandwich bar. Lottie doesn't waste any time once she decides what to do. I felt so proud of her.

4 October 2006

Hi Darling!

Super to get your texts. Another change of hostel! Third time lucky. Manly looks fantastic on internet. Will you take the sandwich bar job? What a great location to work! Well done you!!! Has David found carpentry work? Hope there is loads.

Had one early breakfast this morning at 7 - guest exhibiting at major dairy show at Bath & West. Then two more at 10 (super Irish couple from Co Kerry who gave me a cuddly 'basset' as a thank you!). Just finished rooms. Empty tonight so the 3 of us going to Ploughboy for supper. I have my 2nd life drawing class beforehand. People in the group are all talented artists. Damn! We have an anorexic male model - incredibly difficult to draw. Give me big fat ladies any day! The worst of it all is I have to show my work around at the end. One of my sketches resembled an unbalanced monkey. Ah well, I shall persevere!

Off to Charlton House for lunch on Saturday to celebrate Caroline's 50th. Have got her a voucher for a foot massage & pedicure as that was one of my nicest treatments at Cedar Falls. Jane & Ken and Chris going too so I hope we sit near them. Daddy has to make a speech. He planned on 15 minutes but I've persuaded him to keep it to more like 5... Then a HAMRA folk evening so it will be a busy day. Daddy preaching at Oakhill on Sunday morning. He hopes there will be more in the congregation than the previous turnout of five!

John playing rugby for Wells on Sunday. No idea which team he'll be in but they are short of front rowers. He's thrilled to bits. I'm apprehensive as he hasn't trained much this season so I've told him to work out in the gym.

Your final car insurance payment wasn't collected as your bank balance insufficient - don't worry, I paid it yesterday and bunged £50 into your account just in case anything else comes through. Nat West charged you £38 fee for the inconvenience. What a rip off! I called to complain but gave up on that idea when I realised I was speaking to someone in India...

Daddy and I going to Lynmouth for weekend in early Dec. Staying at Muddy Waters again (slug holiday). John holding the fort... He's been promoted to waiter!

Well, no more news today although I'm bound to think of something as soon as I send this. Ah - Nigel & Sue and Grannie & Grandad delighted to get your pcs!

Heaps of love and huge hugs from us all. Missing you loads but it's great we can keep in touch.

Mum xxxxoooooo

=========

Life Without Lottie: How I Coped (or didn't) During my Daughter's Gap Year

My second life drawing class turned out well. Dave was an hour late – he was delayed in another life session in the Forest of Dean. Phew! No contortionist poses for a while! Two new people turned up and Andrew took the register. As our names were called out, we answered in turn and glanced at Andrew as we each said our 'Yes'. The tapping pencil woman was the only person who didn't look up. She sat opposite me.

Due to the lack of a model, we were told to draw another member of the group. My eyes scanned the room. Who would I select? Who would be less difficult to draw? Someone with lots of facial hair – ah – the dark bearded man in the corner. Andrew went on to say that we had to draw the person opposite us. In three minutes. Oh no! Bugger the time limit - it was the pencil woman I was worried about, for she sat directly opposite. She waved at me with her fingers. If I made a complete balls-up, what would her reaction be? My drawing was awful. Thankfully she never saw it. And I didn't ask to see her attempt of me.

Next we had to draw the person of our choice. Bingo! The dark bearded man was a go situation. But we had to use our opposite hand. What I produced surprised me, despite the fact that beardy didn't sit still for more than a few seconds. How I hate people who fidget! My sketch was not bad, not bad at all. Andrew left the room for most of the time we worked, otherwise, he said, he would interrupt our concentration due to his inability to keep quiet. That was so true. He really did have verbal diarrhoea. But most of what he said was helpful.

Dave arrived at last, said he'd 'driven like the clappers' and stripped off with alarming speed, boots and all. He leapt dramatically onto a table and struck a pose. Charcoal was passed around. I was scared to death as I had never used it before. But I found it a fabulous medium to work with and much easier than a soft pencil to produce great shading. It helped that Dave maintained his pose for 15 minutes. I was supposed to draw his entire body but decided to concentrate on just one side of it. That paid dividends. The result was by far my best effort yet.

As with last week, the two hour session whizzed by. We had to show our work not just to Dave but to everyone in the group. That was hard. I should have wandered around to view my fellow artists' work but I stayed protectively close to mine. Maybe next time, I thought.

I mentioned HAMRA in my email to Lottie. It's our local residents association. Nick is Chairman, Marianne is Secretary and her husband, Norman, is on the Committee. It is a great team, well known for benefiting the area and organising popular social events. The next one is a folk evening, on Saturday.

I also referred to 'slug holiday'. That dates back to April 1993 when we took the children to a holiday cottage in Lynmouth, North Devon for a few days. We were the first party in since it had been closed for the winter. As a result, it was pretty damp and riddled with woodlice. Lottie was only 5 years old and when she discovered a family of the little beasties on the stairs she announced that there were a lot of *'slugs'* about! It fascinated both her and John how quickly they curled up into a ball when they were touched. Hence that particular holiday was called 'slug holiday'. Needless to say we had a wonderful time. Nick and I now escape by ourselves for the occasional weekend in Lynmouth. We don't stay in slug cottage but a smaller one on the same estate called Many Waters. Another word change, we call it Muddy Waters!

The next morning I received an email which stated (for some ridiculous reason) that my last email to Lottie could not be delivered. Maybe she *had* checked her emails and thought I hadn't sent her anything. How awful! I sent her a text to say what had happened and the following short email:

5 October 2006

Hi Lot!

Bloody internet...my last email to you bounced back this morning! Something about being forwarded too many times?! Don't understand it. Anyway, here's a copy! Hope all's well with you both. Party on!

Loads of love and hugs

Mum xxxxxx

=========

Life Without Lottie: How I Coped (or didn't) During my Daughter's Gap Year

I also sent Lottie a Snoopy 'e-card', not from me but from Snoopy. I thought it would be a bit of fun for her to receive something different to my normal emails. E-cards amazed me! I had received a few in the past (birthdays, thank you's etc) but had never sent one myself. Through Google, I found countless sites which offered many different designs and greetings. What's more, the vast majority were free. I chose one of Snoopy in his classic pose on top of his kennel. The whole process from start to finish only took me a few minutes. Excellent!

No texts came in that day. Maybe Lottie had started work? One came through during the night. Could I please call her as David needed the 'tax file number' on his birth certificate which he had left at Manor Farm. Ah! He must be starting work too. I got an email the following morning:

6 October 2006

Hi! All is well in Sydney. Going into the sandwich shop in Manly on Monday about the job. They really want me to work there because of my experience at Greggs - and it's cash in hand! Also signed up with an agency for boring factory work - packing - but it pays really well and they can guarantee both of us jobs. The women's world surf championships start in Manly on Monday so that will be really cool to watch! Had another go at surfing yesterday - still not very good but almost stood up! We both bought wetsuits as the water is freezing. They cost the same as renting them for 3 days. David has a smart black Billabong one, mine is black and fluorescent yellow so I look like a distressed bumble bee trying to surf! Oh well - it was much cheaper than David's so I'm not complaining! Going to get some surf lessons in once earned some money. The new hostel offers private lessons for me and David for the same amount as a large group lesson so that's good.

Weather picking up. Working on the tan but I've got funny stripes from my wet suit! I don't really mind when you call, we're 10 hours ahead. Would be great to here from u. Can't send pictures from this hostel as they lock the computer towers to stop people messing with them. The new hostel we're moving to doesn't have any phone reception inside so I won't be able to get your texts straight away, just so you don't worry. Off to look around the city and harbour now. Will speak to you soon! Lots of love and hugs and kisses xox

=========

What a great email! It really sounded as if they were more settled and organised. I loved Lottie's description of her bumble bee wetsuit! And was most impressed that she had decided to save her money rather than to look glamorous as she rode the waves! I felt much happier.

When I phoned, I got through without any problem. Lottie sounded clear and happy. We chatted for ages about the various hostels they had stayed in, the sights they'd seen, the people, the beaches, surfing, the weather, cocktail hours (obviously a priority!) and work. And I filled her in with the news of us all at home and what we had been up to - very tame compared with Lottie's adventures.

During their train journey, David had spoken to his sister, Naomi (who is currently in Cyprus with her fiancé). She had previously toured Australia and told him in no uncertain terms to avoid going anywhere near the Kings Cross area. Did he take any notice? Of course not! They decided to see for themselves. They did. When they arrived, they had to pass a man slumped down in the corner of the covered entrance porch. He was injecting himself. Lottie said it was the most horrid sight to witness. David complained to the man on reception. He casually replied that once they had seen someone *'shooting up'* a few times they would get used to it. Christ!

I also spoke to David who sounded happy too. As he was born in Australia, he told me that he needed his original certificate in order to apply for jobs. All Lottie had to produce was her UK passport. We agreed how ridiculous this was. Anyway, he said that one of his cardboard boxes stored in the dining room was labelled 'Important Documents'. Inside I would find a green box file which contained his certificate and it should be near the top. He gave me a post office address to mail it to which I double and treble checked. I certainly didn't want to get that wrong. He handed me back to Lottie.

We laughed about how she looked in her wet suit and I wished her good luck with the surfing lessons. I asked her how their money was lasting out. After a slight pause Lottie told me they needed to start work pretty soon for they had rather overspent on tours and cocktails! Plus all youth hostel prices more than double over the two week Christmas period (they increase from $150 to $350 each per week). And they had to book soon (and pay up front) whilst rooms were still available. They'd missed the tour of the 'Neighbours' set in Melbourne; they'd spent the previous evening at the Hard Rock Café which just happened to be serving cocktails, all half price, all night. That was a much better idea, I told her! It was wonderful to know they were having fun but I was a tad concerned that after only six weeks into their year away, they already had money worries.

I felt so proud when Lottie told me she'd got the sandwich bar job which she would probably start on Wednesday. The pay was $14 per hour, cash, and she could more or less choose her own hours. Even better, she'd get a good view of the forthcoming women's surf competition. If, however, the job didn't turn out well, she (and David) could get factory work. They seemed to have everything in hand. I didn't ask if David had looked for carpentry work. Maybe they wanted to stick together for a while. All too quickly the time came to say goodbye, although it helped that I arranged to give her a quick call back once I'd found David's certificate. I went into the dining room to look for it.

Chapter Eight

Lottie's First Job and Farewell to Harvey

It was quite an exercise to locate David's certificate. It was difficult enough to actually get into the dining room and then I had to move several overfilled and very heavy boxes around in order to find the one labelled 'Important Documents'. There wasn't one. Typical David! The only two with labels were marked 'David's CDs' and 'David's cuddly toys'.

I fetched a kitchen knife and one by one opened them up, all eight of them. Sod's law the green box file was in the last one. I felt awkward as I searched through David's personal papers but it had to be done. At least the certificate was reasonably near the top. I called Lottie back, told her I'd found it and would post it to David before midday. When I put the phone down all I could think about was how far away Lottie was and how long it would be until I saw her again. It felt as if I had used up every bit of my energy during those two calls and for the rest of the day I accomplished nothing. In the evening, I ordered a take away for our supper.

You may wonder why I hadn't phoned Lottie more often. She had now been away for six weeks and I had only called her twice. Well, three times really, although I didn't count my last call as we had only spoken briefly.

When she left my heart nearly broke. I struggled to maintain composure. Often I couldn't. I constantly worried about her, and thought of her all the time. My concentration could only be described as pathetic. I felt physically sick and was listless. My alcohol consumption rocketed and the routine of daily chores seemed pointless, although I did them; I forced myself to keep going. My period cycle went completely haywire. Why couldn't I be one of those mothers who took all this in her stride? I was glad I wasn't and didn't.

I was so thankful when, at last, the first week had ended for I could 'tick off' one of the fifty-two which lay ahead of me. It wasn't much but it meant a lot to me. As more time passed, I gradually began to feel better physically and more in control emotionally.

To have phoned Lottie more frequently and heard her precious voice would have dashed any positive progress I had made so far. I had to 'separate' myself for a time. I hoped she understood. I hadn't mentioned this to her; I thought it would be better for both of us to leave that topic alone. And I hoped my decision had helped Lottie too.

I knew she missed us all very much indeed, that was obvious from her texts and emails and our conversations. I needed to settle down to life without her but, more importantly, Lottie needed to settle into life without her family around her in order to get the most out of it. I hoped I'd got it right.

I took a photocopy of David's certificate for his box file and wrote a longish letter to them both. John had taken some photos in Harrods toy department the day they had left and I printed out two of David with Jill and Kim in front of a giant-sized stuffed giraffe and panda. I thought David would like to have them.

I headed down to Wells Post Office. The man behind the counter was most helpful. For the sum of £4.85 (which I thought was most reasonable) he assured me that the package would be tracked all the way to Manly Post Shop to await David's collection, and it should be there within four days. A similar service to our 'poste restante'. Excellent! And a service which I could use in the future to send them letters and parcels.

I got quite excited as I thought about buying presents for Lottie – I so missed our shopping jaunts together when it gave me such pleasure to treat her to a new t-shirt or a pair of jeans or some new make up. When I got home, I sent her a quick text to say the certificate was on its way and it should arrive early next week.

Nick got home that evening in an excellent mood. He had won his case despite a complete lack of believable defence evidence. His client was a down-and-out who had clearly beaten up another down-and-out but had nonetheless been acquitted. It seemed odd that earlier I had spoken to Lottie about similar such characters.

Life Without Lottie: How I Coped (or didn't) During my Daughter's Gap Year

Caroline's birthday party was great. Chris gave Nick and me a lift. Nick sat in the front to offer directions. Being driven anywhere by Chris is a nail-biting experience, from start to finish. She scared the pants off us at one T junction. Nick told her to turn left and said all was clear. Chris started to turn right!

'Left! Left!' he shouted. The car was half way across the road before, mortified, she slammed on the brakes.

'Oh, oh...sorry' she spluttered out, 'I thought you said right!' I won't go into how she manoeuvred the roundabout just before we reached the hotel, but we arrived safely and in one piece.

We sipped fine champagne and nibbled designer canapés on the terrace before we went inside and sat down to an excellent lunch. Nick made his speech which hit the right notes perfectly – and was just the right length. Max also said a few very touching words which Caroline especially appreciated. And Chris, bless her, drove us home without a single wrong turn.

The folk evening was equally good, albeit in the not-so-grand surroundings of the local cricket pavilion, but Marianne and her troupe of helpers had decorated it beautifully. The folk duo deserved their applause. When they did a Wurzels number people started to dance. Nick's solo version of the 'funky chicken' had everyone in stitches. Chris commented that his style was 'quite unique!'

Monday morning arrived. I texted Lottie to say I hoped the Manly hostel was okay and would phone her tomorrow. I received a reply during the night: *'Hi mum! New hostel gt. All v friendly. Got trial in sarnie shop tmoz. Will chk post shop for cert. Loads of love and miss you! Xxx'*

It was fantastic to speak to her again. Nick was at home so he chatted with her also. I asked how the surfing was coming along. Not too well she said! The board often flipped back and hit her on the head. God! But I was relieved to hear that she now really did only go into the sea up to her waist, for the waves were big enough at that depth to get a good 'ride'. And the Manly hostel was the best so far. I said I was glad her job was at the beach rather than in a stuffy factory. Lottie agreed, particularly as a heat wave was expected. David had been offered a job with a house removal company and he could drive the van so he was pleased about that. And apparently the lads cruise the bars after work. I told her to make sure he checked the brakes…

We agreed to speak again in a couple of days so I could hear about her job. I did so hope it was a huge success.

11 October 2006

Hi Lot!

Fantastic to talk yesterday and so pleased Daddy did too. Hope your first day at work went well and the other staff friendly.

John's a bit down. Off sick - came home lunch time yesterday. Wretched sore throat. I'll ask him to phone you later – it would do him the world of good to speak to you and David. Am looking forward to my life class tonight. Plan to repeat last week's trip to the Ploughboy afterwards but that depends on how John's feeling. If there is good food on offer he'll probably make it!

Not much news really. Have 3 lovely US ladies in for 2 nights. They have their own driver! It's great when guests enthuse over everything.

Booked out John's old room (now known as 'The East Room'!) for 4 nights end November - big godly convention at Bishop's Palace. Am chasing up delivery of new bed. It'll be fun getting room ready.

Daddy at home today – working flat out to finish his latest essay. He says that your old Sociology books are a real help.

So sorry Ezetie not enjoying UCL. Hope she can move rooms and get a better room mate. Tell her from me to stick it out til Xmas if she can. It's early days and I'm sure things will improve.

Off to Sarah Hartland's art exhibition on Sat. with Chris. Meeting Caro & Jennie there and having supper out afterwards which will be nice. Wonder what I'll buy?!!!

Well, must away and clean rooms. No hope of washing outside today - damn. Laundry room bursting with wet bed linen and towels.

Loads of love and hugs. Missing you! GOOD LUCK WITH WORK!!!

Life Without Lottie: How I Coped (or didn't) During my Daughter's Gap Year

Mum xxxxxxxxooooooooooxxxxxxxx
=========

Lottie texted me later to say that her first day in the sarnie shop was 'ok'. She'd been out with new friends from the hostel and had a great £4 steak dinner! All good news. She expanded her news by email which arrived the following morning:

12 October 2006

Hi! Just a quick message - on the way to work and decided I'd pop in2 internet café! Work is a lot different from Greggs as you have to use tongs for everything and are not allowed to use your hands, not even with gloves on! Plus they put grated carrot in every sandwich. Very strange! I got demoted from sarnies to the deli counter quite quickly! But never mind they want me back so I can't have done too badly! Going to 'the shark bar' tonight, they do 2pound cocktails on Thurs! It's going to be 35 degrees today so I'll cool off in the surf if I finish early. Going to Palm Beach this weekend – only 20 mins away and where 'Home and Away' is filmed. Anyway, time to go and serve people olives and ham! Will be in touch soon, lots of love Lotty xox
=========

12 October 2006

Hi Lot!

Fab you pass internet café on way to work! Thanks so much for news. Carrots in everything - are Aussies frightened of the dark?!! Fantastic you survived your first day and they want you back! You'll be their 'Deli Queen' by the end of the week!

Great you've found cheap cocktails - another bar! I miss you and David here to mix your famous concoctions. The shaker is sadly redundant but I'll see what we can do this weekend. Daddy in Salisbury on Saturday so maybe when he gets home…

All well - John's back at Strode today. Do text him though and ask him to call you for a chat. He couldn't face calling you - thought it would be too emotional. He really misses you. Off to see Ian in garden, then 3 b'fasts, then change all the beds (groan). Claire here today so at least I have her to help me.

Heaps of love, cuddles, kisses and hugs - big ones!

Mum xxxxxxoooooo

=========

The next morning I was completely shattered to receive this text: *'Got sacked from sarnie job – wanted someone with more experience of the Oz way to make sarnies! Got job in call centre starting Monday. Better pay. David got job there also. Enjoying long weekend now – temp 38!!! Cert. arrived today. David sends big thanks. So nice 2get letter with it!! Will email tmoz with more news. lol. Lottyxxx'*

How dared they give her the sack! I was furious and so sorry for Lottie. I replied: *'Bugger sarnie shop! That's really shitty of them! They should all be shot! Is call centre phone work? So glad cert. arrived OK. Stay cool! lol Mxxx'*

I phoned her but got her answer phone. I left a brief message to say not to worry - who wants to make sarnies the Oz way and it was brilliant she'd already found other work.

Another text came through: *'Its telesales work for a massive catalogue. We take the orders. Should be easy! Gd hours at 8pds per hour! xxx'*

Thank goodness! I texted back: *'Fantastic! Well done you! Can't wait to get yr email! lol Mxxx'*

Friday the thirteenth certainly lived up to its spooky expectations. Lottie got the sack plus I had an appointment at the vet for Harvey. His seizures continued and he had become incontinent.

Even though I expected the worst, I was still taken aback when the vet told me it would be a kindness to put him to sleep. I shakily signed the consent form and said farewell to Harvey whilst I tickled his ears; he loved that.

When I picked up the empty cat box it felt horribly light. Whilst I waited to pay the bill I browsed the adverts on the notice board - it was something to do. I saw one for Siamese kittens, scribbled down the details and phoned when I got home. There were two male kittens left and I arranged to see them the next day. I knew it was rather soon to think of new cats but it seemed too good an opportunity to miss.

Just as Lottie had said, her email arrived the following morning:

14 October 2006

Hiya!

All well here! Getting sacked was very, very embarrassing! I had an answer phone message on my mobile just before I got to work but assumed it would be you or John and ignored it because I had no credit and was a bit late anyway. It turned out to be my boss who said he didn't want me anymore! I went into work, hung up my bag, put on my apron and started doing what I was taught yesterday. The boss came over and said 'Didn't you get my message?' Oh dear! It was so awful and obvious that all the staff knew I'd been sacked but no one told me. Bastards! Apparently they didn't have the time to train me the 'Australian' way of making sarnies (stupid way) so I had to go. I was only paid 50 dollars - less than 4 pounds an hr when promised 6! But I didn't feel like arguing – I just wanted to get out quickly! Spent the rest of the day handing out my CV to different jobs.

Luckily it's been a blessing in disguise as not only am I enjoying a long weekend lying on the beach but I've got a better job working in a call centre! I get 18.50 dollars an hour (about 7 UK pounds) and all I have to do is take phone orders. Start on Monday. David is working with me so that should make it more fun. It won't be nice stuck in an office all day now that we're in the middle of a heat wave, but the job lasts til Xmas so I think we'll stay in Manly til the New Year. All our friends will be here and it's really beautiful and with good bars!

Went out on the town last night and going out again tonight. Hostel facilities aren't great i.e. no internet/bar etc but everything is just around the corner. We've got 2 Welsh friends, 3 French, 2 German, 3 Ozzy and 3 English! David and I have bought a surf board so now we are proper surfers! We got a really good deal and split the cost. Worked out about 70 pounds each. I'll have to send you some pics of us surfing (or trying to!). David has named the board 'Sheila' and it's blue. We are going to keep it until we go to NZ in Jan/Feb as you can sell them for almost as much as you bought them for - second hand beginner boards are in big demand.

I think that's about it for now. I'll head back over the road to the hostel for pre-going out drinks! Lots and lots and lots of love. Lotty xoxox ps. miss u loads!

==========

When I learnt the full story about her 'sacking' it made my blood boil. Lord, the poor girl turning up for work unaware of the fact that they didn't want her any more. It must have been absolutely ghastly. And they'd diddled her out of a fair amount of pay. I was glad she was free of them. How I longed to give her a cuddle and commiserate with her. However, the call centre job sounded good, especially as she and David could work together. I knew he would stick up for her as well as himself. And the work was available until after Christmas.

I so admired Lottie's ability to bounce back after such an awful knock and was delighted she continued to enjoy life, had made new friends and was '...going out again tonight'. Well done her! And she'd clearly started to learn the value of money. I tried to call her but got the ruddy ansafone again. I knew I had to break the news about Harvey and I also wanted to tell her about the kittens. They were absolutely adorable and I had bought them both! I arranged to collect them after Majorca.

Chapter Nine

Call Centres and Teenagers

I sent Lottie a text to thank her for the email and wished her a 'fab' evening out and loads of luck for Monday – she certainly deserved both. My wishes came true when I next heard from her: *'Hiya! 1st day work went v well. Took orders 4 mail order Xmas catalogue. Really easy. Big co. that has its own shopping channel. Didn't Garth's bro. work 4 shopping channel in Sydney? lol Lottyxxx'*

I was so relieved that the new job was a hit. I tried to phone but had to leave yet another message. Damnation to bad signals! I sent a text instead: *'So glad work great – well done! Do give Garth's brother a call. Heavy rain today. 6 days to Majorca, whoopee! lol Mxxx'*

I emailed her very early on Tuesday morning. I woke up and couldn't get back to sleep. I put the heading as 'Bugger sarnies, Call centre rules OK!'

17 October 2006

Hi Darling!

Fantastic to get your email and thanks so much for all your texts. So wanted to speak to you but bloody signal a no-go. Brilliant that call centre has come up trumps and you are working together. I know David will look after you!

Thrilled you've made lots of new friends - quite a mixture! And you've invested in a surf board! Love the name!

Don't work too hard (but play very hard!) and check they pay you the correct amount at the end of the week! And tell Sheila not to hit you on the head!

Heaps of love, cuddles, kisses and hugs. Miss you loads!

Mum xxxooooooooxxxxxxx

=========

Fiona Fridd

18 October 2006

Hi! On a break so a quick email ! Work now soo busy but we get loads of cool free stuff - Snickers bars and flavoured water! I also got a 5 minute shoulder massage from the in-office masseur! Better get back to work! lol xox

=========

    I was glad that Lottie hadn't put her usual 'missing you loads' at the end of her email although she was in a rush. I tried to phone her but couldn't get through so I sent a quick email before I did my shopping:

18 October 2006

Hi Lot! Great to hear from you! Hope the freebies keep coming! Can't get phone signal – will try tomorrow. Just off into Wells.
    Loads of love & hugs etc. Snoopy says Hi! He's very happily cuddled up with Blue Bunny inside Daddy's top hat!
    Mum xxxxooooxxxxxxx

=========

19 October 2006

Hi mum, at work so have to be quick! Just mailing to let you know I'm fine. Significant lack of signal at the hostel so that's why calls don't get through. Weather rubbish! Hope everything ok at home. Will speak soon I hope. lots of love xox

=========

19 October 2006

Hi Lot! Thanks so much for letting me know all well. Nearly the weekend! John's taking me to wine tasting at The Swan tonight. Should be fun! Miss you loads! Tons of love and kisses
    Mum xxxooooooxxxxxxx

=========

Life Without Lottie: How I Coped (or didn't) During my Daughter's Gap Year

The lack of signal at Lottie's hostel was exasperating. Fingers crossed I would be able to speak to her before we went to Majorca. I decided to send her a text about Harvey's demise. I couldn't delay it any longer. She didn't reply, I just got an acknowledgement that my message had been delivered. I hoped that the oncoming arrival of the kittens would ease the sadness I knew she would feel. I also sent her an email:

19 October 2006

Hi Lot,

I am SO sorry I had to text you about Harvey but I thought you should know. It's awful not being able to speak to you in times of need! He went on Fri 13th - the same day I learnt you got the sack and John had missed some lessons. So, three bad things.

Please buy a bottle of champagne (or several massive cocktails) and toast Harvey - and charge to our card. That would be a nice thing to do.

You will adore the kittens. Their names are Tallinn and Riga - what a surprise! They are really tiny and a very pale beige colour with huge apricot coloured ears and stripy tails. I have to keep them inside for two weeks so the kitchen will be an interesting place! I wonder what the dogs will think of them?! If I email photos can you open attachments now?

Torrential rain here this afternoon and skies as black as thunder. I've never seen the barometer quite so low.

Gave two huge beef bones to the dogs, who rushed outside with them and refused to come back in for at least an hour. They got soaked and shook themselves all over the kitchen – and me!

High winds forecast for weekend so hope our flight isn't delayed. Will text you when we arrive. Let's hope the villa is easier to find than the apartment in Nerja!

Do hope to speak to you before we go. Have a wonderful weekend - make the most of it and hope you get loads of surfing with Sheila! Loads of special love and hugs

Mum xxxxooooxxxxxxxx

==========

Five years ago we spent a wonderful week in a friend's apartment in Nerja. We hired a car at Malaga airport and found our way to Nerja pretty easily. However, it took us over two hours to locate the actual apartment! We must have driven up and down every street and alleyway in the town at least twenty times over and asked directions from many locals (in our best pigeon Spanish). Tempers flared and the language inside the car was distinctly blue. The name of our apartment was hidden by a massive shrub! Lottie will remember it well.

20 October 2006

Hi, so sorry to hear about Harvey. I hope it wasn't too upsetting. It's exciting to hear about the kittens though. Do send pics! I think I can open them at work. The job is still going well - had a couple of angry callers but nothing too bad. The weather has picked up so being inside isn't fun but at least it's Saturday tomorrow! How was the wine tasting? Going out in Sydney tomorrow for a 'farewell pub crawl' for someone returning to the UK. Then plan to spend all weekend sunbathing and surfing. I need to keep topping up my tan at the weekends so I don't look pale and vampire-ish like most of the people at work! I hope everything is ok at home. I checked the weather on the BBC website and it looks very wet! Send my love to everyone and missing you lots and lots xox

==========

Yet more attempts to phone Lottie ended in failure. My patience was severely tested. I sent texts but didn't receive any reply. I emailed her the following morning:

21 October 2006

Hi Lot!

It wasn't pleasant at the vet but Einstein was with me which helped enormously. Will take lots of pics of kittens and email to you. You'll adore them! Nick Hunter starts painting the kitchen the day after we get home, so hopefully it will be finished in a couple of

Life Without Lottie: How I Coped (or didn't) During my Daughter's Gap Year

days and I can collect kittens on John's birthday. I've got cat litter supplies ready and waiting...

Sorry you've had some nasty callers - I guess it goes with the job. Just say you can't hear them and put the phone down! I occasionally do that when someone refuses to believe I have no vacancies and is extremely rude. Do hope you get some good surfing over the weekend. Wine tasting was great fun. John looked after me very well. He sampled the reds whilst I stuck to whites. There was some wonderful Cote de Blaye (Daddy's favourite) and I bought a case. Being delivered after Majorca. Daddy did get back in time to go but was too tired. And he's just left for chambers - their AGM today. Quite a week. Can't believe we fly tomorrow! Have SO much to do today!

Jill called last night - all well. She asked if David could contact Mark - apparently he hasn't heard from him and would like a chat. Jill said that Naomi is getting married next June in Oz and you are all going to the wedding! Wow! That will be quite a gathering!

Have a fantastic weekend. Keep Sheila busy. Hope we can speak later. Loads of love and hugs and kisses and missing you heaps!

Mum xxxxxooooooooooxxxxxxxxxx

==========

A bit later I received a text. *'Hi! sorry I missed yr call! have amazin time in Majorca! Off to the bars now. Miss u lots. Lol x'*

I replied: *'Have great pub crawl! Just off to pack! Majorca 78 degrees. Yes! lol + miss u2. mxx00xx'*

As ever, it was fantastic to get Lottie's text. It was lovely of her to wish us a great holiday. The rest of the day was frantically busy. I spring cleaned the Aga (which certainly needed it), filed a vast amount of papers and tidied the whole house. I didn't want to return home to piles of laundry, so I ploughed through the lot and both machines worked at least four loads each. Most of the clothes were John's. I had asked him *not* to leave his washing until our last day at home but, well, that's teenagers for you.

Despite two short downpours, everything dried on the washing line. John's jeans dried on the Aga and didn't require to be ironed. Alas, everything else did. I forgot how many times I carried piles of neatly pressed clothes upstairs and stacked them in the airing cupboard. But it was all done, apart from the dog blankets which I washed and hung up to dry on the ceiling racks in the Laundry room.

Nick and I took the dogs to kennels. He sat in the back with the dogs who clambered all over him. Nick is more of a cat lover and, based on what he said, he obviously didn't appreciate their attention!

The noise of barking when we entered the kennels was horrendous. It was half term week and they were full – apart from a large kennel in the corner reserved for Morse and Einstein. They put their hackles up and raced across the courtyard to the kennel maid who led them into their kennel. But when the door was locked shut, I said my goodbyes and told them to be 'good boys', they cocked their heads at me and looked confused, as if to say 'What have I done wrong?' I felt such a heel, but it was only for eight nights and I knew they would be well cared for.

When we got home I finished my packing. Even John got his packing done which was a miracle. He wanted to leave it until the morning but I put my foot firmly down! He and Will went into Wells for the evening. Before they left, I made them promise to catch the last bus home and set their alarms for 5.15am.

Chapter Ten

Majorca

Our taxi to the airport was due to collect us at the unsociable hour of 6am. Needless to say I found it easy to get up so early. This was our main annual holiday and I was terribly excited!

Nick and I frantically stuffed the last few things into holdalls and Will arrived in great form. John was not. He'd lost the earphones for his MP3 player but, more importantly, couldn't find his geology books which he needed to prepare for a test after half term. Nick didn't help matters at all; he repeatedly told him to 'get a move on!'

At last we were almost ready. Nick did a final check round the house and Will helped him to carry luggage to the taxi. John located his earphones and study books. I turned the Aga temperature down and did the final few pieces of washing up. Lights were switched off, the back door was locked and just after six o'clock the four of us piled into the taxi and headed for Bristol airport. We were off!

After a swift check-in the boys went off in search of breakfast. Nick and I headed for the bar for coffee and a final ciggie. It wasn't long before we heard our flight boarding notice called over the tannoy and we made our way to the appropriate departure gate.

Ten minutes later we boarded the airport bus to take us to the plane but, just as the doors were about to close, a stewardess stepped on. She asked us where the two lads in our party had got to. Oh God! We had wrongly assumed they had taken an earlier bus and were already on the plane. Thankfully we didn't have to panic for long as they appeared at the gate a couple of minutes later and thought it was hilarious that their names had to be called out over the tannoy.

We quickly ushered them onto the bus, ticked them off, apologised to the stewardess (who saw the funny side of it), the doors slid shut and the bus pulled out.

Nick is a terribly nervous flyer. He crossed himself several times before we took off and then reached for my hand. He gripped it firmly and I told him everything would be fine. It was. The flight was soon over – we were only in the air for about two hours – and we touched down smoothly. The weather was fantastic and it was great to peel off some of our layers of clothing. We found the hire car office (a makeshift booth!), collected our car keys and headed for the car park. It was vast but we eventually located the car - a very smart, bright red 4-door Seat diesel. I was pleasantly surprised as the car was a freebie included in the villa rental.

Cases were loaded into the boot and the boys sat in the back, where they proceeded to tuck gratefully into the rolls I'd bought on the plane. I took the driver's seat and tried to make sense of the numerous controls. Thank goodness for symbols, I thought, although there were some I could neither recognise nor make sense of. Nick sat next to me with a pile of maps and directions; a sensible arrangement, as he is an excellent map reader and navigator – my skills in those departments leave much to be desired!

At first I drove mighty carefully whilst I gradually became comfortable with being in a strange car, on the wrong side of the road and on the wrong side of the car. But the Seat was easy to drive, the roads weren't busy and we were soon on the main road out of Palma. The villa company had told me that the journey would take about an hour and a half, but after a couple of wrong turnings (honestly!) mainly due to poor signs, and a quick stop off to buy essential supplies to last us until tomorrow, we arrived just over an hour later.

The villa looked lovely from the outside - a large white three storey building surrounded by beautiful gardens. There was one problem. We couldn't get in! Both the main double metal gates and the side gate were locked. We pressed the bell – maybe our holiday rep. was inside? Nobody came. We pressed again. Without any encouragement, the boys vaulted over the gate and disappeared round the back. The impatience of youth! I fetched the villa's notes from the car, found security instructions and read them. Ah, by the side gate was a box with the keys inside, opened by a particular combination. Nick located the box and turned the numbers to the correct position. Would the box open? No! After countless attempts he finally jiggled it the 'right' way and, hey presto, it flipped open and there were the keys. Phew! I shouted for the boys and we all went inside. It was fabulous.

The villa stood about 100 feet above the marina and had a little green gate at the bottom of the garden. This gave direct access to the sea and to a path which led down to the centre of the marina, filled with an array of sparkling yachts, many of them rudely large. Our swimming pool was crystal clear and flanked by well-tended gardens with sun loungers, a table tennis table and barbeque area. Above all this was a large raised terrace and patio doors which led into the ground floor of the villa.

Cases were abandoned and Nick opened a bottle of wine and a couple of San Miguels for the boys. I found the glasses cupboard and loaded the freezer with more drinks so they would cool quickly. Holiday priorities! We sat down on the terrace and beamed at each other. It was heavenly, although I missed Lottie terribly. This was our first family holiday without her. I imagined her there with us; her happy smiling face, her laughter and how much she would have enjoyed it.

I sent her a text to say we had arrived safely and the villa was fab. I received a most welcome reply the following day: *'Sounds amazing! Stuck in call centre, boo hoo! Going home in 5 mins. Hope ur all havin a great time. Wish I was there 2! lol x'*

After a good rest, much wine and beer and chat, we carried cases upstairs and, bedrooms selected, unpacked and changed into summer clothes. On the first floor were two bedrooms, both en suite and with a large shared balcony. The boys took that floor, thrilled to have so much space. Nick and I took the second floor with a huge double bedroom and balcony and a fabulous marble bathroom. It was an excellent arrangement and everyone was happy.

In the early evening the boys went through the little green gate and down to the marina in search of a good bar. It was a five minute leisurely stroll along a pathway cut through scented pine woods. John phoned me (thank goodness for mobiles!), said they were in a great place called 'The Smugglers', gave me directions, and Nick and I met them there shortly afterwards.

The boys' choice of bar was not quite our cup of tea, so they finished their beers and we moved on to a smart restaurant. The food and service was exceptional and the prices most reasonable, particularly the excellent Spanish wines. And the location, just a few feet from the bobbing yachts, quite enchanting. Armed with our Spanish phrase book we asked for 'la quenta, por favor' (the bill, please). Although the waiters spoke very good English, we wanted to try out our Spanish. They must have been impressed as complimentary Schnapps appeared!

The boys returned to their bar and Nick and I walked arm in arm back to our villa. We took the longer route via the well-lit streets of the town. It would be dark along the pathway and we were concerned we might fall into the bushes! We needn't have worried as the boys told us later that it was floodlit.

The boys got back and were delighted to tell us they had been beckoned by a 'very, very black man' who shouted 'lookey, lookey!' as he displayed his wares. They had bought a stack of pirate CDs from him for the princely sum of ten euros. Most worked, some didn't (!) but it was a pleasure to listen to a couple of them before we all went to bed at the end of a perfect first day of our holiday.

Both boys had the sense to close their patio doors and turn on the air conditioning. Nick and I didn't. The fresh warm night air was too lovely to resist and we left ours (and the curtains) wide open. Alas, the following morning we both sported large mosquito bites – I had one on my upper right arm, Nick had several on his left ankle. Anthisan to the rescue, we tried our hardest not to scratch!

Our holiday rep. paid us a visit and gave us a couple of local maps. Nick and I left the boys still asleep and went into town to explore. There were hundreds of shops and cafés crammed tightly together in a maze of little streets. I was jolly grateful that Nick was with me, otherwise I would have got dreadfully lost. The shops were the most extraordinary mixture of ultra expensive designer boutiques flanked by horrendous 'chav' outlets which sold Spanish tat and not-very-good replica football shirts. There was no street or district differentiation between up and down market whatsoever.

I texted Lottie: *'Sun up here and been shopping. Got 2 great scarves, bracelets + pcs – will send u one so check post shop next wk! Miss u x'*

Life Without Lottie: How I Coped (or didn't) During my Daughter's Gap Year

The boys didn't surface until noon, had a very quick dip in the pool, for the water was cold, and then swam in the sea which they said was much warmer and more fun anyway. After lunch, the boys went into town and Nick and I lazed on the terrace. The sea was perfectly calm, the calmness only broken by the occasional yacht as it sailed by, which sent ripples across into the shore where they lapped musically against the water's edge. A large glass-bottomed pleasure boat came into the marina, turned around and headed out again. It was full of passengers and we waved to each other, which was fun. Late that night, Nick and I shared a bottle of wine on our balcony. We were surprised by a sudden wonderful display of fireworks. I shan't tell you what we were up to when the final rocket went off!

Nick thought we should add a bit of culture to our holiday, boys included, and so we took to the Spanish roads again. We visited San Salvador, a fourteenth century monastery built on top of a hill over 500 metres high. The journey took about thirty minutes, which was a relief as it was very hot and both boys were hung over from the number of bars they'd worked through the night before. When we commenced our ascent the road narrowed considerably and twisted and turned its way up and up. My ears popped several times which was a relief, as they had become somewhat blocked during the flight over. We were glad it was not the height of the tourist season as it was scary enough to negotiate around the occasional car we met, plus two groups of very intense looking German cyclists.

Relieved to reach the top, we parked the car and had a look around. The boys went down some steps to explore the gardens whilst Nick and I made our way towards the monastery. It was an enormous building and from the outside looked more like a fortress than a place of prayer, but we learnt that during the Middle Ages the monks frequently had to fend off attacks by Arab pirates!

The interior chapel, however, was a completely different story. It was incredibly ornate with splendid circular stained glass windows and exuded a wonderfully warm aura of peace and safety. The main altar was huge and impressive. It was made of alabaster, heavily carved, on top of which stood a beautiful statue of the Lady of San Salvador. I thought her face looked so kind and contented.

To one side of the altar was a small recess filled with candles, some lit, some not, below which was a money box fixed to the wall. I put some of my loose change into it (quite a bit actually) and lit five candles – one for each of us and an extra one for Lottie and David. I felt good doing that and asked the Lady to keep us all safe, especially Lottie. I was delighted to learn later that the church is still used for weddings and other special ceremonies and that mass is celebrated there every Sunday.

Upstairs we discovered three of the original priests' cells, each sparsely furnished with an iron bed, a small table and chair and a few old wooden wall hooks. Nick said they reminded him of God camp. The windows were tiny and had iron bars so the cells were pretty dark, but we could see for miles (good for spotting pirates!).

When we stepped outside the glare of the sunshine warranted the quick reapplication of sunglasses. We met up with the boys who had also seen the chapel and enthused wildly about it. This may have been something to do with the fact that the 'lookey, lookey!' man sold more than just pirate CDs, for they had shared a joint during their tour of the gardens!!! By the evening, Will's eyes bore an uncanny resemblance to those of Kha – the wily snake from the film 'The Jungle Book'. This was the beginning and the end of the boys' search for culture during our holiday. We had planned to visit another monastery later in the week, but Nick and I decided to go it alone and left the boys to sleep in after yet another, very late, night on the town.

On the way back I mailed the postcard I had written to Lottie and David. I was assured that two UK rate stamps was the correct rate from Majorca to Australia. I hoped so!

The nearest bar to our villa was The Dolphin, 150 yards up the road and a great place to enjoy a glass or two of ice cold vino before lunch at the villa. It was owned by an English couple who had emigrated with their children some eight years ago. One of their sons helped in the bar, the other one, they proudly informed us, ran 'the best night club' in town. I made a mental note of the name to tell the boys. On the outside, it smacked of the typical Majorcan style with a terrazzo terrace filled with wicker chairs and tile topped tables surrounded by palm trees, bougainvillea and mimosa. White painted archways covered in fairy lights led you up a few steps and inside to the bar.

At the street entrance there was a large stone dolphin, but in the bar there was absolutely nothing even remotely connected with dolphins or the sea, not even a fishing net. It contained an extraordinary eclectic mixture of English and Spanish tat stuffed into every available orifice which ranged from a collection of old violins and gramophones on a rather rickety looking high shelf, to a long clothes airer suspended above the bar festooned with vintage ladies' corsetry! There was a floor to ceiling triple bookcase stacked with both hard and soft backs and a scribbled *'Please swap your books'* sign sellotaped loosely to the front. The first part of the bookcase doubled up as a secret door leading to the loos! And, of course, the ubiquitous huge TV was there - fixed on the wall in one corner and constantly on at high volume. It always seemed to blare out Chris Tarrant's 'Who wants to be a millionaire?'

One evening, after dinner, we sauntered around the town, people and bar-gazing as we went. However, the minute we showed the slightest bit of interest in a certain cocktail bar, a woman rushed out, adorned us with yellow paper Hawaiian garlands and ushered us to a table. It was too late to escape, we'd been knabbed! Within a very short space of time a huge bowl filled with an extremely tall and ornate flower and fruit arrangement was plonked in front of us. Four extra long pink bouncy straws stuck out of it – one for each of us. They were so long that there was no need to move forwards to reach them, but it was wise to keep a gentle hold in case you got poked in the eye!

We sucked and got a mouthful of a delicious ice-cold fruit flavour, albeit rather on the sweet side. I wondered exactly how much actual alcohol was buried beneath all the fruit and flowers which we had been charged over £30 for. We continued until, with some relief, that all too familiar and noisy rasp told us we'd reached the bottom. Will very kindly helped me to the ladies, not because I was pissed but to get there I had to walk over a decidedly ropey little bridge covered with green stuff meant to resemble grass but didn't.

The boys left us in search of a 'decent' bar and Nick and I taxied back to the villa. When I came downstairs the following morning the first thing I noticed were two yellow garlands slung over the back of a chair. I groaned as the memory of the cocktail bar came back to me, but also gave a little smile.

Each morning, two pretty Siamese-cross kittens waited on the terrace to be fed. One was a lovely smokey grey tabby colour and the other was similar, but with a few white stripes across his back. We called them 'Smokey' and 'Bandit'. Bandit had a strange twitch – his head would suddenly jerk to the left or to the right which reminded me of dear old Harvey. He didn't appear to be injured in any way, so maybe he was born that way.

They were always ravenously hungry and consumed vast amounts of Spanish sausage and tinned sardines – the latter which I bought for them at the local supermarket for the princely sum of 10p. I would open a tin for them, scrape the contents out into a bowl and place it at the end of the terrace. I always put the empty bowl straight into the dishwasher. I learnt that if I left it on the ground, it quickly became surrounded by an army of tiny biting ants which required the boiling water treatment. John and Will enjoyed that particular task!

I put the kettle on and made a mug of coffee for me and tea for Nick – our routine early morning drinks. On our first morning, I had used the tap water to fill the kettle. Big mistake. The tea and coffee that resulted was disgustingly salty. In future, I used only bottled water.

I sent Lottie a text: *'Been adopted by 2 adorable little kittens! Reminds me of Crete. Lol mxoxoz'*

Three years ago we holidayed in Crete and were similarly adopted by kittens (although many more than two) and Lottie spent much time with them. She adored them all and practically cleared out the local shop of sardines. Every time I fed the kittens I thought of Lottie and that holiday. God, how I missed her!

In the town, there were several cafés which specialised in Texan food. They all looked decidedly dodgy to me but the boys thought it would be fun to try one. It was the sign on a particular café which read *'Eat as many ribs as you can for a fixed price'* that made their minds up. Outside, it had a giant brightly-painted wooden Red Indian and a photo of John Wayne. Inside, cowboy cartoons blared out from a

Life Without Lottie: How I Coped (or didn't) During my Daughter's Gap Year

widescreen TV. It was so naff! A waiter showed us to a table underneath a 'waggon' canopy, as the weather had turned very humid and the exposed tables and chairs were covered with tiny drops of water. The menu was vast which made me wonder how fresh the food was. I needn't have worried. The steaks Nick and I had were superb. As were the boys' barbequed ribs, piled up so high they were in danger of collapse at any second. They ploughed through the lot with the odd 'delicious' and 'awesome' muttered in between bites and neither of them asked for more! Their choice had been a good one.

The next morning, Nick and I showered as usual and came downstairs. I went into the kitchen to do the washing up. I turned on the tap. No water! I checked the downstairs bathroom. No water there either. I called our rep. on her mobile. She told me the problem was nothing to do with our villa, said in such a way which made me understand that if I had thought of complaining to the villa company, not to bother. That was the last thing on my mind! Apparently there was a burst pipe up the road which was being repaired, although she had no idea how long that would take. I thanked her for her help and hung up. We went to The Dolphin to see if the owners knew any more. They did. They told us that not one but *three* mains had burst and the large Thomson hotel in town was in real trouble. I bet it was!

There was nothing for it, so we ordered drinks, sat on the terrace and tried to forget about water problems. Next door, I watched a man in his swimming pool. He swam up and down non stop and must have completed at least 50 lengths before we left. Rather ironic, I thought. The efficiency of the Palma water board turned up trumps for by late afternoon our water supply returned, albeit in fits and starts and much gurgling from within the pipes. The very best thing was to wash my hands in hot soapy water. I did so several times. The incident made me aware of just how much we rely on a constant water supply and take it completely for granted. It is not until you lose something so essential to life that you realise what you have lost.

We had dinner at a great little café just up the road which we had passed several times. There was no menu and no wine list. The owner simply rolled out a list of choices for both which was limited but excellent. As our holiday was nearly over, cash had become rather depleted so Nick asked to pay by credit card.

'Sorry, cash only please…' he was informed, followed by '…but you visit bank and pay tomorrow.' We all turned out our wallets and chipped in to make up the total, plus a tip. I wondered how many customers had said they'd pay tomorrow but were never seen again.

Two days later I simply had to find an internet café and check my emails in the hope there would be one from Lottie. I was anxious, as I hadn't received any contact from her for five days. I also needed to see if I had any B&B enquiries. I picked up my diary and Nick and I went down to the marina, where I'd previously spotted an internet café with free usage. Nick ordered some wine whilst I signed on. The connection was painfully slow but I eventually gained access to my Inbox. There was nothing from Lottie. Damn. I sent her a brief email to say I hoped she and David were okay, deleted the junk mail, answered two B&B enquiries, and signed off with relief, as the 'computer corner' was confined and stiflingly hot. I joined Nick outside.

On our last day, I texted Lottie before we went into town: *'Just off to do last bit of shopping. Hope all well with you. lol + miss u! mxxx'*

I was desperate to hear from her but there was nothing I could do. As we had an early start the next day, we packed most of our things before we went out for dinner. It was Saturday and the final night of the high season. The town was very busy and awash with 'lookey lookey!' men, keen to sell as much as possible for it was their last chance to cash in. For many places, it was their closing night and they hosted parties and offered cheap drinks.

After dinner the boys went off to the biggest end of season party in the main square. Nick and I wandered around the town for a while before we taxied back to the villa. As we sat on the terrace for the last time, we both agreed that this had been the best holiday we had had for years. Nick even said he would like to return! I was absolutely thrilled, as to get Nick out of Somerset, let alone on a plane, even short haul, is not an easy thing to do.

Next morning, the conversation on the way to the airport was minimal. We all suffered – the holiday was over, plus the boys had

had little or no sleep for the street party had gone on until dawn. We returned the car and the boys piled our bags onto a trolley, but as they pushed it towards the terminal building the bags fell off. After much swearing the trolley was reloaded and we entered, only to discover that we couldn't check in for another hour. The boys gave us a really hard time. They were not happy, not happy at all - they would have done anything to have stayed in bed a while longer. We sat down in a grotty café and Nick went to buy cold drinks. The boys put their arms on the table and buried their heads. Within minutes they dozed off.

Luggage check-in and security check times eventually arrived and we made our way upstairs. The queues were long and whilst we waited an announcement was made. Our plane had been delayed due to fog in Bristol. We all groaned. There was nothing we could do but wait – even longer. Once through security, we split up. The boys went off in search of food, Nick and I headed for the shops to pick up a few small presents to take home. At long last we boarded the plane. As it took off I looked out of the window and whispered with great fondness, 'Goodbye Majorca. Thank you for such a wonderful week!'

Chapter Eleven

Home Again

We finally touched down at Bristol airport. We found Mervyn, our local minicab driver whom we had arranged to meet us, and he soon got us home. I was relieved to be back for it had been such a long day. Luggage sorted, Will thanked us for a brilliant holiday, we hugged him goodbye and he went home. I would miss him as he had been great company to us all.

Back to reality. There was a huge amount to do, and fast, for I had six B&B guests due to arrive within a couple of hours. However, the first thing I did was check my emails in the hope there was one from Lottie. There wasn't. Nick collected the bassets from kennels and it was wonderful to be reunited with them. They looked well, but must have barked for most of the week as they were very hoarse. I sent Lottie a text: *'Hi Lot! Home safely - delayed an hour due to fog. Dogs ecstatic! Early to bed tonite. Busy day tomorrow. Lol mxoxxx.* And another: *Ps. -4 degrees tonite. Bugger! Winter on way! Mxox'*

I had just finished arranging some flowers when the first of my guests arrived. They were from France - a lovely family of four on a house-hunting trip. My next guests, a couple, were also super people. All of them wanted breakfast at 8 o'clock. I noted that down in my kitchen diary and hoped I could cope with six at once on my first morning back. The very best thing about being home was to get back into my own bed. Over the next few days though, all three of us wished several times we were back in Majorca.

Monday morning was a shock to us all. Actually, the whole day was a shock. John returned to college, Nick returned to court and then went on to Bath for his evening tutorial. I struggled through breakfasts and then the decorators arrived. Within minutes the kitchen looked like a bomb site. I called the owner of the kittens and arranged to collect them on Friday. I had hoped for Thursday, but the owner said that Friday would suit her better. That was just as well, for the decorators took longer than they thought.

The absolute highlight of my day was to receive an email from Lottie. At last! I was mighty glad to learn all was well in Oz.

30 October 2006

Hi everyone! Welcome back - hope you had an amazing time! Sorry I haven't been texting. I've not had any credit. Had a really nice weekend - went surfing and spent lots of time on the beach. Work is still boring, David and I pulled a sicky on Friday after a big night out so it was v nice to have a long weekend! I'm back at work. David has now got a job with an air conditioning company (fitting the units) which he prefers. We went to a free bbq for backpackers at the local church on Sunday - the food was really good but the god-botherers were creepily friendly and we sensed it wouldn't be too long before they tried to covert us so, we left after eating!

Better get back to work, would be great to hear all about the holiday! Lots of love and miss you loads xox
=========

I replied before I laid the table for breakfast, even though I knew that would make me late for my guests. Lottie was my priority.

30 October 2006

Hi Darling!

Fantastic to get your news! I thought you might have run out of credit! Glad you had a great weekend. So sorry call centre is boring but at least you've got a job - maybe you could see if the agency has anything better? Glad David's enjoying his new work. Church bbq sounded interesting! At least you got well fed! Let me know the best time to call as longing to have a good old chin wag!

Majorca was the best holiday - even Daddy had a wonderful time, coped really well with the flights and wants to return! The villa was fantastic. The boys swam in the sea a few times but John got bitten by a jellyfish so they used the pool from then on. Daddy got bitten by mosquitoes (we thought of you). The weather was superb - 80 something every day - and we were within a stone's throw of great bars/restaurants and only a 5 minute walk to a fab marina. The boys had a ball. We had dinner together in town each evening and then they stayed on to party. But it's good to be home. Dogs went crazy! John's provisional license has arrived so must book up driving lessons with Colin. Can't believe he'll be 17 on Thursday!

Loads more to tell you but will get this email off so you will hopefully read it before you finish work. I missed you *so* much on holiday. I sent you a postcard which I hope arrives!

Loads and loads of love and hugest hugs. Take care.

Mum xxxxxxxxoooooo

==========

Within minutes I received a text: *'Hi. Thx 4 email. Had gud w/end, weather rubbish tho, rained whole time! Hope all well at home. Miss u loads. Will email tmoz. Lol x'*

I replied: *'Hi Lot! Sorry rainy. Can't be as cold as here! Miss u loads 2! Lol mxxx'*

Tuesday was a little easier, breakfast included, as I had a 15 minute gap between the two groups which helped considerably. The kitchen, however, was hard work. I seemed to clean and shift stuff around for most of the day. At one point I wondered if I would ever regain enough order to produce breakfast the next morning. I did, but only just. The dogs didn't help as they padded relentlessly from one end of the kitchen to the other. They were desperate to catch up on their lack of sleep whilst in kennels, poor things, but their beds kept being moved.

31 October 2006

Hi! Glad holiday was so good and even Daddy enjoyed it!! Do send me pictures! Happy Halloween! Oz pays no attention to it and I was looking forward to toffee apples. Oh well! Work isn't too bad, need to do it anyway – Oz a lot more expensive than we thought plus hostel rent now gone up to Xmas prices. Have moved into dorm to save money. First night was not too bad. We're sharing with Stu (an

English friend) and two girls from Holland. The dorm is clean and tidy although David has already started messing it up! He's back in the call centre - the air con job didn't work out as he was paid less for more hours. We got a 50 cent per hour pay rise yesterday (about 20p). Better than nothing! Calling me this week will be difficult because I don't finish work till 8 and then have an hour's travel back to hostel. The best time to phone would be over the weekend although it would be cool to speak to John on his birthday. I sent him a card. Hope he gets it on time. Better get back to work. Speak to you soon! lots of love Lotty xox
==========

A couple of weeks ago I had almost bought a selection of small ghoulish goodies to send to Lottie but assumed there would be plenty on offer in Sydney. I could have kicked myself. The poor kids now in a dorm - money must be really tight.

I was so excited about the prospect of Tallinn and Riga's arrival. I had bought the necessary supplies for them before Majorca but hadn't yet organised a bed. The wine I had ordered at the tasting arrived and just at the right time, for one of the boxes was the perfect size. I had some spare dog bedding, cut out a piece to fit and decided to put the box on the floor opposite the Aga where the kittens would be nice and warm.

Wednesday turned into an utter nightmare of a day. It started fine; I cooked breakfasts, my guests checked out and the decorators arrived. Then the day took a definite turn for the worse. The tenant in one of our cottages we rent out was due to move on. Since Monday, I had tried to reach him on his mobile but got an automated message which said the phone no longer accepted incoming calls. I also tried to text but with a similar result. Damn. He had obviously 'done a runner'. Nick's trial had been deferred and so we both went to investigate.

The cottage was empty – of tenant that is. As were the wardrobes – his clothes had gone - and his bed. But it was obvious he had left in a hurry for several items remained. These included a sofa bed, a microwave only fit for the rubbish tip, a full kitchen bin which sported maggots, an old tool box and loads of rubbish. Even washing was on the clothes line in the little garden. That went straight into the bin! The kitchen was utterly disgusting but nothing could have prepared me for the state of the bathroom. I had never seen anything quite so repulsively filthy in my entire life. Furthermore, if I had bought the house, the first thing I would have replaced would have been the lavatory. It was indescribably dirty with caked faeces smeared all over the pan, seat and lid, both inside and out. I heaved several times, put a hand over my mouth, opened the window as wide as it would go and bid a hasty retreat to check the bedrooms.

The double bedroom was dirty but empty, thank goodness. The single bedroom likewise apart from some rubbish in one of the cupboards but when I pulled a lager poster off the door, a huge hole stared back at me. The bloody tenant had obviously put his fist through it. I went back downstairs, told Nick what I'd found and he went to see for himself. He couldn't believe the state of the bathroom either.

Nick measured up for a new door and we headed home, thoroughly depressed at the enormous task which lay ahead. And we only had an incredibly short space of time to get the cottage ready for viewings as my 'to let' advert would appear in the local papers within 24 hours. Bugger!

Luckily, the sunshine of Majorca had boosted my energy. I certainly needed plenty. Armed with a basket loaded with many 'serious' deep-cleaning products, several scourers and cloths and an industrial pair of high-up-the-arm rubber gloves, I spent the whole of that afternoon at the cottage. I scrubbed and disinfected the kitchen until my hands and arms ached and my eyes stung from the fumes of the cleaning products. The oven was the worst. I got through bottles and sprays of every description plus several tough scouring pads and gallons of hot water before eventually the grime and the horrible stench of stale greasy burgers was gone.

My tenant had obviously smoked heavily but fortunately only downstairs. The walls and ceilings were dreadfully stained and I had to get my decorators to paint the whole lot. The final result was fantastic. The rooms were brighter, clean and smelled wonderfully fresh again. I polished all the inside windows and those on the outside I could reach, washed down all the woodwork and hoovered the carpets before I called it a day.

I was mighty proud of what I had achieved and sent Lottie this text: *'Hi lot! Thx 4 email. Glad dorm not too bad. John's card arrived y'day - he was thrilled, saving 4 thurs. will call you then, early. lol mxxx'*

She replied: *'He shouldn't have opened it already! Oh well. Glad he liked it. Almost finished work, its been a long day, taken over 500 orders. Everyone going mad for Xmas! Lol x'*

I sent another: *'He didn't open it! Saving 4 Thursday. 500 orders, wow! Bet yr glad wk is over 4 today. Have gt evening. Lol+hugs mxxx'*

Will and his parents were due round for an informal fondue supper. My kitchen was still in complete disarray. I cleared the table as best I could, turned down the lights and lit candles to help create a more inviting atmosphere.

We had a great evening and showed them our holiday photos – on John's pc – and recounted some funny stories of Majorca. The number of empty bottles in the kitchen the next morning was disgraceful.

It was John's seventeenth birthday! I collected his presents and cards which I'd hidden in the dining room. He had an early start at college and by the time he surfaced there was just enough time for him to open them. His favourite card was the one from Lottie and David. Lottie had written a lovely letter inside to her 'little bro', and David had wished John a great day and to make sure he had 'several tinnies'.

Then a text arrived: *'Hi mum! Wish John a happy birthday! Still at work. Don't finish 4 another hr + got no battery. Will charge up wen get back 2 hostel in about 2hrs. x'*

Lottie's timing was perfect! I replied: *'He's just opened your card and says big thanx! Will phone later! Lol mxoxox'*

John also sent her a text, much longer than mine.

Thankful that I had decided to close for B&B until next week in order to settle the kittens in, I left the decorators in full swing and returned to the cottage and to the ghastly prospect of cleaning the bathroom. Ian was already there, busy in the garden which was badly overgrown. Yesterday I could easily have burst into tears but today, when I saw the kitchen restored to its original pristine condition, I was more determined than ever to give the bathroom the same treatment.

It was hell and worse. Fortunately, spirit of salts dissolved most of the grunge down the loo so that was a positive start. Thick rubber gloves were a godsend. I scrubbed and scrubbed until my efforts were rewarded and not a moment too soon. Hooray! The state of the loo had definitely improved, all apart from deep down the bowl, so I poured more spirit of salts inside, closed the lid and would pop back tomorrow to scrub it again.

I then hit the wall tiles. I sprayed them with lime scale remover and left it on (for twice as long as the instructions said) to eat its way through the dark orange stains before I scoured them, and the bath, with bleach and cream cleaner and rinsed it all off with hot water from the shower over the bath. This I had to repeat twice. At last the tiles, taps and bath gleamed.

Next, on to the basin and finally the linoleum floor which I never thought would clean up but it did, and well. I had forgotten it was pale green! I collected my cleaning stuffs together, looked around the bathroom and grinned with satisfaction. I would gladly have challenged anyone to find bacteria in there now!

Nick took the garden waste to the local tip. Little did he know that one of the shrubs that Ian had pruned was a serious skin irritant. Ian wore gloves but Nick hadn't and he developed a beastly itchy rash on both hands. Anthisan came to the rescue yet again. Poor man, he got some strange looks in court, for the rash took four days to subside.

The cottage was almost ready for viewings. It was time for the nice bit – the addition of those important extra touches in order to make the house look more inviting to prospective tenants.

I bought green plants and fresh flowers and collected up a few items from home – scented candles, a couple of hand painted bowls and some bath and shower products in designer bottles. Ian made up two pots of winter pansies and cyclamens for either side of the garden door. All done, I locked up and went home.

My efforts were quickly rewarded for the next morning I showed two nurses around, they loved it and, four days later, moved in. The extra touches had worked.

I called John on his mobile. He and a couple of mates were in town and I met them at Tesco. John chose a chocolate birthday cake, two huge pizzas and some garlic bread for his birthday supper plus, of course, a case of lager. I felt guilty as I hadn't had time to make him a cake myself, which I always did on family birthdays, but he seemed delighted with his 'Tesco finest' cake. When we got home, the boys disappeared with the cake and lager into the Snug.

I felt left out. It was my only son's seventeenth birthday, I'd seem him but briefly that morning and, now he'd got his lager and his mates, I was surplus to requirements. I sat down at the kitchen table, grateful that the dogs wanted my attention.

My mind went back a year to John's sixteenth birthday, when Lottie and David were here, and we eagerly waited for him to return from school. They had put up a 'Happy Birthday' banner outside the back door and mixed an incredibly potent cocktail especially for John, which he had to down in one as soon as he got home. The house was filled with laughter and loud music and we had a wonderfully happy evening.

A far cry from tonight, I thought. How I wished Lottie and David were here now. I hoped Nick would be home soon. It was too late to phone Lottie, for it would be the middle of the night in Manly. I swore inwardly at the time difference.

I felt really guilty because I hadn't phoned her this morning when I said I would, so I sent her this text: '*Really really sorry didn't call earlier. Had 2 clean cottage - left in horrendous state + tenant buggered off....! Lol + hugs mxoxx*'

The decorators had finished the kitchen and made a marvelous job of it. My task was to return everything back to its rightful place. That was simple enough, but the process took ages and it wasn't long after the ten o'clock news that I went to bed, happy that order was at last restored and happy that tomorrow was the day I could collect the kittens.

Chapter Twelve

Arrival of the Kittens

Before I collected the kittens I had to do a big shop. As I neared the check out, I noticed a display of Advent calendars, the ones with a chocolate behind each window. I bought three, one each for John, Lottie and David. If Australia didn't recognise Halloween, I thought, maybe they didn't have Advent calendars and no way would I be caught out again. I also went to the Post Office and posted a present to David as he would be twenty-one in two weeks' time.

That done, with great excitement I drove over to Midsomer Norton to collect the kittens. They had grown so much since I had first seen them! But they were still tiny and rubbed affectionately against my leg whilst I wrote out a cheque to pay for them.

It was extremely difficult to tell the difference between them, but one was very slightly darker and I decided he would be 'Riga'. I popped him inside the cat box and spared a fond thought for Harvey, who had been the last cat to use it. Tallinn climbed up and sat on top of the box. He was obviously ready to go!

I asked the owner if the kittens had a nice Siamese yowl. She said not yet, but it would come. That disappointed me but not for long. When I carried them to my car, as soon as I switched on the ignition they both yowled loud and clear and continued to do so all the way home. It was fantastic!

The kittens were incredibly brave when I first introduced them to Morse and Einstein. I put the box on the floor and let the dogs sniff around it for a while before I opened it. They had a shock when the kittens emerged and promptly spat at them. Tallinn dotted Einstein on the nose. He yelped and bid a hasty retreat to his bed, but Morse chased the kittens round the kitchen until they sought refuge behind the fridge. When they came out, I scooped them up and put them into their bed opposite the Aga. That was not one of my best ideas. They immediately jumped out and this time shot behind the boiler. At one point their yowls were so loud the noise closely resembled peacocks!

When John returned from college and saw the kittens for the first time, he immediately fell in love with them. It was wonderful to see such a hunk of a lad handle them so gently and tickle their ears whilst they purred at him. I was glad of the help, for the kittens were as quick as lightning, and to exit the kitchen without them in hot pursuit was quite a task!

Chris and Janine called in after work. Janine took photos of them with her mobile and sent one by text to Lottie. Dinner that night was interesting, for the kittens were terrible thieves – typical Siamese. We rescued what we could and bid a hasty retreat into the Breakfast room where we ate in safety, but with yowls of protest from next door.

Early the following morning I emailed Lottie:

4 November 2006

Hi Lot!

So sorry not to have emailed sooner. It's been one hell of a week here! Big mistake having 6 guests in as soon as I got back from holiday! The kitchen repaint was a nightmare - took 4 days and everything was upside down. But all done now apart from a few small things which Nick H will finish on Monday.

It took me two days to clean the cottage. I have never seen such filth. Got new tenants which is a great relief. John had a good birthday and was delighted with the card and notes from you both. He got mostly money (great for driving lessons). Daddy and I are fine but wish we were back in Majorca! It is SO cold here now. The bed up the side of the garden has been completely replanted with roses and perennials and loads of spring bulbs in between so next year it should look really colourful.

I collected the kittens yesterday. They are absolutely fantastic! Very affectionate and very brave with the dogs although they yowl and spit at them! Dogs really gentle with them (but they chase them lots!) and constantly wag their tails. Tallinn is the boss - very haughty and confident but so affectionate. Riga is smaller and his fur is rather on the thin side so he looks a bit pink. Daddy and I thought he could take over as the hairless cat you always wanted. Janine and Chris popped in to see them and Janine texted a photo to you. I'll take lots over the weekend and email on, together with holiday pics. Sorry I didn't call last week but will do so at weekend. Will be fantastic to speak again!

I've posted a parcel to David for his birthday - a little something inside for you too. Hope everything arrives in one piece! Do let me know.

Well, it's just gone 7am and I have 4 baskets of ironing to plough thro – hardly any of it got done this week so am very behind. At least no B&B's to worry about and Daddy and I look forward to a quiet weekend. Hope you have a great one and a good rest after taking all those orders.

Loads and loads of love and hugest hugs. Miss you lots!
Mum xxxxxxxooooooooo
==========

A few minutes later I received a text from Lottie: '*Hi. Got email. Can't receive pictures on my fone. Kittens sound really cool! Had gud w/end, weather rubbish tho, rained whole time! Hope all well at home. Lol x*'

I sent her a text back: '*Sorry rainy. Cant be as cold as here! Kittens such fun and putting dogs in their place! Miss u! Lol mxxx*'

On Sunday afternoon, we buried Diesel's ashes under the clerodendron tree in the lawn together with his red collar (which still had some of his white fur around the buckle) and Lottie's special note in the little brown envelope. How I wished she could have been there in person.

8 November 2006

Hi Lot!

How's things? Do hope weather better. Went into Greggs on Monday - girls send their love and miss you lots. I bought one of their yummy steak slices.

Dad's got a new hotmail account and has emailed you to check it works – particularly to Australia and back!

The kittens continue to enchant us all and their different characteristics are emerging. Tallinn loves being cuddled, Riga not so much. Has my Majorca postcard found its way to you yet? Hope David's parcel arrives soon. I know Daddy emailed you to say we'd buried Diesel. I planted some snowdrops around his tree. It will be lovely to see them come up next year – the start of Spring!

Carnival on Friday and poor Daddy will miss it as he's at God camp all weekend. Chris Thomson and his (new) girlfriend are coming to stay but they'll have to sleep on the floor as the bed I ordered for John's old room still hasn't arrived. I've had countless arguments on the phone with the supplier! It's due on Friday and I will be amazed if it actually turns up. Bumped into Penny – Rhys loving Uni but comes home often as he's smitten with the same girl he brought to your leaving party – the one with train tracks. Daph popped in for coffee this morning. She and Andy have sold the church and bought a house in Mortehoe - where their little flat is. It will be sad to see them go but Daph promised me there will be a good party beforehand!

Loads of fireworks were set off this weekend which poor Einstein hated. He shook constantly and was even off his food. John didn't have a birthday party on Sat - we were worried the kittens may have got out but he went to a firework do at Joe's farm which he said was tremendous. He came home on Sunday looking decidedly pleased with himself. Must have been a good night girl-wise!!!

Well, time to feed the kittens again. Its already pitch black outside and only 5pm! John's just got home and sends his love to you both. We've had horrendous fog for the past 3 days and rain today - miserable. Hope work not too bad. Loads and loads of love and the biggest darned hugs ever! Miss you heaps and heaps.

Mum xxxxxxxxooooo

=========

Lottie had received Nick's email and, much to his delight, sent him this lovely reply:

Life Without Lottie: How I Coped (or didn't) During my Daughter's Gap Year

9 November 2006

Testing testing! I hope this reaches to you. All well here. Still working hard in the call centre - it was Melbourne Cup yesterday and everyone dressed up in their Sunday best and we had a buffet (not boo-fay as Mum would say!).

Cats sound great. I hope God camp isn't too dull! Is everyone there still really odd? I'll be thinking of you sitting in the back of the Range Rover with your wine carrier and a packet of fags!

Missing you loads, it feels really strange not being at home for birthdays and other special occasions but I'm thinking of you lots. Got to get back to work now, more old women ringing up to order size 24 swim suits. Groan!

Lots and lots of love and kisses and hugs xox

==========

I laughed out loud when I read the bit about 'buffet'. I cannot bear to hear the word pronounced like a train buffer and the children love to tease me about that, and about my absolute hatred of other certain words such as 'front room', 'toilet' and 'serviette' all of which make me cringe. Sometimes (often when they were younger), Lottie and John would repeatedly chant 'serviette' at me when I ask them to put 'napkins' on the table, in my opinion the correct word to describe what you use to dab your mouth with whilst eating, whether it be the crisp starched white linen variety or simply a piece of kitchen roll. I make no distinction! The reason behind this? I put it down to my upbringing and being fortunate enough to attend Cheltenham Ladies' College, known by those who know as 'CLC'.

I texted Lottie to ask if it was a good time to phone her. I received no reply and decided to call her the next morning, early. Just as I was about to pick up the phone, it rang. I always expect bad news at that time of day, so was gob smacked when I answered it and heard, 'Surprise, surprise Mum!' It was Lottie! She certainly had surprised me! I told her I'd call her back but she said there was no need for she had been given a freebie ten minute phone card. It wasn't, for a minute later we got cut off.

I called her back. Nick was about to leave for a trial in Portsmouth and then on to God camp for the weekend, so I handed the phone over to him so he could talk to her first. Then Lottie and I spoke for ages. It was fabulous and I was on top of the world for the rest of the day.

Interestingly, she told me that with the exception of beef, food in Australia is much more expensive than in the UK. Even a cheap loaf of white bread costs £2! And three small battery-farmed chicken breasts £5! Spirits aren't cheaper either (a litre of vodka costs £20). You can only buy the proper brand names - supermarkets don't sell alcohol at all so the discounted 'own brands' we get over here are not an option. Furthermore, alcohol can only be purchased from 'Bottle Shops'. They've tried kangaroo meat a few times as that *is* cheap and we giggled about 'Skippy steaks'! Lottie said it tastes a bit like beef but sweeter, although it is very rich so you don't want to eat it too often.

I asked if she wanted me to post a pot of Marmite to her, for Lottie cannot exist without it. But no, she said it was available, as were most food items found at home, although David got upset one day when he asked for tinned oxtail soup – his favourite. The shop assistant had never heard of it and gave him some very strange looks as he attempted to describe the ingredients!

I was delighted to hear that my parcel had arrived (unlike my postcard) but they couldn't wait until Monday and had opened it already. I spoke to David and he was thrilled with the Simpsons goody bag and cash – and his singing card. He expressed surprise that his pressies weren't wrapped up with my usual silver foil – I told him that a twenty-first birthday warranted proper paper! I rarely buy wrapping paper. Silver foil doesn't require sellotape and both my family and friends expect it.

Lottie was delighted with her white chocolate money. She loves white chocolate. And she was really pleased with her lip salve as hers had run out. But most of all she was so grateful for the cash, something they are both very short of. It had already been spent – on surf boards! David had traded in 'Sheila' for a smaller one and Lottie had bought her own board. It was bright pink and she had named it 'Priscilla'! I shrieked with laughter and told her I couldn't wait to see the photos. I was so sorry they were pretty broke and asked if they needed any clothes – no, they were fine, Lottie said, just short of money. I said I would send some more as soon as I could.

They were to finish work in the call centre on 17 December, but hoped to return between Christmas and the New Year and for a couple of weeks in January in order to save more before they flew to New Zealand. Lottie reminded me that 'Lord of the Rings' was filmed there and they wanted to explore, as she so sweetly put it, 'hobbit land' and climb some mountain or other featured in the film. And bungee jump. I told her to tell me about *that* after they'd done it, not before! I said I'd phone again next week, which Lottie was clearly pleased about.

As ever, I found it so hard to say goodbye and I sensed that Lottie did too. I went into the kitchen, made myself another cup of coffee and sat down at the table where I dreamily recalled our conversation, several times over. I was abruptly brought back to reality by a knock at the back door. A parcel had arrived which needed my signature. It was some godly study books for Nick. Autograph given, I took a deep breath in and, with mixed emotions, started my daily chores.

I was thrilled that I'd spoken to Lottie, but sad because she was so damned far away. I also didn't relish the fact that Nick wouldn't be back until Sunday afternoon. 'Keep busy girl!' I told myself. I did.

As predicted, the bed didn't arrive. Chris and his girlfriend did, late afternoon. It was great to see Chris again, and to welcome Sal who was lovely. I have known Chris and his family for years. We spent an excellent holiday in France with his parents, Nigel and Debbie, a couple of years ago.

The Wells carnival was due to start at 7pm. The kids had decided to head into town beforehand and visit the fun fair. Unfortunately, only John went. Both Chris and Sal had developed bad stomachs so they stayed here and watched TV in front of the fire. That was such a shame as they had specifically come up to see the carnival. Chris had seen it before but it was the first time for Sal. Nevertheless, they had a nice evening but had gone to bed by the time I returned from supper out with Hils; I had decided to give carnival a miss this year.

Fiona Fridd

Accompanied by my family and friends, I have attended the Wells carnival many times. It is an annual event and enormous fun. The city is packed and the atmosphere is fantastic; everyone is in 'carnival' mood and cheer as the floats pass them by. Some of the floats are so big that they occasionally get stuck as they manoeuvre their way round the narrow streets. This only adds to the fun. Money is an important part of the carnival and many thousands of pounds are raised each year for worthy charities and causes. Special collection floats form part of the procession into which onlookers throw their loose change. If you watch from a high window you are not left out - a long 'drainpipe' is held up to you in order to collect your pennies!

My evening out with Hils was memorable. We met Jane and Ken for a pub supper. Afterwards, we phoned for a taxi only to be told there would be a wait of at least an hour; the carnival had just ended and the roads were gridlocked. We took up Jane and Ken's offer of a lift back to their house to have another drink and taxi home from there later.

Ken had his 2-seater sporty job with him. It was raining. Jane volunteered to get in the back and somehow managed to contort her body enough to squeeze it into the incredibly small space. Hils got into the front and I sat on her lap. I had to bend my neck down painfully low in order to fit under the soft top and how I got my left leg inside in order for Ken to shut the door I just don't know.

It was dreadfully uncomfortable for us three girls but all full of booze we saw the funny side of it and got the giggles, egged on by Jane's repeated shouts of expletives from the back. Someone farted. Our giggles turned into hysteria. The vibration of Hils laughter made my body bounce up and down and my head smacked against the roof. Ken pressed the button to open it. It slid back and my neck popped up like a spring, grateful for the release.

More shouts from Jane. 'Shut the ****ing roof Ken, I'm getting soaking wet back here!' So was I but that was infinitely preferable to my torturous neck position! Relief was short-lived for Ken did as Jane demanded and the roof glided back over us.

'Are we there yet?' I asked. More laughter as we had only moved 200 yards! Then Ken put his foot down. Yet more expletives from

Jane as the turbo kicked in and she was forced backwards, except there was no backwards for her body to go. I was grateful I could only see out of the side window for the hedgerows passed me by at an alarming rate.

But Ken got us back safely, helped us out of the car and we ran inside out of the rain. Ken opened a bottle of wine which disappeared rudely fast. Shortly afterwards our taxi arrived, which was probably just as well. It dropped me off first and then continued down the hill to take Hils home.

John and one of his mates, Phil, were still up and I joined them in the sitting room for a while. I don't remember what time I went to bed, suffice it to say I left John to lock up the house. The following morning when I staggered downstairs, the doors were locked but most of the lights had been left on all night.

After a mug of coffee and a couple of much needed paracetamol, I got dressed and laid the table. As luck would have it, my guests had ordered breakfast late so I had time to recover before I had to face the frying pan. Bacon and eggs over with and table cleared, I drove Einstein over to Julie's for a shampoo. On the way home, my car hit a large stone. I checked the tyres and they seemed fine. However, a couple of hours later when it was time to collect him, I could hear a strange 'thump, thump' noise as I reversed down the drive. The nearside front tyre was as flat as a pancake. Luckily, Lottie's car had been returned yesterday after its service, so I drove mine back into the garage and used hers.

That afternoon, before new guests arrived, I sank gratefully into the Snug sofa for a nap. In the evening, Nick called me after a long day of godly lectures and duties. At lunch break, his group were told to return by 2pm for an organised walk around the town. He and another student had hot-footed it to the nearest pub and returned at the time instructed only to find that the walk had started early. It took them a while to locate the group! Furthermore, before his final evening lecture, he had nipped outside for a ciggie. But like the walk, that session also started early so he was caught out yet again.

I asked if he had a decent bedroom. 'A bit cell-like' he replied, 'and some distance away from a bathroom.' Poor Nick, but at least he was now in the back of the Range Rover with a bottle of wine and a ciggie, the latter which he accidentally stubbed out on the inside of the window whilst we chatted. It was dark but he didn't want to draw attention to himself and so hadn't turned on the interior light. I'd be jolly glad to have him home tomorrow.

Before I went to bed I emailed Lottie:

11 November 2006

Hi Lot!

Here are a few pics of Tallinn (silver collar) and Riga (red collar). They sleep either in the salad bowl or on top of the boiler, but the bowl is their favourite spot! They continue to enchant us. Einstein was washed today and smells wonderful, but if he gets the chance he still scoffs the contents of the cat litter tray. Yuk!

John went to the carnival last night. It chucked it down but he said it was a good one. Chris and his bird stayed here as they had a tummy bug – and chucked it up! Hils and I had sups with Jane & Ken at Waldegrave Arms. Head wasn't good this morning. By the time you get this, David's 21st will be over. Ah! Hope he can remember some of the celebrations!

Getting late so off to bed soon. Just spoke to Daddy at God camp. They had a walk scheduled after lunch but it started early and he was still in the pub! He's looking forward to coming home tomorrow. John's got a rugby match and I'm cooking roast beef for us all in the evening.

Heaps of love and kisses and cuddles. Hope you get some amusing orders today!

Mum xxxxooooooooooxxxxxxx

=========

Chapter Thirteen

Rugby and Rats

On Sunday morning, I drove John down to the Wells rugby club for his match. I wished him good luck and he said he'd phone me when the game was over. We would all have lunch together before Chris and Sal had to catch their bus back to Plymouth. I received his call just after 1.30pm.

'Hi Mum,' he said.

'Hi Johnny,' I replied. 'Did you win?'

'No,' he said, 'and I think my nose is broken.'

Shocked to the core, I asked 'Oh God darling, are you all right?' an incredibly stupid question, but it just came out. John told me he was 'okay' but had been advised to get checked over by a doctor as quickly as possible.

'Is someone looking after you? What on earth happened?' I asked.

John assured me that the first aiders had been great and he was with John, his coach. But nothing, absolutely zero, zilch, could have prepared me for his description of what had occurred. Towards the end of the match, completely out of the blue, one of the opposing team's supporters had run onto the pitch and without hesitation punched him hard in the face. Initially blind to the pain, John had tried to go for the man but his team mates (and several of them at that) held him back. How I wished John had got him! I told him I'd be down straight away.

When I collected him, he looked dreadful. He had a white piece of wide strong tape across his nose which was heavily encrusted with dried blood and still oozed. His top lip was badly swollen and cut. There was blood splattered on his clothes and on his arms and hands and he was very pale and shaky. My nerves were shattered, both at the state he was in and from the horror of how it had happened.

I tried my best to compose myself, gave him a big but very gentle hug and squeezed his hand. My motherly instincts of protection were intense. I was desperate to provide comfort. Although he was incredibly brave and stoic, which his coach commented upon, I knew he needed that hug. His coach was a brilliant support and said he'd never encountered anything quite so shocking. He also said, with great delight, that the assailant had been marched firmly into the clubhouse and detained by members of the Wells club.

I helped John into the car and we drove home. Fortunately, Nick was on his way back from God camp and only ten minutes away. Just before I'd collected John, I'd called him on his mobile and filled him in.

When he returned, the barrister walked in; God camp was forgotten. He told me to take photos of John (for evidence). My hands shook as I held the camera. Nick took John to the local hospital in Shepton Mallet where he was quickly attended to. He was told that his blood pressure and pulse were both 'well up' and he should get plenty of rest. His nose wasn't actually broken (which apparently rarely occurs) although it had sustained a very nasty bang, and he had 'whiplash' to his neck as a result of the force of the blow.

When John came home, I helped him take his rugby shirt off without his nose being touched and he went upstairs for a very welcome shower. I took his mouth guard out of its box to wash it. It was covered in blood. I got the shakes again.

I telephoned the Police to report the incident. The female officer I spoke to was most sympathetic, told me not to worry and would arrange for an officer to interview John later in the day.

I was impressed with the way John handled the meeting. Although his voice was shaky and at times raised, he remained calm and gave a clear account of the attack and a description of his assailant. The interview ended after a very long two hours and many cups of tea, by which time John was absolutely exhausted and in increasing pain from his whiplash. I gave him some more painkillers which he gratefully swallowed down with a pint of Ribena.

We hugged each other for a long time. We both needed to be close and I nearly cried when John thanked me for my help. I kissed him goodnight and he went to bed. A little later, Nick went upstairs to check that he was okay. He was fine, he said, just sore and very tired. We retreated to the kitchen. I leaned gratefully against the Aga and welcomed its warmth. I took several deep breaths in an attempt to relax and slow down my pulse rate. Not much luck there. Nick poured us both a large Cointreau. And another. They helped. We talked about John's attack for a long while. It gave us some solace to share our thoughts and concerns but neither of us slept well that night.

The next day John stayed at home for some essential rest and recuperation. He was still in pain and looked very pale, but he put on a brave face. I made dental and physiotherapy appointments for him.

The Wells rugby club contacted me, as did the RFU headquarters in Twickenham; John's assault had been referred to their Child Protection Officer for a full enquiry. The Wells Journal, our local rag, called and wanted to run the story.

For most of the day I was busy with paperwork and phone calls. That was a pity because Keir and Ann arrived for a three night stay and I felt sorry I couldn't spend as much time with them as I had originally planned to.

Phone calls continued for the next few days. John saw his dentist who said that his mouth guard had saved his front teeth. The physiotherapist commenced treatment for his whiplash. The local rag came out and several friends phoned to express their disgust at what had happened and to wish John a speedy recovery. It was wonderful to have Keir and Ann with us, but their visit was marred by John's misfortune. Still, we had a lovely time and I was sad to see them go.

Some weeks later, we discovered that John's assailant was the opposing team's official coach! He received a caution from the Police and the RFU banned him from any further involvement with rugby, for good.

An email came through from Lottie that day. I hadn't told her about John until I knew David's birthday celebrations would be over.

16 November 2006

Hi! Had a great weekend and did loads of surfing. I got a surfing injury on Sunday. I was wiped out by a wave and my surfboard came back and the fins hit me in the side. I now have two nice big bruises! David's birthday went really well, we threw a surprise party for him at the hostel and then 20 of us went out for steaks at one of the really good pubs, plus cocktails and fizzy wine! I bought David a stripy cover for his surfboard which he's really pleased with. I got your text message but not till yesterday. That's mad! Poor John! I can't believe a spectator would do that, it's awful! Wish John to get well soon from me and David. Have to keep the message short as it's really busy in the call centre today with orders coming in thick and fast. Will speak to you soon, lots of love xox
=========

I found it eerie that both my children, thousands of miles away from each other, were injured within a few hours of one other. I hoped Lottie's bruises would soon get better, but I hoped even more that no more waves would 'wipe her out'. I was delighted to hear that David's birthday was such fun – good old Lot for organising a surprise party. She takes after me in that department for we are both masterminds at arranging anything along those lines. I replied:

16 November 2006

Hi Lot!

Fantastic hearing from you and SO pleased weekend and D's birthday went well. Poor you getting hit by Priscilla. Do take great care surfing - it was a weekend of injuries indeed. My nerves are shot! John's on the mend so please don't worry. Wells club are being fantastic.

Life Without Lottie: How I Coped (or didn't) During my Daughter's Gap Year

Am posting a parcel to you today (I wonder what it is?!!!). Can you accept UK cheques as presents? Keir and Ann would like to know. Loads of love - will call you within next couple of days.

Mum xxxxooooooooxxxxxxxx

=========

When I phoned I only got the ansafone. I received this text the following morning: *'Bruises much better, ready 2 get back out surfing this w/end! Glad John OK – send love. Yep, cheques would work, that'd be great! So glad its Sat tomoz, no work! Missin everyone lots xx'*

I replied back: *'Hi Lot! TGIF! Watch those waves! Can I phone now? Lol+miss u too! Mxoxxx'*

No reply came through, so I guessed her phone was either out of battery or out of signal. I left a message and asked her to text me when it was a good time to call. I hoped that would be soon. I went into Wells to buy a bed for John's old room. I'd had yet another blazing row on the phone with the supplier, who refused to give me a refund and told me he was about to go out of business anyway. With less than a slim chance to receive either the bed or a refund, I bought another one for £20 less which was delivered that afternoon. I kicked myself for not having used my local bed store in the first place but a lesson was learnt, albeit the hard way. Sometimes it pays *not* to use the internet for shopping!

Back in the summer, John had entered a competition on the rugby Six Nations website. The prize was two tickets to every England rugby match in the 2007 tournament. Not only that, two nights bed and breakfast accommodation in 5 star hotels and return transport were also included. He won! The timing was perfect, for John had something to divert his thoughts away from his assault. He also had to think about who to take to each match. Nick and I were over the moon for him.

Saturday was interesting. I only had one B&B room booked out, unusual over a weekend. I checked my diary and made a mental note of their names (Peter and Karen) in order to welcome them personally. When they arrived I didn't mention Karen by name but I did call Peter 'Peter', both when I shook hands with him and when I served them tea and biscuits.

Five minutes later, there was a knock at the door. Another couple turned up who said they were booked in for the night. The man introduced himself as 'Peter'. My heart sank. Luckily I had a spare B&B room and showed the second 'Peter' and his partner upstairs. They then joined Peter and Karen for tea.

But Peter and Karen *weren't* actually Peter and Karen. They politely told me they were called Ray and Gill! Having jotted down 'Peter and Karen' in my diary I had thus assumed they were the first couple to arrive as I hadn't expected anyone else. Thankfully, they all saw the funny side of it. I was mighty glad I hadn't booked out the second bedroom.

My guests retired to their rooms to unpack and have a rest before dinner. Shortly afterwards, the phone rang. Nick answered it. He had a brief conversation at the end of which I heard him say, '...don't worry, we'll be up in a minute'. I wondered what on earth was the matter. Nick told me it was Karen on the phone – from her bedroom. Apparently she was dreadfully allergic to feathers and wanted us to change the duvet and pillows! Karen met us at the bedroom door in an awful state. Her eyes and nose were streaming and she was scratching both arms which were already covered in big red bumps. We changed the bedding as quickly as possible and I offered them both a complimentary glass of wine.

Karen looked horrified.

'Oh no!' she said, 'I couldn't possibly...I've just taken an antihistamine!'

'All the more reason to have one!' I replied. Peter jumped at the chance of a drink and managed to persuade Karen to have a small glass. I rushed downstairs and filled two glasses to generous proportions. The following morning, Karen was better, breakfast went well and both couples said they had had a super stay and would return. I haven't seen Peter and Karen again, but Ray and Gill have been back several times.

On Sunday lunchtime, we had drinks at Jane and Ken's. We met Ken's daughter and son-in-law and their dog - a terribly old and doddery Alsatian. It went missing. Ken and family went into the garden to search. Jane returned briefly and I asked if we could help. She said no, it would be best if we went home. Just before she rejoined the search party, Nick announced that the dog had probably crawled under a hedge to die. That was not one of his most tactful comments!

As soon as we got home the phone rang. It was a local smallholder who told me that John had almost been shot. Oh great, I thought. What on earth now?! The farmer explained how he had a plague of rabbits on his land and had instructed someone that afternoon to shoot as many as possible. Just as that someone was about to shoot a big fat rabbit, out popped John and his mates from behind the hedge.

Afterwards, John told me they had decided to walk home from the bus across the fields. I repeated the niceties the farmer expected of me and hung up. Nick thought it was hilarious.

That evening, Jane phoned to say the dog had been found – twenty miles away! It had jumped into a truck and not been discovered until the driver had reached the end of his journey.

New B&B guests arrived, just for the one night. They were a young couple and obviously much in love. Nick asked if he could help with their luggage.

'No, that's okay,' replied the young blond piece as she lifted out a small sponge bag from the car. 'This is all I've got.' Nick told me he winked at her before he showed them up to their room. I ticked him off for that. They came down for breakfast *very* late the next morning and ate the lot. Their bed linen required a very hot wash!

20 November 2006

Hi! Sorry didn't call/text over the weekend, it's been really hectic and my phone ran out of battery and I didn't have time to charge it. Been surfing all day everyday and then fri and sat night went to big house parties and last night went to the pub to watch a band which was really good.

Spending so much money, just been told we're getting sacked straight after Xmas because they won't need us anymore, plus our shifts start drying up next week as they're cutting down the Xmas orders. It will be nice to have some more time off but we'll prob have to reduce the amount of time we spend in New Zealand. We also have a new plan - we might do the East Coast first and buy a camper van with some friends and then do New Zealand once we've saved up enough. We're also thinking about spending the last month or two in Asia and do Thailand, Malaysia, China etc as it's a lot cheaper than Oz.

Weather great but a bit hot - 40 tmoz! Rubbish having to be inside but it would be too hot to stay outside for long anyway. We have a rat problem in the hostel. They've taken up residence behind the work units in the kitchen! The owner is sorting it so hopefully we will be ratless soon! Can't think of any more news, got to get back to work now and to lots more old people wanting to order very large swimming costumes! Speak to you soon and lots of love xox

=========

I called Lottie and got straight through. I couldn't believe my luck! As ever, my heart skipped a beat when I heard her voice. The rat situation sounded dreadful. There were obviously many as Lottie said she had seen them eat out of the kitchen bin and run along the corridors. How disgusting!

David had offered to remove the kitchen units. I told Lottie in no uncertain terms to ensure he did no such thing and to leave that job up to the hostel owner. I had visions of him being attacked by half poisoned rats and ending up in A&E. I made her promise not to prepare any food in the kitchen until they were well gone and to inform environmental health if the problem persisted.

The amount of partying they were doing was obviously not helping cash flow. Lottie said she'd check the post shop in a couple of days to see if my parcel had arrived. I didn't tell her about the cash I'd slipped inside with the advent calendars. I wanted that to be a surprise. I asked how the surfing was going.

'Fantastic!' she said. She could now stand up for all of six seconds! But Priscilla may have to go in favour of a slimmer board as her arms aren't quite long enough to paddle effectively.

I conjured up a wonderful picture of Lottie paddling madly to 'catch a wave' without much success.

I emailed her the next day:

21 November 2006

Hi Lot!

Fantastic to speak yesterday! Appalled by the rat situation. For heaven's sake, don't use the kitchen and keep well out of their way.

It's hard being broke - I remember my student days (ah!!) and the struggle to make ends meet. But as long as you're happy that's all that matters. Exciting news about maybe touring the East Coast and a great idea to see a bit more of the world on your return journey. I loved your story about 'Goon' wine!

Have actually started my Xmas shopping! Waterstones have taken over Ottakars and they have an awesome selection of books, so bought a few pressies there. My 'little book' has begun!

HEAPS of love and hugs from us all. Miss you loads. And watch out for them rats!

Mum xxxxooooooooooooxxxxxxxxxxxxxxxxxxxxx

=========

Lottie told me that 'Goon' wine is the nickname for the cheapest wine available. It is dirt cheap, in both senses of the words. It comes in a plastic box and the ingredients are listed on the back. As well as grapes, these include fish bones, dairy products and an array of non-pronounceable chemicals! Needless to say, Lottie and David bought a box but won't be buying any more. She said it made her think about the roughest Somerset 'Scrumpy' cider, rumoured to have dead rats at the bottom of the fermentation tanks – perfectly preserved!

That reminded me of when Nick and I met at Oxford and we used to drink Scrumpy out of a plastic barrel which Nick brought back from Somerset after the holidays. It was all we could afford and got us drunk and fast. We would leave the last couple of inches in the barrel for that was always extremely cloudy and full of 'bits'. How our stomachs survived I will never know!

My 'little book' appears every Christmas. I buy a new one each year and write in it a list of all the people I have to buy presents for and, as my shopping progresses, what I have bought them. I keep it in my handbag. I have brought Lottie and John up to respect ladies' handbags and *never* to look inside them, but I know only too well that when they were little the temptation to take a peek was sometimes too strong for them to resist. They never confessed to this but I think that when some of their presents were unwrapped on a certain Christmas Day, the contents were not quite such a surprise as they should have been.

I can remember one Christmas when I was little and firmly instructed by my parents *not* to go into the cupboard in the Drawing Room. I couldn't resist either. At the back of the cupboard, covered in a big blanket, I found the most wonderful dolls house in the world that every little girl dreams of. It even had little light bulbs! But my discovery completely and utterly ruined that particular Christmas Day for me. I never went on the hunt again. I hoped that Lottie and John's first peek inside my little book would be their last. Maybe I shall find out one day.

Farewell party – Manor Farm

Blue Bunny and Snoopy at Easter

Nick and me

David and Kim - Harrods

Nick the barrister

My birthday with Norman, Nick, Beryl and Keir

John, Will and Nick - Majorca

Welcome to Perth

David with 'Sheila'

Lottie with 'Priscilla'

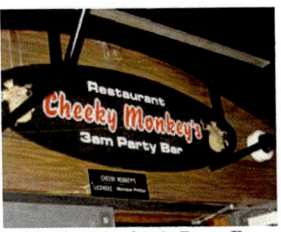

Cheeky Monkey's Party Bar

Great Ocean Road

Manly Youth Hostel – Card Game

Christmas Day – Manly Beach

The Train

The Yacht

No more beer!

Cocktails!

Oz Day

Camp – Fraser Island

Fraser Island group

Windswept Lottie

Lottie in Bali

Lottie with Skippy

Heli Flight – Mini Sammy

Cairns – Shampoo Waterfall

Apostles

Byron Bay

Hong Kong

Hard Rock Café - Sydney

Sparticus

Sydney Opera House

verge, the car ended up at a very strange angle as we were on a slope and, with a lurch, the engine stalled.

He panicked and muttered 'Shit, shit' as he tried to restart the car, but the engine stalled again. He'd forgotten to shift out of gear and had taken his foot off the clutch. The other driver pulled in to a field entrance to let John pass.

'Keep calm, keep calm!' I said and tried desperately hard not to sound as panicky as he did. 'Put your foot on the clutch, go into neutral!' He did it.

Then he couldn't get the car into first gear. Horrific grinding noises emanated forth as the seconds ticked past. The other driver smiled at us knowingly. John tried to appear as if he was totally in control and sorry for the hold up - he waved at him in rather a nonchalant way. That had quite the opposite affect - his actions were a complete giveaway that he hadn't much of a clue.

At last John managed to get the car into gear but took his foot off the clutch too quickly and stalled. He tried again – and again – and each time the car lurched forward and straight back again. After at least eight attempts, we finally moved forwards but at such a rate that we shot out of the verge and headed straight for the other car.

'Left! Left!' I screamed.

John pulled the wheel round just in time and we passed the man, his smile now long gone. John said 'I think I need some practice with hill starts.' That was the understatement of the year! I made him drive *very* slowly to the end of the road, where I insisted we changed places and I took the car home, despite John's best pleads to have another go. I had had quite enough for one day and headed home the safe way, my way.

I sent Lottie a text and told her I had survived, but only just! She replied and said to get in extra wine supplies. She emailed me a couple of days later:

24 November 2006

Hi! It was great speaking to you the other night. Still haven't heard from John but I suppose that's boys for you! Tell him good luck with drivin lessons and to look after Mr. T!

Chapter Fourteen

Driving

I was in Tesco when I received a text from John: *Just got back in, drivin is amazing! See u later. John x'*

John had had his first proper driving lesson. I called him at home. He was ecstatic and said that it had gone really well.

'I got up to 60!' he told me.

'Good God, John!' I exclaimed. 'Didn't Colin tell you to slow down?!'

'Er, yes, he did actually.'

When I returned, he begged me to take him out in 'Mr. T' – Lottie's name for her car. Boy! I needed a drink afterwards! We only went up and down our local lane twice. That was quite enough. The first time was a complete white knuckle ride. John revved up the engine so much in between gear changes that I honestly thought the poor little car would explode and each time it leapt forward at an alarming pace. Instinctively I pressed my legs hard against the front of the car – at imaginary brakes. How I wished for dual controls!

'Slow down!' I shouted, 'and keep both hands on the steering wheel!'

He careered around a corner – in the middle of the road.

'Keep left!' I yelled.

John swung the car into the verge and back out again.

'Christ, boy! Slow down now or that's it'! Thankfully he did. I wondered how on earth Colin had kept his cool.

To begin with, the second trip down the lane was a little less hair-raising, although my heart raced like a formula one car (bad analogy!), my palms were sweaty and I kept both fingers firmly crossed. Damn it, we met a car coming in the opposite direction.

'Slow down and pull in a bit,' I said, for the lane was certainly not wide enough for two cars to pass. John pulled too far into the

Life Without Lottie: How I Coped (or didn't) During my Daughter's Gap Year

Your postcard from Majorca arrived yesterday! Better late than never, it looked beautiful. Can't wait to get the parcel with the pics etc in it!

It's been really hot and humid. We've had forest fires in the suburb that we work in so the sky is a funny yellow colour and smells pretty smokey, but don't worry, they're nowhere near us.

The weekend is supposed to be even hotter so will spend lots of time on the beach and work on my tan! Hope everything is ok at home and send my love to everyone. I'll check the post office again on Monday to see if the parcel has arrived. lots of love xox

=========

24 November 2006

Hi Darling!

Forest fires must be awful. Hope they don't spread. Don't sunbathe too much - watch out for premature wrinkles!

The religious group I expected this weekend is not so - couldn't be more different - they are 'Stargate' fans attending a convention in the Bishop's Palace, complete with stars from the show and an auction of memorabilia. So Manor Farm is full of geeks! All are ladies, apart from one rather earnest young lad who doesn't say much but I think he's enjoying himself. The ladies obviously are - breakfast is a noisy affair! Daddy keeps rattling on about Doctor Spock and the Vulcans, even though he knows that's 'Star Trek' speak, and repeatedly chants 'Neep neep' in front of the guests which makes them howl with laughter! We have made some lovely new friends amongst them, particularly an ex wine buff from Denver called Pat.

As you didn't mention rats, I assume they've gone? Have posted two large Christmas parcels to you (tee hee!!!). Do open them as everything is individually wrapped. Don't lose the envelopes inside!!! Let me know when they arrive.

HAVE A WONDERFUL WEEKEND!!! Will be thinking of you. Loads and loads of love and hugs.

Mum xxxxxxxooooooo

=========

Fiona Fridd

The parcels contained 'fun' Christmas presents, cheques for Lottie and David (their main presents) and a little stocking for Lottie filled with a mixture of luxury and practical items. It gave me enormous pleasure to decide what to buy. I had to be careful not to opt for large, heavy or fragile items, but this made the selection process all the more interesting and I love a challenge.

For Lottie's stocking, I bought Clarins mascara and lip gloss, and two pairs of 'Sloggie' mini briefs which I knew she liked. I found the sweetest red felt stocking in Bastins. Sticking plasters, safety pins, face wipes, paracetamol, chocolate reindeer noses (thanks Tesco!), and a couple of other small things completed the pressies.

I got David a packet of instant Oxtail soup and a bar of Dove soap – his favourite (he hates shower gel!). And for them both, a mini Christmas pudding and a packet of custard mix.

I went to the Post Office and bought two of the largest jiffy bags they had and picked up two customs declaration labels. I returned home in great spirits, delighted with my purchases and looked forward to wrapping everything up.

I got organised. I emptied all my shopping bags out onto the kitchen table and sang to myself happily as I collected together sellotape, scissors, silver foil and a pen. I found some gold and red Christmas labels left over from last year. That was a relief as I had forgotten to buy any! I wrapped everything neatly in foil and wrote separate labels for Lottie and David and some joint ones – for the Christmas pudding and custard.

I'd bought gold and red shiny ribbon and tied this around the presents to make them look pretty and scoured the ribbon ends into curls. I didn't stick on any bows for I knew they would get squashed in the post and look awful.

All presents wrapped and labels attached, I put the non-stocking items into one jiffy bag, added in a few photos of the kittens and our Majorca holiday, sealed it up with brown parcel tape and addressed it to Lottie, c/o Manly Post Shop. I then started to stuff her stocking.

It hit me when I was about half way through. I was totally unprepared. At first, my heart rate increased, then I went hot and my spine prickled from top to bottom, the same reaction when a

Kitchen - Manor Farm

Fishing boats - Bali

Riga in salad bowl

Morse & Einstein with Joann (guest)

Me with my kids - Glastonbury 2007

Fraser Island

Tigers – Australia Zoo

Life Without Lottie: How I Coped (or didn't) During my Daughter's Gap Year

teacher has squeaked chalk across a blackboard. I felt shaky, my lips began to tremble and I started to cry.

With a desperate voice, I stammered out 'Oh Lottie, I don't want to have to post these presents to you; I want you here with me for Christmas!' It was a useless plea, I knew. I had lost control.

Both dogs waddled over and looked quizzically as if to say 'What's wrong?' They nuzzled against my legs. I crouched down and gratefully cuddled them both until my sobs began to subside and I did my best to wipe the tears off my face with the palms of my hands. I took several deep breaths. The worst had passed and I regained my composure.

With the odd sudden intake of breath, I completed Lottie's stocking and popped two cheques inside the Christmas card which we had all written the night before. I placed everything carefully into the second jiffy bag and then made a split second decision. Without further ado, I grabbed both parcels and drove back into town. I went straight to the Post Office and posted them. I felt much better once this was done.

That weekend, I was kept busy in the mornings with my 'Neep neep' guests. The afternoons were wonderful. Nick and I had time to ourselves and took things a little easier, which was much needed by us both.

We chatted to one another, read, did the Saturday Telegraph general knowledge crossword, a weekly ritual (well, we attempted it), listened to good music and in the evenings lit the fire in the sitting room, swiftly accompanied by two fat bassets and two tiny kittens.

At last the four of them had settled down. It was a lovely picture to see them curled up together, especially Tallinn who lay on top of Einstein's tail and played with it each time it wagged, a frequent occurrence!

The following week when I spoke to Lottie I was absolutely horrified to learn that one of my parcels had arrived but had been opened by Customs, all the presents unwrapped and a large 'Quarantined' sticker slapped on the jiffy bag which the authorities hadn't even bothered to re-seal. Lottie said she was amazed anything had arrived at all! I was terribly upset – not only had Customs confiscated some items but they had also denied my darling daughter the pleasure of opening the presents herself and discovering the surprises inside.

Damn them! The Aussies are strict about food being taken from one state to another, she told me; at stop offs during their long train journey between Perth and Adelaide, they had been firmly instructed to 'leave any food items behind' before they re-boarded the train. So, maybe my food presents were the reason behind the ravaged parcel, although it seemed that only the Christmas pudding and custard had been taken. David's soup had arrived and he was thrilled to bits with it.

I told her that John had posted his present separately, so they should also look out for his parcel, as well as my second one and we agreed to speak again next week. This time, after we'd said goodbye, the anger I felt towards Customs replaced the normal feeling of loss. I was fuming.

The next day, I was delighted to receive not one but two emails from Lottie:

29 November 2006

Hi, was great speaking to you! Thanks so much for all the things you sent me! I can't believe the Xmas pud was quarantined! The pics of the kittens r so cute, they look so white! Hopefully the other parcels will arrive soon. I've got a half day on Thurs so I'll go check the post office then. Glad to report all rats have gone and kitchen is safe to use again.

David and I might be buying a camper van - one of our friends in the hostel is a mechanic so he is going to have a look at it first. It seems great though and comes with a stove, tent, table/chairs and plenty of cutlery and pots and pans. So watch this space!

We have to look for new jobs as we have only been given 5 shifts each for the whole of December. Not good. Hope to speak again soon! Lots of love and missing u loads xox

==========

29 November 2006

Life Without Lottie: How I Coped (or didn't) During my Daughter's Gap Year

Just a quick update on the campervan situation - we bought it! Our mechanic friend said it needs about 200 pounds worth of work so we managed to knock the price down from 900 pounds to 550! What's even better is that it's worth about 2000 pounds! The couple had to sell before they leave Australia so we got a really good price! It even has a roof rack for our surf boards!! Once you take the mattress out it turns into an 8 seater so we can go on trips with our friends. Another bonus is that we've got a safe parking space behind the hostel. I'll send some pics on.

Day off tmoz so will sort that out. lol xox

=========

29 November 2006

That's fantastic news! I am SO thrilled for you! Wow! I think the best accessory **by far** has to be the board rack!!! What a great deal - well done! Just make sure you get it fixed properly before using. Please! Do send pics soon!

As ever, wonderful speaking to you. Am so sorry the Xmas pud went missing. What a pity. The big parcel on its way has your stocking in it and two important envelopes for you and David. I hope they arrive intact. The smaller parcel is from John and is wrapped up in proper Xmas paper! He did it all himself, even what's inside the present. Maybe it was the silver foil. Dad said the X-ray machines wouldn't like it so I won't use that again.

All well here. Weather is mild but oh so wet. Bottom of road completely flooded and water mighty deep! V high winds 2 nights ago - so much so that a tree by George's farm fell across the road and blocked it.

Had hair cut yesterday - much needed - so I feel glam! Having lunch with Jennie at Andre's new bistro (was Chapels). So glad you got the pics of kittens etc. They are incredible! Now eating like horses, growing fast and their fur darkening slightly, particularly Riga's. I've nicknamed Riga 'Riggs' aka Lethal Weapon as he behaves just like Mel Gibson - mad as a hatter!

A week on Friday we go to Appledore. Fab! And I've just booked flights to Palma early March and 5 nights in an amazing apartment with a huge sunken bath. John staying at home which he's fine about. I'll get Ian to move in and supervise whilst we're away.

So relieved to know hostel is rat free and that forest fires have died down. I had visions of you waking up to find a rat peering down at you amidst a room full of smoke!

John's had his second driving lesson. Having sups with Caroline, Jane, Kay etc. tomorrow. Yes, you guessed – going to Mendip Inn! Pet & Peter spending Xmas with Grannie & Grandad and we're joining them for lunch on Xmas Eve which will be nice.

Heaps of love, miss you SO much and wish I could see you in the camper van! Have loads of fun sorting it out and making it lovely - I know you will. If you need me to send any bits for it just let me know - and I won't use silver foil!!!

Mum xxxxxxxxxx

=========

Over the next few days, every time the boiler fired up it made strange whooshing noises. When these escalated to almighty bangs (which made the kittens run for their lives), I had it serviced. Then the Aga decided to play up. I could smell oil in the kitchen, just a vague whiff at first, but by the evening it reeked and when I checked inside the workings, large yellow flames leapt out at me. I immediately switched it off and called the engineer first thing the following morning by which time the Aga was stone cold, as was the kitchen.

I was put down as an 'emergency visit' and, that afternoon, the Aga engineer arrived. He serviced and cleaned the inside workings before he fired the beast up again. All was well, or so I thought.

The following morning, when I came downstairs, the wretched thing had gone out and flatly refused to relight despite my several attempts to do so. I was put down for another 'emergency visit' and hoped it would be soon.

Fortunately I only had two breakfasts which could be cooked on the hotplate. I hoped my guests wouldn't both want 'full English' and the engineer could rectify the problem later. He couldn't. My poor Aga required a new thermostat which wasn't in stock. I had to wait until Monday. As a result, the kitchen remained freezing cold all weekend and I had six guests in.

Breakfasts were an utter nightmare, not helped by constant yowls from the kittens who strongly objected to being shut inside their pen. The last thing I wanted was for either (or both) of them to burn their paws on the hot plate.

4 December 2006

Hi hi! Just sent off Xmas cards and bits and bobs - the cut off date is tomorrow so hopefully they will be with you in time.

We took the van on a road trip up the coast last weekend. It rained non-stop and there was a massive storm. I've never seen anything like it! Luckily we took plenty of alcohol and sat in the van and got drunk. It was good fun as there were five of us but then the tent flooded (David and I slept in the van) and our friends got soaked and we ended up leaving the camp site at 8am. The tent next to us got blown away! We're going on another road trip this weekend – depending on the weather as the tent isn't waterproof!

I collected another parcel today which had my stocking in it! V exciting! It also got opened by customs so I don't know if anything is missing. Still no sign of John's parcel, but I got an envelope from Ganda and Ann. Please thank them from me!

Only three days of work to go! Yay! All work is drying up for Xmas so will be difficult to find work to keep funds up. Hope to speak to you soon and lots of love Lotty xox
=========

Christ! They'd opened her stocking as well! I was livid. If Customs had nicked the Clarins mascara, they could shove it right up their xxxxx!

4 December 2006

Hi Lot!

Fab hearing from you! Road trip sounded interesting! Glad alcohol came to the rescue. Better luck next weekend. Must be great having your own wheels. We had horrendous storms and high winds on Sat night - noise woke me up - but no trees down and Manor Farm still as solid as the rock it stands on. Thrilled your stocking has arrived but am furious it was opened. Do hope everything's there. No peaking now!

All news when we speak.

Loads of love, Mum xxxxxxxxooooooooooxxxxxxxxxxx

==========

I made several attempts to phone but, like so many times before, only got as far as Lottie's ansafone. Five times I left her a message, the last of which was highly garbled due to my frustration. I decided to retry tomorrow; the poor girl wouldn't appreciate any more messages from me today! But tomorrow only gave the same result, and the next day too. Damn, and blast it! Still, we kept in touch by text which was great although I did want to speak to her before Nick and I headed down to Appledore for the weekend. That was just not to be. I was entirely at the mercy of the mobile phone networks to provide a decent enough signal, which they didn't – all week. How I despised them.

Chapter Fifteen

Appledore

Nick and I had stayed in Appledore earlier in the year. It was our first visit there and we had fallen in love with the place, and thus we had a good idea of where our cottage was and found it easily. The outside didn't look up to much but I recalled the brochure's description and felt reasonably confident that the inside would be lovely. It was perfectly awful and damned cold!

Without further ado I sent the same text to Lottie and to John: *'Arrived safely in Appledore. Cottage naff! Off to pub for supper. lol Mxxx'*

'Naff' was the understatement of the year! I wouldn't have called it a cottage at all. To me, the word 'cottage' conjures up a picture of a pretty little house, old and with character, with an open fire, an exposed beam or two, a cosy feel. Ha! Ours had absolutely none of these, well, apart from a ghastly black plastic beam across the ceiling of a very dated kitchenette. The walls were paper thin, the windows were the cheapest money could buy, as were the dark red see-through curtains which hung sadly skewed due to a pathetic lack of sufficient hooks. There was no central heating system to speak of, just less than luke warm night storage heaters and a perfectly frightful two bar electric wall-mounted heater in the sitting room – the focal point - above which was the most disgusting cardboard faded picture of Venice in shades of dismal browns and greens.

On the plus side, there was a half decent three piece suite and a lovely view of the sea (discovered in daylight the next morning). For hot water, we had to switch on the immersion heater and for all electricity, we had to push £1 coins into a meter which was positioned so high up the wall that we had to stand on a chair in order to reach it. Determined to be warm and not plunged into sudden darkness, we emptied our purses and came up with eight coins. During the weekend we fed the damn thing with many more.

Fiona Fridd

There were two bedrooms, both furnished courtesy of charity shop left overs from the 1960s, more see-through curtains in an uninviting steel grey colour, and tiny puce pink bedside lamps. We decided on the one which overlooked the sea. The bathroom opposite was icy cold. When I sat down on the loo for a welcome end-of-journey pee, with zero warning I was immediately jettisoned to the left and nearly fell off! When I lifted the seat I discovered that the fixings were broken, save for one hanging in there for dear life. From then on, I treated that seat with the utmost of respect and, if I was careful, managed to get the jettison down to a gentle slide.

We didn't locate the immersion heater until the next morning. Instead of waiting for it to heat the water, we decided to use the electric shower over the bath. That was a laugh. I would like to think of us as 'intelligent' but it took us at least twenty minutes to work out how to get hot water out of it and then we were either scalded or iced. So much for my dream of sharing long and luxurious baths full of sexy smelling bubbles surrounded by candles!

We spent as little time as possible in that bathroom. But we made the most of it – we were away from home and on our own – and that was just perfect in itself.

Over the weekend, Lottie and I exchanged texts. I didn't hear from John at all – typical of a teenage boy – but he had a short conversation with Nick on how to make the volume work on Nick's laptop so we could actually listen to the CDs we'd brought with us. We caught the bus into Bideford and sat at the front of the top deck. It brought back fond memories of my young teenage years when a group of us, all giggling girls, would scamper upstairs to knab the front seats and chatter incessantly whilst we tried to eye up any good-looking boys at the back. This time, all the other passengers were on the lower deck. We held hands and had an elevated view of houses; their quaint chimneys, a couple of belvederes and the sea beyond as the bus bumped and swung its way into the town.

Once in Bideford, we ambled around its charming narrow cobbled streets and stopped to browse inside a couple of secondhand bookshops before we headed for the pannier market at the top end of town. There were many stalls and it was very busy.

Nick got a great pair of shoes for a tenner and bought me a lovely pair of gloves. I thought fondly of Lottie as I chose the pink ones.

When we left the market, Santa drove past us on his sleigh. He waved at the crowds and shouted 'Ho, Ho, Ho!' We waved back and shouted 'Merry Christmas, Santa!' I squeezed Nick's arm, for it was yet another reminder that Lottie would not be with us this Christmas.

We were hungry and so headed back down towards the quay to Quigley's Irish Bar & Restaurant. We had had a super lunch there during our last visit and decided to return. In typical Irish fashion we were greeted with 'Good evening!' by the barman and shown to a table big enough for us to spread out the Saturday papers we'd bought earlier. We ordered food and drinks and had a go at the crossword. We laughed at the simplicity of certain clues and groaned at the complexity of others we couldn't even attempt.

After lunch we both lit cigarettes with my lighter as Nick's had run out. He discarded it in the ashtray. Shortly afterwards, he asked for the bill and paid a visit to the gents. I flicked my ash into the ashtray. Immediately there followed an enormous 'Bang!' as clouds of black smoke and ash were suddenly hurled into the air, landing all over me and the table. Nick's lighter obviously wasn't empty after all.

I let out a loud scream and instinctively threw my arms in the air and the barman rushed over to me, just as Nick re-appeared. It was hilarious and, I thought, could only have happened in an Irish bar. I grabbed my napkin and tried my best to wipe the ash-ridden table into a pile whilst I apologised profusely. Nick took some notes out of his wallet and put them on top of the bill.

'I hope you've left a good tip!' I said. The waiter burst out laughing. So did we. We wished him 'a very Happy Christmas' and left, still laughing. On our way back to the bus stop we called in at a newsagent and bought not one but two new lighters, just in case.

The entire weekend was heavenly and we forged an even stronger love for one another. But Monday morning came and Nick was due back in court. Thus, at 5.10am, in the pitch black and pouring rain, we packed up the car and headed home. The first thing I did was to check my emails. There was one from Lottie!

10 December, 2006

Hi! Hope you had a good weekend and John didn't leave the house too messy! The weather here has been great but now we're in the middle of another massive storm! Surfed all weekend - we discovered a new bay just around the corner from Manly which isn't so choppy and better for surfing. I've got a new job starting tomorrow in a deli in the mall down the road. Hopefully it will go better than the last deli/sandwich job! I hope my parcel has arrived. I've found a good internet café so I'll send on new pics. Not much else to say. Life at the hostel is still great and everyone in at the moment is really nice. Missing you all lots and lots, especially leading up to Christmas. It's starting to get quite Christmassy here but not the same without the cold weather, although there's a lot of spray snow in shop windows. That looks a bit odd when its 35+ degrees outside! lots and lots of love xox

==========

11 December, 2006

Hi Darling!

Fabulous to get your email! Thanks so much! Appledore was a wonderful weekend of pure escapism. We bussed into Bideford on Sat, found some lovely shops and ended up in a great Irish bar for lunch. It's so hard not having you here - I know just how you feel - but glad to know the Aussies have spray snow!

GOOD LUCK with your new job. Can't possibly be worse than the must-have-carrot place with the shitty manager. And good that it's close by. Let me know how it goes!

Forgot to tell you - the dogs and kittens sent you a little present which I hope got through. It was in one of the two large jiffy bags but I can't remember which one. Will let you know when *your* parcel arrives! Can't wait!

Have a fantastic week; hope the storm blows over soon. VERY wet and windy here but meant to brighten up later.

Missing you loads and loads and sending tons of love and hugs. Need a chat soon!!!

Life Without Lottie: How I Coped (or didn't) During my Daughter's Gap Year

Mum xxxxooooooooooxxxxxxxx
=========

A postcard arrived from Lottie. It was such a lovely surprise to find it amongst a wad of Christmas cards in our post box. The picture was of Manly Beach which looked fabulous with clean white sand and the clearest blue skies and sea, interrupted only by huge white rollers. At the edge of the sands was a cluster of low apartment blocks. Above these, Lottie had written *'We live here!'* and drawn an arrow which pointed down at one of them. What a fantastic location for a youth hostel, I thought.

Her postcard read: *'Happy Christmas!!! I hope you all have an excellent day and drink lots and eat loads of yummy food! I will be thinking of you lots and missing you millions! We will be sitting on the beach drinking fizzy wine and having the traditional Aussie Xmas bbq! Love you all so much. Lotty xxx'*

David had added a note at the end: *'Merry Xmas. Lots of love David xoxox'*

My stomach knotted. The run up to Christmas without Lottie was bad enough and I hoped that Christmas Day would not be too difficult. I knew that Nick and John experienced similar feelings, but I was determined to do everything I could to make the day as happy as possible, for all of us.

I scanned the postcard picture into the computer and set it as my new background. To receive something hand written from Lottie way outshone her texts and emails. It was so much more personal. I decided to write her a letter in long hand. I knew it wouldn't get to her before Christmas but I knew she would appreciate it more than computer or mobile contact, as I did.

14 December, 2006

Hiya! Glad the house didn't get burnt down or anything whilst you were away! I think there was a parcel from the animals - I'll check when I get back. The new job is going well - I'm working in a large organic supermarket which is really cold because of all the fridges but everyone seems friendly and all I have to do is slice cheese and meat so that's not too bad! Got a text from John yesterday which was nice. Wish him good luck in his mocks from me!

David had a little accident last night - the fridge in the hostel was stuffed full and when I opened it a bottle of wine fell out onto his foot and broke (the bottle not the foot!). David got quite a big cut on his foot. We went down to A&E this morning to get it looked at and to make sure there was no glass left in it. David is fine but he has to keep a bandage on for 3/4 days. Could you please pass on the message to Jill and get her to call David so he can let her know he's alright. Apart from that no other dramas! I've got the day off today which is probably just as well so I can help David hop round the hostel! Back to work tomorrow. The weather is getting a little too hot for us now. Missing you all lots and will email again soon! lol xox

=========

I have never known anyone quite so accident prone as David. Even during their farewell party at home he not only fell off the front porch but also twisted his ankle when he careered down the water slide. The latter injury resulted in a visit to A&E. Fortunately he was so pissed when he fell off the porch that he didn't do any serious damage. He was very lucky, as he landed with a fair wallop. I phoned Jill and told her about the latest incident. Needless to say she wasn't surprised. Before I settled down to the daunting task of writing our Christmas cards, I replied:

14 December, 2006

Hi Lot!

So sorry to hear about the foot - typical David! Glad he got it checked and a proper dressing applied. Did you need to use your medical insurance? Have spoken to Jill and she will call him soon. She's fine, sends lots of love and is very excited about their forthcoming trip to Cyprus (although Kim wants to stay at home to watch TV!).

Your parcel has arrived! I've taken off the customs label so that Daddy and John won't know what's in it. Can hardly wait to open it on Christmas Day!

Daddy in Bristol on a new case (won yesterday's which he said was a miracle). Bugger - just seen the time. Must wake John up and rush him down to catch bus! Will finish this later...

Back again... Decided to do my shopping after I'd dropped John off. Tesco was heaving - nightmare Christmas crowds already. I queued for ages at Post Office, then did bank, pet shop and filled up with petrol. All exciting stuff for a Thursday! It was great to come home and find Claire had almost finished cleaning the house. Incredibly warm here (12) but incessant rain so her clean floors won't last long once the dogs have run in and out a few times! Kittens are growing so fast. Will send on more pics soon.

Thrilled the new job is good. Don't catch cold with all those fridges about. What's the pay like? Good timing that you have today off so you can help David.

Will call you soon and keep texting. Missing you tons and tons and thinking of you lots and lots! Do tell David I hope his foot gets better quickly and he can return to surfing soon.

Huge hugs and love and more.

Mum xxxooooooooxxxxxxxx

==========

I tried to phone Lottie many times but couldn't get a signal. God, I hoped that didn't happen on Christmas Day. I battled my way through Wells and actually finished my Christmas shopping. Carol singers were in the Market Place and I joined the group around them, grateful to put my shopping bags down for a while. After I had listened to 'In the Bleak Midwinter' (ironic, as it was sunny) a boy who can't have been more than five years old began a solo of 'Little Donkey'. He had a quiet voice and was obviously terrified but sounded quite enchanting. Probably due to nerves, his voice cracked up. I felt so sorry for him as his face blushed a deep cherry red colour. One of the adult singers gave him a swift prod in the back and the little chap struggled his way through to the end of the song.

I started to clap; I just couldn't resist. Others quickly followed suit which caused the lad to blush even deeper but he managed a smile. I gave him the thumbs up sign, picked up my bags (which seemed a good deal lighter than before) and jostled my way back to the car.

At the weekend, John held on to the stepladders whilst Nick climbed up and through the hatch into the kitchen roof. It was time to get the decorations down! I had reluctantly agreed with Nick not to put quite so many up this year because of the kittens, but once I had almost finished, the house looked lovely. The usual pine swag was looped across the mantelpiece above the fire in the sitting room which I adorned with small decorations and a string of tiny white fairy lights. One tree was put in the usual corner and festooned with decorations, many of which were made by Lottie and John from their junior school days. Our Christmas 'star', years old, was placed on the top. A second, bigger tree was put at the end of the main entrance hall. I decorated this one only with red and gold baubles.

On the top, with great pride, I placed not the usual and accepted star or angel, but the special fun decoration Lottie had insisted we use when she was a little girl and has been used every year since – a see-through white rubber gecko with a long tapering tail and a bright red ribbon which she had tied around his neck! Needless to say it has never failed to prompt some very peculiar looks from my guests over the years, but none of them have ever made any audible comment!

I sent Lottie a text: *'Decorations up! Gecko in place! Hope D's foot better. Miss u! lol m xxx'*

She emailed me a couple of days later:

18 December, 2006

Hi!

All well here, thanx for texts! I can picture my gecko up! The weather is boiling so it's quite nice working amongst fridges. I'm doing 7 days this week but finish early on Xmas Eve and a load of us are going down the pub. The job is a bit boring but not as much as the call centre!

Had a really good bbq Sunday night and a bit of all day drinking, just like Sunday at home! It reminded me of summer in the garden.

Life Without Lottie: How I Coped (or didn't) During my Daughter's Gap Year

David's foot is on the mend. He's still hopping around so no work for him till after Xmas. Glad my parcel arrived. I'm afraid it's nothing too exciting - I just thought you'd like a few aussie things! I got an email from Grandad to say he's posted me a cheque so I'll have to go check the post office! The hostel is covered in decorations but it still doesn't feel that Xmas-y.

I met someone I used to go to school with at Wells Cathedral on Manly beach! His name is Simon and he was in my tutor group for 3yrs! He's out here travelling too and is doing a sailing course. We're going to go for a drink sometime this week. So strange to meet someone from home!

The prop shaft on the van is knackered so we need to get that fixed but it should only cost about 70 pounds. Our mechanic friend is going to help us find a good garage to sort it out.

Hope to speak to you very soon, missing everyone lots and lots! I'm free for phone calls after 5.30ish our time every evening. When I speak to you on Christmas Day I'll be finishing my day when yours is starting! lots and lots of love xoxoxoxoxoxoxo
=========

I maintained contact with Lottie by text until finally, albeit days later, I actually got a signal and spoke to her. That lifted my spirits. Lottie told me she'd traded in Priscilla for a smaller board. She hadn't named the new one as yet but described it as 'baby blue' in colour and 'narrower and shorter than Priscilla' and her surfing had much improved. Great news! She mentioned the camper van. I said I hoped they managed to find a decent (and trustworthy!) mechanic to repair the prop shaft and warned her that I thought it would cost much more than £70 for a 'proper job' to be done. But Lottie didn't take much notice as she was so excited about the prospect of heading off in it to the East Coast with a group of friends towards the end of January.

How I love the enthusiasm of the young – oblivious to the worries of reality until they actually happen. She and David are sleeping in the van twice a week. Lottie explained this was to try it out before their trip. I think what she really meant was they needed to escape the hostel dorm. from time to time for some privacy.

Lottie was thrilled that her parcel had arrived, and even more so that her gecko was on top of the tree for another Christmas. I told her I wouldn't have changed it for the world. She laughed when I recounted how the kittens had made a beeline for the tree and already knocked it over twice *and* pulled off some tinsel and several decorations in the process! I laughed with her. That was wonderful and I felt so close to her. She told me she had sent local postcards to family and friends as an alternative to Christmas cards, which I agreed was a much better idea. We laughed some more when I said how I had licked down in excess of one hundred envelopes for the cards I'd sent out, which had left me with a mouth like the bottom of the proverbial parrot cage.

As we chatted on, I missed her more and more. I was desperate to say 'I wish you were here...' and '... if I win some money I'll fly you both home for Christmas' but I didn't. That would have been cruel. I realised how important it was for Lottie to enjoy Christmas in Australia and I didn't want to unsettle her as I knew she missed home much more than usual.

We talked on about all sorts of things, which included how weird it was that she had bumped into Simon, Christmas parties and, of course, the weather. Their beach barbeque on Christmas Day would depend on that and I said I really hoped it would be a super day – and I was sure it would be. With Christmas nearly upon us, to say goodbye was much harder than the last time we spoke. I emailed her that afternoon:

20 December, 2006

Hi Lot!

Really wonderful speaking to you again! Bet you'll be pleased to finish work for a few days. Gosh, you do work hard. But then so do we. Guess we've set that example.

Delighted your new 'baby blue' is better for surfing. Hope David can get back to it soon. He must miss it heaps. His foot should quickly heal once you've plastered it with liberal amounts of iodine!

Daddy posted a big cardboard box to you today - for your birthday. Inside is a copy of the Wells Journal - thought you'd like to

Life Without Lottie: How I Coped (or didn't) During my Daughter's Gap Year

catch up with local news! And maybe Simon would too.

All my cards posted (and mouth recovered - phew!) and all presents wrapped, although I forgot to put a tenner out for the dustbin men so hope our bins get emptied next year. Daddy forgot the recycling boxes today - he put them outside the back door but they never quite made it down to the gate in time. All I can say is I'm thankful it is winter!

Cats and dogs fine, altho Einstein's right ear a bit red. Have put drops in and will keep an eye. Cats disappear down their tunnel now but litter tray still in situ. Not for much longer I hope. They have grown so much, especially Tallinn. Riga loves to rub noses with me!

Well, must go and greet new guests - their taxi driver just called to say he was lost but only down the road so will arrive any minute.

Huge amounts of love and hugs. Miss you enormously!!!

Mum xxxxxxooooooooxxxxxxxxxx

=========

21 December 2006

Hi! Great talking to you yesterday too! Looks like we'll be having an 'English Xmas' – rain is forecast. So maybe it won't be spent down the beach but in a bar. Going to a 'beach' party in the pub on Saturday night - you have to wear hula skirts etc so should be good fun! We went out for cocktails and to a karaoke night last night. It was hilarious. People were so drunk. One guy fell asleep half way through his song and two gay guys did 'Girls just wanna have fun' complete with a dance routine! What's Christmas number 1 at home in the charts - is it something like the Tellytubbies?!

We're going to meet Simon later in a rooftop bar which overlooks the beach. Missing you lots and lots and speak to you soon, millions of love xoxox

=========

21 December, 2006

Hi Lot!

Weather crap here too - freezing fog is so bad that all internal UK flights cancelled and many European ones also. Heathrow have put up huge marquees to house the hundreds of delayed travellers. How perfectly awful, especially at this time of year.

Karaoke sounded such a laugh! So far, Number One is Take That with 'Patience', followed by Cliff Richard with '21st Century Christmas'. Now you know!

Have a great time catching up on news with Simon. Venue sounds wonderful - I suddenly felt desperately in need of a rooftop bar!!!

Daddy just left for a case in Gloucester. John arrived home with 4 mates last night - all still asleep in Snug & Cider Room. End of term - hooray! B&B guests due down any minute so must go. Have fun!

Huge love and hugs, missing you millions too!

Mum xxxxoooooooooooxxxxxxxxx

=========

The following evening, just before I went to bed, I sent Lottie this email. I was now actually really excited about Christmas, only a couple of days away.

22 December, 2006

Santa is on his way - he leaves early to get 'down under' in time! I wonder what he'll bring for you?!!!!

Huge love and hugs.

Mum xxxoooooooooooxxxxxxxxx

=========

Chapter Sixteen

Christmas and New Year

On Christmas Eve morning, this text came in: *'Hi mum! It's absolutely pissin it down! Massive storm, road flooded where van parked. Van OK but other cars up to windows in water! Not quite how I pictured Xmas!'*

What shocking conditions!

24 December, 2006

Hi Lot!

Just got your text and can't get a reply through. Must be the weather. What bad luck! Don't worry – I'm sure storm will pass soon.

Glad you're okay and van not afloat! Stay on high ground and hole up in a good bar. We'll all phone you later. Can't wait! Make sure your phone is fully charged!

Huge love and hugs

Mum xxoooooooxxxxxxxxx

=========

Nick, John and I gathered round the phone. I crossed every finger and toe and pleaded madly for a signal. Also, that Lottie would pick up the other end and I wouldn't get her ansafone. I was desperate to speak to her. It would be Christmas Day in Sydney in a couple of hour's time and I just had to wish her 'Happy Christmas' now, in case I couldn't get through tomorrow.

I tried my best to think positive as I punched in the numbers. No one said a word. I knew it was important for Lottie to talk to us too, especially to John because she hadn't spoken with him at all since she'd left home. I respected that that was John's way to cope with her absence, which he felt most deeply.

'It's ringing!' I said, but it rang and rang and I was convinced her ansafone would cut in at any second. Then there was a click and Lottie answered with a cheery 'Hello!'. The background noise of people's laughter and the thump thump of loud music was terrific. She said she was in a bar and would go outside in order to hear me better. I waited. It seemed ages until she said 'Hello' again, but when she did, her voice was clear and the connection great.

We exchanged Christmas wishes and love, I said I'd think of her as she opened her stocking and promised to call again tomorrow. I was very tearful as I handed the phone over to Nick. Then it was John's turn. He spoke nervously at first and rather awkwardly and it was obvious he struggled to cope with the emotion of their first conversation in four months. But soon he chatted and laughed freely as he and his sister caught up with each other's news. Nick and I slipped out of the kitchen so he could speak in private. He was on the phone for nearly twenty minutes! I hadn't seen him look so happy for ages.

Nick and John left for lunch at Norman and Beryl's. Unfortunately, I couldn't join them for I wouldn't have been back in time to welcome my new guests. Whilst they were away, I picked a selection of greenery which I arranged behind pictures and around the top of my grandmother's long case clock. Then, in between rain showers, I took the bassets out across the fields. When I got back, an overwhelming stench of poo hit me. To my horror I discovered that one of the kittens had crapped, not in their litter tray but on one of the dogs' blankets.

'Oh Shit!' I said, literally, but before I had time to grab the kitchen roll, Einstein wolfed down the lot. 'Arghhh!' I screamed at him. 'You filthy dog!' I chased him outside and slammed the door shut behind him. I grabbed both kittens, chucked them down the cat tunnel and slammed that door shut too. Morse waited, somewhat nervously after my outburst, for his biscuit treat. He would have a long wait this time, I thought; I had far more important matters to attend to.

I picked up the soiled bedding only to be met with a large wet patch on the wooden bed frame underneath. I groaned. The bloody cat had pee'd as well. I marched off to the laundry room where I stuffed the blanket into a machine and programmed a 'hot wash' with 'extra rinse'.

Back in the kitchen, I washed and bleached the soiled bed frame before I let Einstein and the kittens back inside. I tried my best to ignore Einstein as he licked his lips with glee. I hoped he wouldn't get diarrhoea – that's all I needed over Christmas! He looked at me expectantly for a biscuit. 'No way!' I told him. But that was not all. With incredible speed, Tallinn made a beeline for the dogs' bed and without further ado crapped on the other blanket. Little bugger! At least I now knew who the culprit was. I rubbed his nose firmly in his 'deposit' and, as he squirmed and yowled in protest, once more chucked him down the cat tunnel. Alas, Einstein wolfed most of that lot down too. I screamed again only this time much louder. Both dogs ran for the back door. That was a wise move.

I swore repeatedly as I dealt with the second blanket, then I let Tallinn back in and poured myself a glass of wine and sat down for a while before I prepared the Beef Wellington for our Christmas Eve supper. As soon as I'd placed the fillet on the chopping board the kittens jumped up beside it. I quickly pushed them down and threw them a tiny snippet each – up the other end of the kitchen. Their speed was phenomenal. I pitied any mice that got in their paths in future! I popped them both into their cage so I could continue undisturbed. The bassets dragged themselves out of bed and enjoyed the odd snippet too.

As I worked, I so wished Lottie could be with us for tonight. The four of us had spent twelve Christmas Eves at Manor Farm and this, our thirteenth, would be the first one without her. I tried to imagine her celebrating, as in Sydney it would now be Christmas Day. I went into the Study and sent her the following email. I felt pretty low.

24 December, 2006

Hi Lottie!

MERRY CHRISTMAS to you and to David!!!***!!!

DO HOPE weather improves and you have a **wonderful** BBQ on the beach - complete with loads of fizzy wine!

Daddy & John have gone to Grannie & Grandad's for lunch. I'm doing the usual Beef Wellington for tonight. Hils is joining us which will be lovely. Champagne on ice. We shall toast you several times over!

Missing you loads. Drink and eat plenty - that's an order to you both! Hopefully we will speak again later.

All love as always, especially for today.

Mum xxxxooooooooxxxxxxxx

==========

My guests arrived. I felt so sorry for an American man who had severe back pain and went straight up to his room for a lie down. I took up a tray of tea and shortbread, for which he and his wife were most grateful. Three days later, when the surgery re-opened after Christmas, he was even more grateful to see our family GP. He told me he had pleaded 'Help me! Help me!' as he had staggered doubled up into the consulting room. Help was given in the form of opiates. They took a while to 'kick in' he said, but certainly did the trick.

Nick and John returned after an excellent lunch, although Pet had a virus and hadn't eaten a thing. Nick asked her if it was of the sore throat variety. 'No' she told him, 'projectile vomiting'. Thankfully, she was not smitten during their visit.

When I recounted the disasters with Tallinn and Einstein, John burst into laughter and disappeared upstairs to wrap presents. Typical, I thought. Nick wondered if Tallinn had left 'presents' for Einstein. 'After all,' he said, 'that cat has often witnessed Einstein devouring the contents of the litter tray.' He was probably right, but it wasn't much help. I thought it could be a hormone problem and the sooner the kittens were castrated the better, particularly Tallinn whose balls had now developed into the size of large grapes. I called the vet and was given an appointment for 8th January. I jotted it down in my kitchen diary in large letters.

We had a super evening. The beef was delicious and we pulled crackers and laughed at the stupidity of the jokes (aren't they always?!), donned party hats and swapped cracker presents.

Life Without Lottie: How I Coped (or didn't) During my Daughter's Gap Year

Somehow you never end up with the right one. I was delighted with Nick's earrings and he was similarly delighted with my miniature screw driver set – perfect for repairing jewellery and watches.

There was more laughter as Hils swapped her racing car with John's handbag mirror. The mood was good. Nick made a toast to Lottie and David and wished them a Happy Christmas. 'Here! Here!' we replied and chinked glasses. The room fell silent for a few seconds.

After dinner, John met up with some mates for a pub crawl. Soon afterwards, Hils took a taxi home as none of us wanted to stay up too late. Best laid plans... Desperate to escape the enforcement of a family reunion, the younger of my two B&B couples returned. Nick got two more glasses and yet more wine was opened and consumed. Although we enjoyed their company, we were glad when they finally left us to it. We did the washing up, well, most of it, and stuffed the three stockings which hung by the fire. That was fun, but the absence of Lottie's stocking left a huge hole.

When I went up to bed, I gave Snoopy a longer cuddle than usual and as I snuggled down I whispered, 'Merry Christmas Lottie! I love you!'

* * *

I woke up just after 7am. It was Christmas Day! I left Nick asleep and I went downstairs. I hugged the animals, wished them a happy Christmas and gave the dogs a squeaky toy each (their usual presents) and the kittens a table tennis ball which they immediately chased across the floor. My guests were due down at 9am for 'continental' breakfast (I don't offer cooked breakfast on Christmas Day).

Nick and John appeared and we opened our stocking presents accompanied by continuous and loud squeaks from the dogs' toys as they were lovingly nibbled. When wrapping paper was discarded, the kittens pounced on it and had the time of their lives. It was pandemonium but a perfect start to Christmas and I loved it all. There is something so special about stockings and I was so pleased I had made one up for Lottie. Several times I thought of her and hoped she'd got as much pleasure out of this year's as in previous ones.

I had an idea. 'Let's open Lottie's parcel now,' I said. We usually opened presents after church, but I thought it would be nice to open Lottie's whilst just the three of us were there. I fetched it from under the tree in the hall and gave it to Nick to undo. Although I already knew what was inside, the contents were still a lovely surprise. There was a fabulously painted real boomerang, a shot glass (perfect for my evening sip of Cointreau), a lovely Aborigine tea towel and a beer can cooler with 'G'day mate!' written across it (perfect for John). Plus a note which Nick read out:

'Here are just a few fun Aussie goodies! I've also included most of the pics since Melbourne. It was a bit of a rush getting them in the post by Xmas deadline so will send more on ASAP. The cylinder thing is a stubby holder – you put your beer stubby/can in it to keep it cold. I also wanted to send an Aussie beer and kangaroo jerky but customs wouldn't allow that! Missing you all lots and lots. Lots of love Lottyxxxxx'

We hugged one another in silence. The physical contact and the knowledge that we all felt the same helped a great deal.

Much to the kittens' annoyance, Nick cleared away the paper. He couldn't stand the noise of the squeaky toys any longer and so took them, with the dogs in hot pursuit, into the kitchen.

I went upstairs to get dressed – breakfast was due in fifteen minutes!

That over and my guests out for the day, Nick and John went to the Christmas Eucharist service at Wells Cathedral. They would pick up Janine on their way home as I had asked her to join us for lunch. Whilst they were out, I prepared lunch and then went upstairs to clean the guest rooms. I started in the South Room.

To my dismay, the young couple had left it in a god-awful state. The bed and the floor were littered with discarded paper and bows and several items of clothing, both dirty and clean. The duvet and bedspread were in a crumpled heap in the corner. I couldn't see any pillows so I guessed they were buried underneath. Their suitcase, open, was on the bed and the contents spilled out. I stuffed everything back inside, closed it and shoved it under the dressing table.

Life Without Lottie: How I Coped (or didn't) During my Daughter's Gap Year

I collected up the rubbish, picked up the clothes and tried my best to sort dirty and clean before I placed them neatly on the shelves. Bed cleared, I made it up. I then replaced used mugs, teaspoons and glasses with clean ones, replenished stocks on the tea tray and in the mini-fridge (most of the chocolate bars had been scoffed), tidied books and magazines, matched up odd shoes and sprayed a few of blasts of lavender polish about (well, it was Christmas Day!).

Bedroom done, I hit the shower room. All I can say is it looked like it had already been hit.

'Bugger it!' I muttered, 'Here goes!' In record time, I cleaned, replaced towels and mats and tidied make-up and matched up tops with bottoms. I checked my watch. Christ! Nick and John would soon be back from the cathedral. Whilst they had sat down for most of the past couple of hours, I had worked flat out! And I still had to clean another room, change out of my old clothes, do my hair, refresh make-up and put the beef in the Aga. Argh!

At least my other guests had not only made their own bed (and beautifully) but both their bedroom and bathroom were immaculate. I adored them!

As I slung the beef into the Aga I heard the Range Rover on the gravel drive. With no time to change let alone tidy my hair or refresh my make-up, I welcomed them all and Nick got the champagne out of the fridge. I certainly felt I deserved some. We took our glasses through to the sitting room, where Nick lit the fire and it was fabulous to at last sit down - and to feel the bubbles on my nose as I sipped. I prised the kittens out of the tree for the umpteenth time and we started to open presents.

There were gasps of joy as we opened 'just what we wanted' and absolute hilarity as a totally useless and inappropriate gift was revealed (isn't there always one?!). The kittens left the tree alone in favour of the paper and I returned to the kitchen to check on the beef. More presents were unwrapped and Nick jotted down who'd given what for the forthcoming task of 'thank you' letters. He did a brilliant job.

At last I found the time to pop upstairs and freshen up before, finally, lunch was ready. To be honest, I was now so full of champagne that I'd gone past caring whether or not lunch was a hit. But it was, even the reheated mashed celeriac which I'd forgotten to serve last night! None of us had any room left for Christmas pudding, not even for the oh-so-tempting stinky Stilton, although we did manage some Turkish delight and after dinner mints.

We left two exquisitely happy bassets to wolf down a mixture of choice remains and returned to the fireside, where we sank gratefully into the sofas to ease our swollen bellies. It was gone 9.30pm before we had both the inclination and the room for Christmas pudding and brandy butter. The Stilton remained untouched until Boxing Day.

In the evening, Lottie texted me:

'Happy Xmas! Thank u so much for all my presents! I love the tamagochi and all the little stocking gifts and the fruit cake and everything! Give John a big thank u and hug for the dollars and ten d album! It's really cool! We listened to it on the beach. Weather turned out to be really hot in the end! The hostel owner put on a big lunch for us and in the evening we had a party on the beach and drank lots of fizzy wine. Missing u all lots and thinking of u round the fire with the cats climbing the tree! Lol xxx'

I was thrilled that she had had such a lovely day and the weather was sunny after all, just like I'd said it would be, and I was so grateful that the hostel owner had taken the trouble to provide lunch. John was delighted with the reference to his cash and his CD.

'Let's give her a call,' I said. 'It's early morning there but she's obviously awake!' I didn't wait for a response - I started to dial. Someone obviously smiled down on me as I got through first time. That made my Christmas.

'Hi Darling!' I said. 'Just got your text.'

'Happy Christmas, Mum!' Lottie replied. 'And thanks a million for my presents!'

'Oh, you're more than welcome, and thank you so much for yours! The shot glass is being christened with cointreau as we speak!'

I heard all about their delicious lunch and the beach party that followed. She sounded so happy and I was incredibly grateful for that.

'How's the hangover?' I asked.

'Um, not too bad!' she said.
'Don't worry, darling,' I told her, 'I'll have one in the morning!'
We both laughed. I asked how David was.
'Oh, he's fine...he's just gone off for a surf.'
When the sun is up and a great surfing beach is on your doorstep, who wants to stay in bed, I thought. We said our goodbyes and I handed the phone over to Nick. Then it was John's turn and I was delighted to hear him laugh and joke with his sister. Twice in two days!

That night, it was pure pleasure to climb into bed. I was exhausted but happy. Happy because we had all had such a wonderful Christmas at home, and happy because it seemed as if Lottie had also had an equally wonderful, although very different, celebration in Sydney. The three of us had missed her like crazy but I thought we coped amazingly well.

On Boxing Day, I printed out our Christmas photos and put them into a large envelope together with several cards people had sent to Lottie, some of which I knew contained cheques, both for Christmas and for her forthcoming nineteenth birthday on 11 January. I also enclosed a letter I had written, and then posted it as soon as the Post Office reopened.

It seemed that New Year's Eve was upon us in a flash and countless times I tried to phone Lottie, but couldn't get a line. I received no contact from her, not even a text, so she probably had the same problem.

Throughout the day I sent this text but each time it was refused: *'Happy New Year! Cant get thro by phone + texts being returned – system overload! Hope this makes it. Lol+hugs. M+d+j xxx'*

Boy was I grateful that we had all spoken to her on Christmas Eve *and* on Christmas Day. We'd been so lucky! My text didn't get through until 2 January, when I quickly received a reply. Lines were open again!

'Hi! Just got yr txt! Hny 2! Tried calling + textin U2, network 2 busy. Had a good nye, watched Sydney fireworks from Manly waterfront. Hope u had a good 1. Off 2 the Blue Mountains 2day. Go do sum slight seeing. Lol x'

It was wonderful to resume contact and I just adored her *'slight seeing'* spelling. Poor Lot must have had one hell of a hangover! Blue

Mountains – sounded fabulous! I would look them up. I also received this email which had taken two days to reach my Inbox:

31 December, 2006

Hi! Happy New Year! Most people from the hostel have gone into the city for new years to watch the fireworks but about 10 of us have stayed behind in Manly to watch the fireworks at midnight. You have to get into Sydney before 10am to bag a spot on the side of the road and you're not allowed to drink. There isn't transport back to Manly till 6am new year's day and it's going to rain all day - so we decided to give it a miss.

Instead I think we're having a mini party in the hostel and going down the beach or the pub and before midnight we'll walk round to Manly point where you can see the Sydney fireworks in the distance.

What's happening at home for New Year?

One of our friends we met in Perth has come over to see us and we're all driving up the east coast late January/early Feb. Tonight should be good fun! Will speak to you later! Missing u loads and lots of love xxxxxxxxxxxxxxxxxxxxxxxx

=========

New Year's Eve came, complete with a fresh set of guests. I welcomed a young couple from Manchester, and an older couple to celebrate their wedding anniversary as well as the New Year. They'd asked me to buy them a bottle of champagne and put it in their minibar. I did so, and attached a little card and gave them a box of handmade chocolates.

Yesterday, John had gone down to Devon with a group of mates to stay with Ed, but Manor Farm remained lively to say the least. As soon as the young couple arrived, they threw more than the occasional snipe at one another and the husband always managed to have the last sarcastic word. He told me they had been married for two years.

'Lovely,' I commented, but in the back of my mind I wondered how much longer their marriage would last. They didn't look like they would hit a 60th anniversary together, that was for sure.

Life Without Lottie: How I Coped (or didn't) During my Daughter's Gap Year

They drove into Wells to have a look around, so I saw them again albeit briefly when they returned to shower and change for the special dinner they'd booked at our smart local pub/restaurant, The Slab House Inn. The name dates back to the time of The Black Death when a huge stone slab was placed across the road outside the pub. This served as a quarantine barrier against the infected folk of Wells. Kindly local farmers left supplies of food on the slab for the sick to collect.

When their taxi arrived, much to the annoyance of the driver, I had to dig them out of their room. I knocked on their bedroom door, the husband opened it and looked rather annoyed at my intrusion. He was barefoot, still in the jeans he'd arrived in and had a champagne bottle in one hand and a full glass of the stuff in the other. I could hear the shower so his wife wasn't even washed, let alone dressed. I groaned inwardly.

'Oh!' I said. 'I see you're not quite ready.'

'Yeah,' the husband replied. 'We'll be down in a minute.'

Impossible, I thought and added as nicely but as firmly as possible, 'Do be as quick as you can – the driver is waiting.'

He raised his eyebrows, looked down at me and closed the door in my face.

'Wanker,' I thought. It was a full fifteen minutes later before they came downstairs – in jeans. What they had on top wasn't much better. I was aghast at their total lack of effort to 'dress' for the occasion and pitied their fellow diners. To save any further delay, I darted through to the hall, opened the front door and ushered them outside as quickly as I dared.

The taxi driver had started to walk down the path towards us. He looked livid. I mouthed 'sorry' to him from behind the couple, to whom I wished 'a lovely time' and thankfully closed the door. My other guests went out for dinner shortly afterwards. They were ready well before their taxi arrived.

With the house back to ourselves, Nick and I looked forward to a quiet celebration. Well, at least it started that way. We feasted oh-so-decadently on delicious caviar and fine champagne followed by humungous tiger prawns, which Nick stir-fried in liberal amounts of ginger and garlic and the best of olive oils, and then took a break before we had lobster as our main course. We spoke fondly of Lottie and 'Larry'.

After dinner, with an hour to go until midnight, we snuggled down together to watch Jools Holland's 'Hootenanny' on TV. Bugger it if the young couple returned early and joined us. They didn't bother to ask if we minded. They were as drunk as skunks and had obviously had a pretty major tiff, for they ignored each other completely; not a pleasant atmosphere for New Year's Eve.

Neither of them removed their coats, although the wife pulled off her scarf and flung it over the back of a chair, and missed. She didn't notice or, if she did, disregarded it. She sat down on the carpet, an action taken by the bassets as a firm invitation to join her. She seemed to love their attention, slobbers and all. She looked up.

'We had mooore champagne!' she said with a decided slur and switched her attention back to the dogs. She proceeded to tickle them, fairly roughly, and threw Morse's tennis ball across the room, where it hit the wall and narrowly missed one of my prized watercolours before it bounced back and was caught by a jubilant Morse. Much to his delight (and to my disgust) she continued to throw the ball for him and screeched with glee every time he caught it and brought it back to her for more. I was only sorry that Morse was so quick at that trick!

The intimate and peaceful evening that Nick and I had so far enjoyed was over. The only saving grace was the fact that, in between the prawns and the lobster, we had engaged in a not short spell of wanton passion. Thank goodness we hadn't left it any later!

Her husband stretched himself out across the sofa from where he stared disapprovingly at his wife and let out a huge sigh. Nick started to chuckle. I dug him in the ribs.

'How was dinner?' I tentatively enquired. I wished I hadn't, for the husband proceeded to rattle on about what a wonderful restaurant it was and detailed each and every course. Then he went on to say how amazed he was when the chef had taken the trouble to leave the kitchen and approach him personally. He sat up, proudly puffed out his chest, leaned towards me and said, '...and he only spoke to *me*, complimented *me* on my *excellent* choice of red wine... and that was *soo* good, oh wow, a really *deep* colour, and rich and velvety smooth, so velvet and gorgeous I had to order *another* bottle!'

I wished I had a piece of velvet to stuff into his mouth there and then. Nick chuckled again only this time I didn't prod him. Completely undeterred, the husband continued,

'I had this HUGE meringue thing for sweet… filled with fresh raspberries and blueberries and homemade ice cream – well it must have been homemade as it was SO good – and a rich toffee sauce poured all over the top. Oh, and sprinkled with pecans and pistachios.'

I felt sick. His voice reached fever pitch as he added,

'Then we had liqueurs, several in fact!'

That was obvious! All I managed to say during his rendition was the occasional 'Mmm' and 'Lovely'. I dared not look at Nick whose laughter had by now made the sofa vibrate. The room fell silent. Nick and I concentrated on the TV in the vain hope that they might get the message and leave us alone. But more was to come, and worse.

The man suddenly flicked his hand nonchalantly at his wife and came out with 'She wants a baby!' He made it sound as if it was the most ridiculous request he had ever heard. His wife gave him a thunderous look before she resumed her attention to the dogs, who were now so excited they had begun to race around her, tails tucked in tight.

'In fact,' he continued, 'that's about all we spoke about during dinner!'

I now understood why they had returned so early. Shit! I grabbed my glass of wine and took a big gulp before I managed an 'Oh dear'.

He went on. '…and she wants one NOW!' He threw his arms up in horror before he continued.

'When we got engaged we agreed to leave it AT LEAST five years.'

At this, his wife spat out at him 'It was TWO actually.'

Oh Lord! Nick went into the kitchen to open more wine. When he returned, after he'd been there long enough to open two whole bloody cases, he plonked the bottle on the table. I didn't offer either of them a drink, determined not to do anything to encourage the continuation of their presence.

'She said we agreed only TWO!' He hadn't realised that Nick had heard this just before he beetled out of the room. Nick pulled his specs down and held them as they rested on the end of his nose. He peered at the man over the top of them and, with all seriousness but with a slight smile, said,

'These things can take time, you know.'

I nearly cracked up.

'Pfff, chance would be a fine thing!' came the husband's quick reply.

Nick gave me one of his lecherous looks as if to say 'I've had the chance tonight!' I dug him in the ribs again and stifled my giggles at the thought of what we'd got up to earlier.

I grabbed the TV remote and turned the volume up.

'Oh, I love this song!' I exclaimed, although I didn't, desperate for anything to divert the attention away from babies. Nick burst out laughing.

'What's funny, mate?' the husband asked. This merely encouraged Nick's laughter. I turned the volume up some more and started to sing along to the music.

'Sorry,' Nick replied as he regained some form of composure. He had to shout in order to be heard above the noise of the TV. 'It's nothing to do with, er, what you said; it's just something I thought of.'

At this point, my other guests returned. I could have kissed them. They picked up on the awkward atmosphere and only stayed with us long enough before they went to bed to say they'd had a brilliant time and wished us a happy New Year. Sensible people, I thought.

It was back to the four of us. The wife, who was now flat on her back with the dogs on top of her, drooled out,

'All men are the same,' she said. 'All they want is sex...not a babeee.'

She started to snivel. To my horror, Morse began to hump her arm.

'Morse, get off!' I commanded.

'Oh, oh,' she said, 'I don't mind, they're so gorgeous and so (she paused and looked daggers at her husband) faithful!'

Fuck a duck, I thought, although I bet her husband wasn't thinking of ducks.

'Yeah, yeah!' he slurred, 'that's what you women all say..."too tired, I've got a headache".'

There was another awkward silence. I took a large swig of my wine.

He carried on, unperturbed, 'I had a dog once. He was a huge beast!'

Oh no, please let's not hear about his dog! But we did. At least babies had been forgotten.

At two minutes before midnight, the wife managed with some difficulty to extract herself from the dogs. She staggered to her feet and announced that she was going to bed. At last! I thought.

She wavered from side to side and looked dreadful with her mascara badly smudged, eyes half closed and hair a complete mess, thanks to the dogs' treatment.

She stared at her husband for a while as if to say 'join me' but he made no effort to move. I was appalled. She headed upstairs. He said nothing. I did. I grabbed the moment as I went into a blind panic at the thought of having to suffer his presence any longer.

'Oh, you must go up too! You have to be together at midnight! …she's your wife! …and it's almost New Year!'

My efforts were useless.

'Nah!' he replied, totally uninterested. 'I'll see her later…tomorrow.'

Nick tried his best too but his words also fell on deaf ears. The expletives which spun inside my head disgusted me. I silently accused the wanker of every word. And so midnight arrived with the three of us as Jools and his guests whooped and embraced and pulled party poppers whilst fireworks exploded in the background. I wanted to whoop and laugh too, but I didn't. Nick and I quietly hugged and briefly kissed. Neither of us got up to shake hands with the wanker. We merely exchanged our happy New Year's, and swiftly. I turned to Nick.

'May I have a Cointreau, darling?' I asked.

'Of course you can. And I'd be delighted to get one for you!' he replied, and headed off to the kitchen at incredible speed. I was left with wanker, fortunately for a shorter period than Nick's previous visit to the kitchen. He returned in record time, bless him. He knew.

'Ah well' I said. 'That's it for another year!'

I turned off the TV and pretended to yawn, which turned into a real one. Nick yawned too. Still the message didn't get across.

'I must put the dogs out,' Nick said.

Oh God, don't leave me alone with him again, I thought. The husband got to his feet, gave a big long stretch and said, 'I think I'll head up to bed now.'

Such was my relief that I shot out of the sofa, kissed him on both cheeks and wished him a happy New Year. I didn't mean it for an instant. Before Nick and I turned in, we spent a quiet ten minutes or so as we finished our drinks after an extraordinary end to the previous year and a not particularly inspired start to the new one. But we laughed as we recounted certain conversations and expressed our pity for the man's wife, who seemed quite a sweet girl.

I tried to call Lottie but to no avail. Then I called John. At least I had no problem in reaching him but he was only a mere 150 miles away. I thought he sounded remarkably sober. He told me he had been to several pubs and clubs, had had an 'awesome' night and would catch the train back some time tomorrow. I passed the phone over to Nick. It wasn't until John got home and I mentioned how in control he sounded on the phone that he told me with a wide grin on his face that he was 'absolutely rat-arsed' at the time!

Chapter Seventeen

A New Year Begins

4 January, 2007

Hi! Happy New Year! Tried texting you loads of times over New Year but messages kept getting rejected and then I ran out of credit, even though you didn't get any of them! Picked up the birthday parcel and envelopes you sent me. I haven't looked at the customs sticker to keep it a surprise and I can't believe all the money I've been sent!

Do say a big, big thank you to everyone! I've bought postcards to write thank you notes. I banked the cheques today but it takes 3/4 weeks for them to clear which is ok because that will be about the time we head out of Manly. I loved all the Xmas pictures! The kittens look so much bigger and so naughty! It's sweet how they curl up with the dogs and everyone looked like they were having fun!

New years was great here - we spent the day in the bar drinking cocktails and then went out for a really good Italian. After that we played drinking games and then went down to Manly wharf to watch the fireworks, but arrived too late and missed them! Oops! But at midnight we could see the Sydney fireworks which were great! And then we went to another bar...

On the 2nd a few of us went to Palm Beach where 'Home and Away' is filmed. It's not as impressive as it looks on TV so we camped at the next beach along (Whale Beach) which was much nicer. The next morning we headed to the Blue Mountains and saw the Three Sisters and Echo Valley, both of which were amazing and beautiful but it was really wet and foggy so we'll go back for a better look before we leave. I've added a few pics. I hope they get through! I had to do loads of resizing to get them to fit in the email. The last one is us and all our friends on the beach on Christmas Day.

Lots of love to you all and hope to speak to you soon! Missing you loads! Xox

=========

4 January, 2007

Hi Lot!

Fantastic to get your email and the fab pictures! It was awful not speaking over New Year. Hardly surprising as I expect the whole world had the same idea. Your celebrations sounded a real blast. So pleased your birthday pressies have arrived. Don't take any notice of what I put on the customs label - I lied! Ha! Ha! Am thrilled about the cheques you got! Disgraceful they take so long to clear.

Pictures of the flood looked like Armageddon! The van was lucky to escape - she looks smart. Do you have a name for her? Love the grill bar on the front. Is that to keep Skippys off?! Hope you've had the repair work done. Great pic of you surfing - plse send more! And I loved the group beach snap – now my desktop background! You all look so tanned and happy. Good luck getting another job. What happened to the supermarket one? Hope D gets something soon too so you can save up more for your trip. Both cats being neutered on Monday. Dogs are blooming.

No more news I can think of at the moment. Will keep trying to phone.

Huge love, hugs and kisses and missing you so much!

Mum xxxxxxxxxxoooooooooo

=========

The following day, Nick sent this email to Lottie. When I read it, I thought she would find it a welcome change to receive something intelligent rather than the usual gossipy news from me!

Dear Lottie,

Here's one I was thinking about earlier: Do Australian compass needles face south? And the non-magnetic end of the needle painted red to make it look as if it is pointing north? What do people your side of the world say about that one? My guess is that Australian compasses are fixed to make them look as if they are pointing north. Or, do Australians have different compasses altogether with, say, green for south? Don't know why I thought about this. Oh, I've remembered, it's because I've heard that in Australia you can get world maps which show Australia upside-down on the top of the world. This would blow your mind if you'd had a few smokes.

Thinking of you both, with love, Daddy.
=========

Lottie replied:

Hi Daddy! I asked the owner of our hostel about the compasses and she just stared at me blankly (she's a bit odd!) so I'm not sure if they are different. As for the maps, I've seen ones with Australia at the top - they look very strange!

Anyway, it's great to hear from you. Nothing new and exciting to report here. Had a chilled weekend as the weather was rubbish so watched films and mooched around the hostel. Went fishing! It was quite fun but didn't catch anything.

I think Australians lie about having great weather all the time! It said on the news that this is the worst summer Australia has had in 10 years! Just our luck! Looking forward to my birthday although I will miss you and home. Lots of love and missing you and hope to speak to you soon! Xox
=========

The day arrived for the kittens to be 'done'. I felt guilty when I dropped them off at the vet. I told them to be 'good boys' and drove home. Whilst I was out, an email had come in from Lottie. All thoughts of what the vet was about to do vanished from my mind as I concentrated on her latest news:

8 January, 2007

Hi! Just thought I'd send you a quick message! I've sent off all my thank you cards. Had a good weekend, it rained quite a bit so relaxed in the hostel. Still looking for a job.

I'm not sure what the bar on the front of the van is for but because it's parked on a slope it bangs on the ground every time we move it! Getting the prop shaft fixed soon and starting to sort things out for the inside. I'm going to try and make some curtains – hopefully won't be a disaster! There are three of us travelling up the East coast – Stu, who we met in Perth is coming along and he has the same van as us! I think a couple more people might join us but we're not sure as everyone wants to see different things.

Hope to speak to you soon - missing you lots and lots! Looking forward to my birthday and opening my parcel! I think a group from the hostel is taking me out for supper which should be fun! xox
==========

I replied by text and said I would email all news tomorrow. I spent the rest of the morning catching up with urgent household chores put off from the weekend and in the afternoon I collected the kittens. All had gone well. It certainly looked that way, although Tallinn was still a bit doped up. He snuggled down in between Einstein's paws and went straight to sleep. Riga, on the other hand, seemed totally unaffected by the whole procedure.

9 January, 2007

Hi Lottie!

Great to get your email and news! Snap - won't stop raining here either and it is *so* dark - haven't seen sunshine for days. Good for you finishing thank you cards already. I've done mine and John almost there... Glad to hear van getting fixed. Well done having a go at curtains. I'm sure they will turn out fine. A little tip - cut them out on the floor, it's much easier than on a table which is never big enough. Great that Stu is travelling with you. It must be difficult getting people together - I can understand everyone wanting to see and do different things. Oz is too big!

John got a 'B' for his Business Studies mock - fantastic. He has his first (of 2) real AS module tomorrow, the second one next week. Julia and John (my cousins from Glasgow) popped in for a sandwich lunch today. They're staying with friends near Castle Cary.

Life Without Lottie: How I Coped (or didn't) During my Daughter's Gap Year

It was lovely to see them and catch up on Scottish family news. One of Gavin's twin boys is studying medicine and Ganda has given him the set of bones which he used when he learnt anatomy! Posted off a small 'happy new year' pressie to you yesterday. Got John the same and he's thrilled, so hope you are too. The mystery will be unwrapped soon!!! Also forwarded on a Christmas card from Heather & Andy. Had a lovely long letter from her and she and family are all well.

Hey ho – you're nearly 19. Wow! Bet you're excited - great that a crowd of you are going out. Have a ball. Will call you on 11th - and probably 10th just in case can't get through on your big day. Daddy back at Bath for his evening tutorials and a new essay set so he's busy. He has a church meeting tonight and I'm out with the girls tomorrow. Stewart here on Thurs evening so I'm looking forward to a quiet night in together on Friday! Nick Hunter is painting your shower room. I'm trying to put my hands on a new wall unit with higher shelves so lotions and potions will actually fit on them.

Both cats were 'done' yesterday. They were also micro-chipped. That wasn't cheap! Today they are back to normal and chasing each other around. I hope Tallinn has got the message…

Well, need to go into Wells for a few things. Missing you so much and thinking of you loads! Make sure you have cocktails on your birthday - complete with sparklers! Try and get hold of some fireworks and DO take pics!

Loads of love and hugs and will speak very soon.

Mum xxxxxxxxxoooooooooooox

PS Snoopy says Happy New Year!

=========

The following, evening when I returned from my supper out, I tried to call Lottie, for in Australia she had already turned nineteen. Sadly, I only got her ansafone. I wished that tomorrow, when it would be her birthday in the UK, I would have more success. A few minutes later my mobile beeped. It was a text!

'Happy Birthday 2 me! Thank u soo much for all my presents. They all fit really well. The dressing gown is so nice and fluffy and the clothes so pretty! Thank the animals for my bracelets 2, well picked! And more money. Wow!

I'm rich! Thank u! Missing you all lots, it's going 2B 38 degrees 2day so I don't think I'll be doing much. Havin a party 2nite + cocktails! Lol x'

I replied: *'Happy Birthday to you darling! Thrilled everything fits! Have a wonderful party. Will keep tryin 2phone. Huge hugs. Lol mxxx'*

11 January, 2007

Darling Lot

*** **HAPPY BIRTHDAY!!! WOW!!! 19 TODAY!!!** ***
=======================================

Many happy returns! Do hope you had the most **fabulous** day. We thought of you so much. Everyone sends birthday greetings. Daddy's just phoned you but had to leave another message. What a bugger! Won't give up tho - you have a mother who is a descendant of Robert the Bruce...!!!

Again, HAPPY, HAPPY BIRTHDAY!!! Missing you loads and sending thousands of hugs and kisses and mountains of love. Party on!

Mum xxxxxxxxxxoooooooo
=========

Later that day, another text came in.

'Hi! Sorry I missed your calls. I had a great b'day. 20 of us went out for Thai + then back to the hostel where David had organised surprise cake, banners, balloons + party hats! Then we went out 4 drinks which was fun! Wish I could have spoken 2 u tho. Hope 2 speak soon! Miss everyone lots. Xx'

Well done David for the efforts he had made to make Lottie's day special. And what a huge group for her birthday supper! Lottie must be popular, I thought, with great pride.

I couldn't get a signal all day and by the end of it I nearly screamed. Life could be so cruel at times. All I wanted to do was speak to my daughter on her birthday – whether I managed it on Sydney or UK time didn't matter. Was that too much to ask?

Throughout the day, the emptiness I felt without her grew. I thought of her almost constantly and particularly at 2.29pm – the actual time of her birth and when my life changed forever, for the very, very better. I remembered being in the delivery room and my tears of utter joy as the midwife announced, after a difficult birth, 'Fiona, you have a beautiful baby girl!'

I had indeed. She was the most beautiful baby in the world and I knew, from the first moment I gingerly held her to me, that I would love her and protect her forever – for eternity. During supper that night we all raised our glasses to Lottie and wished her a happy nineteenth birthday. It was the best we could do.

On Saturday morning I came downstairs to find bodies strewn across the sofas and the floor of the sitting room. The room reeked, both of stale bodies and stale beer. I opened the window and someone stirred as the icy cold air hit them. With difficulty I made my way through and managed not to stand on anyone. However, the mess hadn't come as any surprise to me, for John had brought some friends back last night. He had stood across the kitchen doorway and asked me if they could stay over.

'Of course they can, darling!' I said. '...no B&Bs in so anywhere downstairs.'

'Ah, thanks Mum, that's really cool. Cheers, cheers!'

He then proceeded to usher in no less than six mates! I didn't realise there would be *that* many, but I welcomed them all. They'd been here several times before and were good lads, and I much preferred them here rather than in the town after the pubs had turned out.

The only problem was, I *did* have B&Bs in! Thankfully it was only the one, a lady called Jackie, due down for breakfast in about an hour's time. As there wasn't the remotest chance of the lads being up and out by then, like me, she too would have to negotiate her way over and around them in order to reach the breakfast room. I hoped she would understand and that the room smelt a bit fresher by then!

Desperate for a room for the night, Jackie had phoned me long after John and his mates arrived. She explained that she had worked late and felt too tired to face the drive home. I thought it only fair to mention that my seventeen-year-old son had a few friends here. She said that wouldn't bother her – she had a boy the same age - so I took her details and gave her directions. She arrived twenty minutes later. I discovered that she was also a regular visitor to Lundy Island and so we compared notes on the place and the pitfalls of teenagers' behaviour. We had much in common!

When she came down for breakfast, I apologised for the state of the sitting room and gingerly asked her if she'd slept well.

'Like a log!' she told me.

With great relief I said, 'Oh, thank goodness! I was worried the lads would disturb you.'

'Didn't hear a thing!' she replied.

Jackie checked out and the boys eventually stirred themselves once I'd wafted a plate of bacon sarnies under their noses. That works a treat, every time.

I have a press cutting on the wall next to my Aga which I read in *The Observer* magazine, many years ago. It appealed to my sense of humour and so I cut it out and put it into a clip frame. It reads: *'Anyone who tries to make a bacon sandwich with brown bread has missed the point completely and should be sent to sandwich hell.'*

I couldn't have put it better myself. I hate it when I am specifically asked for a 'brown' bacon sarnie by my guests. Fortunately, it rarely happens.

15 January, 2007

Hi Lot!

Thanks so much for email. My screen decided to conk out overnight so I accessed it via Dad's laptop. Although I did not delete it, it disappeared without a trace! Bloody computers! Do send again or another message as I only read it quickly before I dashed out to buy a replacement (now installed and very smart).

The chief witch of cleaning houses should be shot – line her up with the others! Am so sorry you had to go through that. Do hope you find a decent job soon. What's David doing?

All fine here. Dad on hunt sabotage trial, John's final exam on Wed. Guy off to India soon. Had lunch with Hils yesterday. She sends love. She said she was on a diet but proceeded to devour a massive plate of bangers, chips and peas! Good for her!

Do you have a date to go up East? Hope you've found someone to fix the van. How are the curtains shaping up?

Missing you loads and sending huge hugs, kisses and masses of love. Will keep calling - we WILL speak soon!

Mum xxxxxxxxxooooooooooxxxxx

=========

Although I couldn't remember everything in Lottie's email, I did remember exactly what she had said about her most recent job as a cleaner. It had started out well – both the pay and working conditions (in 'pukka' homes as she had put it) were good. However, after three days, her female boss (whom Lottie said was a complete dyke) went in for the kill. Not only had she tried to touch Lottie up, but relentlessly sent her suggestive texts. I could well imagine what David had to say about that! The filthy cow, I thought, and another one destined for the firing squad. Lottie resigned, but the texts continued so she turned her mobile off – for 48 hours. That had done the trick.

17 January, 2007

Hi!

Haven't got a definite date for moving but Mark and Hannah fly over in 5 weeks time so we'll stay here until they arrive.

I've got a great new job! Yey! V sign to the mad cleaner! Am working for an advertising company in the city and the job I've been put on is for Oxfam. Basically, a team of about 5 of us are sent to busy locations in Sydney to try and rally support for Oxfam. For every person I sign up I get fifty pounds! I had to go for my second interview today and I was picked from just under 50 people in total! They said I should make at least two hundred pounds a week and I could probably manage four hundred, which is an amazing wage for a backpacker! I've got my first training day tomorrow starting at 7:45am so I have to get the early ferry. I'll have to get up at 5:30 - groan. That will be a bit of a shock to the system!

Anyway, hope to speak to you soon!!! I have to go and sort out my documents for tomorrow. Tell John very good luck in his last exam and if he's already done it tell him to have a drink on me! Send my love to Daddy and say hi to Hils and everyone!

Lots and lots of love xox

==========

I was delighted that Lottie had found another job, and one which paid well and sounded good, particularly as it was for Oxfam. The spacko cleaner was forgotten. The remainder of my week was uneventful apart from my temper which, due to more failed attempts to speak to Lottie, reached boiling point. In addition, my mobile refused to send any texts. Was there some sort of conspiracy against me? It didn't help that Nick had meetings every evening and on Friday afternoon went off to God camp. I'd hardly seen him during the week and now wouldn't see him again until Sunday afternoon. Some weeks went like that. I hated them. At least John's exam had gone okay and Lottie had what sounded like a great new job.

19 January, 2007

Hi Lot!

Your email came in just in time for John to read it before he left to sit his exam. Your good luck wishes worked! He phoned to say it went okay. He's delighted. I'm relieved!

Many congrats on getting the Oxfam job out of so many applicants - well done you! Hope you sign up lots of people and earn loads of money!

Thanks so much for all your texts. Sorry I haven't replied but my stupid mobile refuses to send any. Bloody thing. In desperation I got Daddy to text you from his mobile which worked fine so it looks like mine's buggered. Have ordered replacement. Hope it's easy to work - I hate getting used to new ones. In the meantime, I'll text you from John's phone.

Have a great weekend. I'll keep trying to phone. Missing you so much and sending mountains of love!

Mum xxxxxxxxxooooooo

==========

By early evening I felt mighty pissed off with the world and so I was delighted when Chris and Janine both popped in for a quick cuppa after work. We hadn't met up since Christmas Day and it was great to get together again.

Both cats were asleep on top of the boiler. One of them suddenly let out a very strange noise - half yowl, half hiccup. We turned to look. It was Riga. His neck was stretched forward, he stuck out his tongue and began to retch for all he was worth. Obviously desperate to expel whatever had made him feel bad, he did so, and with the utmost of success. A stomach full of half-digested kitten food burst from his mouth, cascaded over the edge of his blanket, down the front of the boiler and splattered onto the floor below.

Chris was nearest to him. With a shriek of dismay she jumped up, grabbed the kitchen roll and started to mop up, but such was her distress she only made matters worse. Chris is a great animal lover and a staunch vegetarian. Any story of any living creature's suffering, let alone her actually witnessing such, turns her into an absolute jelly and renders her utterly useless. I was now on my feet too for the dogs had made a beeline for the vomit. I had to try and remove their two black noses out of it, and fast.

'Back to bed!' I commanded.

I was ignored. However, it was now apparent that Riga hadn't been that successful for something red hung out of his mouth.

'Oh, Fi!' Chris cried. 'Look, look! Oh God, what is it?' She was now so distressed she had to clutch the boiler for support. 'Someone do something...you must do something! He can't breathe! Quick! Quick!'

I knew exactly what it was. When our postman has more than a couple of letters for us, he secures them together with a red rubber band. When I remove the band, the kittens adore playing with it until, much to their annoyance, I prise it off them and bin it. I must have missed this one!

Whilst Janine attempted to assure Chris that Riga was *not* about to choke to death, I quickly but gently pulled the rest of the band out of his mouth. He retched, sat up and shook his head. He jumped down and went over to the water bowl and started to lap.

His throat must have been sore! I threw the band into the bin and vowed to be more diligent with their future disposal.

Janine opened a bottle of wine. We were all in need of a drink and, unlike the cat, needed something a tad stronger than water, Chris most of all! The 'quick cuppa' turned into a two hour session; a great start to my weekend.

The next week had an even better start. First thing Monday morning I received an email from Lottie, but when I read it her news shocked me to the core:

22 January, 2007

Hi hi!

Been ages since we've spoken - must chat soon. I've found a spot by the right side of the window in our room where I get one bar of signal!

I've quit the Oxfam job. It turned out that working for them basically means you're a glorified promotions girl and to get people to sign up they tell you to make guys think they can sleep with you! I was told to say stupid stuff like 'Hey guys, why don't you come and talk to me, I'll make it worth your while'. How degrading. Plus, I didn't make any sales and I got into Sydney at 7am and stood on street corners until after 7pm! I have found new job in a café but it doesn't start till Sunday altho they may need people later this week.

Australia Day on Friday! Apparently it's a really big event in Oz. A group of us are going into the city to watch the boat races and the tall ships coming into the harbour and have a picnic (with fizzy wine of course!).

Then in the evening there's a big firework display over the bridge so that should be good! Apparently its tradition to be drunk before midday so hopefully I'll make the fireworks!

We might take a boat tour to watch them from the water as the deal is 'all you can drink and eat...' Nothing else exciting to report. Anyway, must dash as almost run out of internet credit! Missing you all lots and lots! Xox

=========

Good God! I could hardly believe what Oxfam was up to! I was appalled by the scam they openly operated to lure totally unsuspecting young, pretty girls into such a ghastly position on the expectation of high potential earnings. Oxfam was turning them into nothing less than prostitutes!!! Thank goodness Lottie had quit that job in a hurry. She was certainly experiencing life of the very worst kind, I thought, and I wondered if the powers that be at Oxfam were aware of the situation. I decided to make some enquiries. First, I replied to Lottie:

22 January, 2007

Hi Lot!

Oxfam are absolutely disgusting. I am so sorry for you - it must have been just awful but at least you quickly discovered the truth and quit. I hope you told them to shove it up their arse. They should all be shot. I'll NEVER donate anything to Oxfam ever again! I'm amazed at the speed with which you've bounced back - and got another job! Hurray for Lot! Oz Day sounds really good fun, especially the boat trip (and the fizzy wine picnic!).

Glad weather's good. Crap here (wet & windy) so breakfast BBQ didn't happen. We watched a v depressing TV documentary on global warming last night. Apparently we're headed for more extremes – flash floods, strong winds, boiling hot summers and little or no hope of any more 'white' Christmases. Bang goes Scotland's winter sports income. It'll soon have to advertise 'Come rapids-riding in the Highlands'!

Daddy enjoyed his weekend at God camp but was pleased to get home. His group had to put on the main Sunday service - in the New Zealand Methodist style. I conjured up a wonderful picture of them all beating chests and slapping thighs as they chanted around the altar in their frocks!

Not much news here either, although kittens v entertaining. Last night they charged around the sitting room for at least an hour and dived under cushions, jumped on the dogs and climbed the curtains! It was hilarious. Jill called in the middle of it all and we were on the phone for ages. I don't think Cyprus worked out as well as she had hoped. Kim has refused to go back – ever. What a pity. I hear you'll be in Oz for Naomi's wedding. Wow! That will be some party! Jill's still worried about David's foot so do get him to call her. Did you buy any iodine? Fuss, fuss!

Had 2 businessmen booked in for 4 nights this week but they've cancelled as job put on hold. Bugger! Still, less housework to do.

For some unknown reason, the ivy on the archway over the garden gate has died. Ian's dug it out so I'm off to Rocky Mountain to buy some new climbers. Hope they take quickly. Your viburnum has loads of new buds on it!

Put the Oxfam episode behind you, have a great week and a fab time on Friday – I'll be thinking of you! Bet the fireworks are amazing. My new mobile arrives soon so texts will resume once I've worked out how to use it.

Huge hugs, love and kisses - the works! Miss you *loads*. It will be wonderful to speak again.

Mum xxxxxxxoo

=========

It wasn't until months later that I discovered just how badly affected Lottie had been by the Oxfam job. At the end of her second day of standing on street corners she had phoned David in floods of tears. He and Stu hot-footed it into Sydney and found her in a dreadful state. All she wanted to do was come home there and then and quit the remainder of her gap year. They took her out to a bar where they all got completely smashed and she decided to stay on. Since Lottie had been away, I seem to have condemned most of her employers to the firing squad. I wondered how many more would suffer the same fate before she returned.

Chapter Eighteen

A Difficult Week

My new mobile arrived. At last, I could text Lottie again! The only problem was, the buttons were ridiculously small and I couldn't see what the hell I was doing. What's more, I quickly discovered that the blasted thing was incredibly complicated, well, it was to me anyway.

To say I was disappointed would put it mildly, particularly as the mobile had come highly recommended by the salesman. The stupid man had assured me that the buttons were big and easy to read. Ha! Not only that, I had to listen to him prattle on about how his bird had the same model and how she thought it was 'the most amazing mobile ever'. I rapidly came to the conclusion that she was stupid too.

Still, all was not lost. Nick's contract was up for renewal and he was thus entitled to a new mobile but didn't want one – he was quite happy with the one he'd got. In addition, John's all-singing-all-dancing mobile had met an early death a couple of months ago when it fell into his pint of beer. Nick had refused to replace it so John had bought himself a cheap secondhand model with none of the fancy gizmos he was used to. John positively drooled when he clapped eyes on my new mobile and was thrilled to bits when I said he could have it. I couldn't get rid of it quick enough. I ordered a new one for Nick which I kept for myself. This time I made absolutely sure that the salesman knew *exactly* what I wanted – and it arrived on the following day.

With more than a degree of trepidation, I opened the box. A Nokia 6085 stared back at me. It was fantastic! A flip up phone with big buttons and clear numbers and letters. What's more, it was a doddle to use and even had a built-in camera, rocket science to me but within ten minutes I'd managed to take photos of the cats and dogs, and good ones at that. Needless to say, Lottie received many texts from me that day. I was like a child with a new toy.

26 January, 2007

Hi Lot!

Happy Australia Day! Just called you but with all the celebrations and noise going on, I doubt you heard your phone! Hope you had a wonderful time - can't wait to hear all about it!

Linzi moving to Glasto soon - into a new house opposite the hospital – the one I took David to when he did his ankle in.

I've bought two pine shelf units and a big mirror from her for your shower room. At last - shelves that will take tall bottles! So hard to get.

Alice is on reception at White Hart but off to France soon. She sends her love.

Had supper with Daddy & John at City Arms on Wed. Drinks at Con. Club first - Pat sends regards to you both. Lovely evening, especially as Daddy had meetings every night last week, was away all weekend and yet more meetings this Mon & Tues. He, John and Andy are off to Lundy soon for 3 nights – by helicopter, not the ss sick bucket! They're really excited.

Young Morse is 2 on Tuesday! Will get him another tennis ball. Poor Claire spent most of her time yesterday throwing his old one for him which is now decidedly ragged.

On Friday there's a 'horse race' night in South Horrington which should be fun. I've sponsored a race (The Manor Farm Scramble) and named the horses, one of which is 'Lottie's Choice' which I shall bet on! Others are 'Inspector Morse', 'Big Bear' (David will like that one!) and 'Italian Stallion'. Well, got to have a laugh! Stallone's making a final 'Rocky' film - awesome at his age!

How's work in the café? Do hope it's going well for you.

Missing you enormously and sending mountains of love, hugs and kisses. Will keep phoning!

Take great care and have fun!

Mum xxxxxxxxxooooooooxxxxxxx

=========

Life Without Lottie: How I Coped (or didn't) During my Daughter's Gap Year

I was worried about Einstein. Over the past two days he had been sick and had the runs, although the sickness had eased yesterday. Einstein is a dreadful scavenger. Most times when he pinches stuff out of the refuse bins I catch him before too much has reached his tummy. On walks, he goes straight for badger shit, eats it and then delights to roll in what's left behind. There is nothing I can do about that. At least he can no longer get at the cat poo – the litter tray now stands on an old table by the back door.

But first thing this morning, when I let him and Morse outside, he passed some blood. As soon as the vet opened, I was on the phone. I got an appointment for late morning. Within five minutes of my call, the receptionist called me back. They had just received a cancellation – could I bring Einstein down now?

Poor Nick – I rushed him out of the house midway through his first cuppa.

As I turned the sausages the phone rang. Typical! I have lost count of the times when I have been in the middle of a crucial part of breakfast and someone wanted to speak to me. It was Nick.

'Hi, darling,' he said. I thought he wanted to check if I needed any shopping done on his way home.

'Hi,' I replied, as I moved back to the Aga with phone in one hand and fork in the other. 'I'm just doing the sausages. How's Einstein?' There was a pause before Nick continued. That worried me.

'Um, he's got to stay in. They've err, found a lump.'

'What?' I shrieked. 'Where? Oh, my God!' I went hot, then cold and my stomach did a nasty flip. I flung the fork onto the worktop, sausages abandoned.

'On his tummy. They can feel it. It's the size of a tennis ball.'

'Oh, God! He must have something stuck!' I said, and desperately wracked my brains to think of what on earth he could have eaten.

'That's what the vet thinks but they want to x-ray him...then they'll give us a ring. They may need to open him up.'

'Oh, poor Einstein! When will we know?' I felt sick.

'Late morning,' he said. 'They'll x-ray him when surgery's finished.'

'Oh, Nick, the poor dog.' Nick realised I was panicky and said what he could to try and calm me down.

'He's fine, don't worry. He went off with the vet quite happily. I just thought I'd phone you…thought you'd like to know now.'

'Oh, yes, yes! Um, when will you be home?' I needed him.

'I'm just going to pop into Tesco and grab the Saturday paper, and then I'll head back.'

'Oh good. Could you pick me up a packet of Mayfair please?' I thought I may need extra supplies.

'Yes, of course,' he replied. 'Now don't worry!'

Too late, I was frantic. It was also too late for the sausages. They were burnt. I slung them in the bin, grabbed some more from the fridge and started again.

It helped that I had guests in. I had to be my usual cheerful self and act as if nothing was wrong. Somehow I managed to pull it off but all the time my mind worked overtime.

I wanted to cry. What if it *wasn't* something Einstein had eaten? What if it was a tumour? I thought of his dreadful start in life. This just wasn't fair. Hadn't the dog been through enough already? All I could do was wait, and worry.

I broke the news to John. He was devastated, gave me a hug and disappeared back to his room with the instruction to let him know when I heard something.

Waiting is not my strong point. By 11.30 I had paced the kitchen countless times and all the while willed the phone to ring. Bloody thing never does when you want it to.

I reached the point where I couldn't stand the wait a moment longer and called the vet, only to be told that Einstein hadn't been x-rayed; the surgery had gone on longer than usual but I should hear within the hour. I did. The news was not good.

'Hello, Fiona?' It was Ian, our vet. My stomach lurched horribly as I waited for the worst.

Pleading to every known god in the universe for good news, I nervously replied, 'Yes. Hello, Ian. How's Einstein?'

'Well, we've done the x-ray. It clearly shows up a round lump but I can't make out what it is.'

'Oh God! What happens now?'

'Well, he hasn't been sick and hasn't passed any more blood, so rather than open him up now, I think we should let him rest quietly for a little while, see how he gets on and then make a decision.'

'Oh, okay. Will you give me a call?'

'Yes, of course. Don't worry, we'll look after him.'

An hour later, Ian called to say that Einstein had passed more blood and he wanted to open him up without further delay. I gave my consent for him to do whatever was needed. But I also said that if what he found looked hopeless, not to let Einstein wake up. As much as this hurt me, I couldn't bear the thought of his suffering being prolonged. The worst of it was, I hadn't even had time to say goodbye to him such was the rush this morning.

The wait was ghastly. All I could manage was to lie on the sofa with a glass of wine, the TV on (although I couldn't concentrate on it) and the phone right next to me. Nick offered me something to eat but I wasn't hungry. Morse and the cats jumped up to join me and we all cuddled up together. They say that stroking your pets helps to alleviate worry. Whoever 'they' are, they are right.

An hour passed by, and another. Then it stretched into three, by which time I knew that whatever Ian had found must be serious. Nick assured me that if it was *that* bad, we would have already heard, so at least Einstein was still with us. At last the phone rang. I hesitated to answer it, terrified at what I might hear, and waited for the third ring before I pressed the button to take the call.

Einstein was alive! But only just. Ian said he was 'a very sick dog' but had survived a huge and absolutely necessary operation; if he had waited any longer, it would have been too late. Ice cold shivers ran up and down my spine. He went on to say he was amazed by what he had found. The lump was not in Einstein's bowel – there was nothing trapped at all - it was actually at one end of his spleen which had become twisted and infected. Furthermore, the spleen was six times its normal size - it was over two feet long! The poor dog, I thought, he must have been in excruciating pain for some time and I hadn't realised.

At least there was no sign of a tumour. That was good news. Ian had taken the decision to remove the spleen completely, a risky procedure, but he knew that Einstein was strong and wanted to give him the chance to pull through. I will forever be in his debt for that crucial decision. He said that the next few hours – and the next few days – would be critical. Amongst a string of possible fatal post-op complications, peritonitis could set in. Ian had done everything he could and now, we just had to keep our fingers crossed, him included. I thanked him profusely. He said he'd call me later with a progress report. Once again, I waited by the phone.

With all my heart, I hung on to the fact that despite everything Einstein had so far survived. And later, Ian had good news. He told me that Einstein had sat up and had a drink of water. Christ! I thought, that dog has resilience – and an obvious iron will to live. Eighteen months ago, we had rescued him from a life of hell and welcomed him into our home, a home he obviously wanted to come back to. I felt very humbled by that. I quickly passed the news on to Nick and John, we recharged our glasses and I made an emotional toast.

'To Einstein! Please get well and come home soon!'

Ian had also told me that he'd call me first thing in the morning and I could visit Einstein, just for a few minutes. My enormous joy at the thought of being reunited with him was quickly overshadowed by the strong possibility that he wouldn't last the night. Nick stayed up with me until the small hours. We talked only of Einstein - and how he just *had* to pull through. He did. He survived the night and Ian had taken him out on the lead. I was amazed he could walk at all!

I arranged to visit him at 10 o'clock. I felt as nervous as hell and arrived on the dot. Ian took me round the back of the surgery to the kennels and there was Einstein, sitting up in his cage. He looked simply dreadful, but as soon as he saw me he wagged his tail. I nearly cried. Ian let him out and he gingerly tottered towards me. I got down on my hands and knees and gave him the gentlest and biggest cuddle you could imagine whilst silent tears rolled down my face. I couldn't help it.

Ian looked so understanding and quietly talked me through the surgical procedure he'd performed. I must confess I was in no fit state to take much of it in, but I certainly got the gist of the supreme urgency involved and the utmost care and dexterity Ian had taken.

As far as I was concerned, the man was an angel. What had caused the problem was a bit of a mystery. Ian said it could have been as a result of gastro-enteritis and Einstein being sick, although he hadn't been *that* sick. We would never know. The important task to concentrate on now was to help him get better – and continue to keep our fingers crossed.

'You can take him out for a little walk if you like,' Ian said.

'Oh, yes, that would be great…if you're sure it's all right?' Ian nodded. Terrified that something may go wrong, I added 'Can you come with us?'

'Yes, yes, of course' He turned to Einstein. 'Come on then, boy! Off we go!'

Blow me if the darling dog didn't spend a penny as soon as I led him onto the grass.

'Ah, that's good,' said Ian with a smile. 'He didn't perform for me earlier…he must have felt embarrassed.'

I was gob smacked by the total understanding this man had of animals. He was a very special vet. I slowly led Einstein back to the surgery and, without being prompted, he put himself back into his kennel. Clearly, the walk had exhausted him. I removed his lead, gave him a kiss, stroked his ears and Ian closed the door.

When I got back into my car and pulled the door shut, I burst into tears. It was several minutes before I composed myself enough to bung the key into the ignition, switch on the engine and drive home.

When I arrived, Morse jumped and howled with delight for he could smell Einstein on my clothes. It was pathetic to see him stare at the door for his pal, to no avail. That evening I spent most of my time with him – and his tennis ball. It was the only way to successfully distract him from continuous whining and searching.

The following morning, I was more than delighted to receive a happy email from Lottie:

29 January, 2007

Hi!

Sorry missed your call on Oz day! Had an excellent time - went to Hyde Park to watch some bands and then down to the harbour and sat in beer gardens in the sunshine! Then we went to the bottle shop and bought some drinks to have in the botanical gardens (next to the opera house) which were really pretty. By that time it was about 10pm and we decided to head back into Manly because we had all spent way too much money in the city! It was such good fun though, there was so much going on in the harbour. There were loads of tall ships decorated like pirate boats and a huge Royal Navy ship display and they fired their guns!

Started new job yesterday which went fine. It was so busy but apparently it's only like that on Sunday so that's ok. I've got to work 4pm til the end today which is usually about 11pm, huff!

David and I have bought walkie talkies for the van! Stu has one too so we can communicate on the road! They have a 3km radius! We can tune into what other people are saying and even into the channel the police use! Mark and Hannah fly into Sydney on 21st Feb so we will leave for up the coast absolute latest 30th. Not a bad plan as we can both get more work in so we don't have to work once we've left - fingers crossed!

Still practicing on my baby blue board! I haven't named it yet though, any ideas? David's traded in his board. The new one is mainly yellow and called 'Custard'! I'm getting better at surfing - I can now go sideways but can't go up and down the waves like the pros!

Good to hear everything is great at home. The horse race sounds like really good fun! Wish John lots of luck in his theory exam! The day I passed mine, Bill ran away with that woman from the internet. That seems like ages ago!

Missing you lots and hope to speak to you soon! Wish Morse happy birthday! lol xoxox

==========

I felt awful that Lottie had no idea Einstein was so ill. I saw him again that afternoon and he was a little stronger. I chatted with the nurses for a while. One of them told me they had nicknamed him 'Miracle Dog'. He was indeed. She also said that he could probably go home tomorrow afternoon but I was to call first, at lunch time, to check that it was still okay. Overjoyed, I sang all the way home. I was given my usual exuberant welcome by Morse and crouched down to cuddle him.

'Morse! Guess what? Einstein should be home tomorrow – on your birthday!'

When Morse heard Einstein's name and picked up on the excitement in my voice he started to charge up and down the kitchen. That made me laugh! He was such a sweetie. What a wonderful present for him – for all of us – to have Einstein home again. In the evening, I replied to Lottie's email. I didn't mention Einstein; it was still early days.

29 January, 2007

Hi Lot!

Great to get your lovely newsy email! Thanks so much. And delighted Oz day was such a blast! So glad new job is okay. I remember when I was nursing, donkeys years ago (gawd!) - I absolutely loathed the late shift. It made the day seem so long. Great you've got walkie talkies! And a good range too. Your surfing skills sound amazing - I'm proud of you Lot!

Everything's fine but not much news. It's just that time of year. Two lots of guests in which is good – I'm swamped by bills! Daddy's at his tutorial. He has a great new case coming up soon. I'll email results of the horse race night - should be a laugh. Hope your horse wins!

Am attaching new photos of cats and the East Room (amazing change from John's former pit!). Have already taken a couple of bookings over Easter which is good.

Well, that's it for today, darling. Take care and have a good week. Hope work isn't as busy as Sunday. If I don't manage to speak to you this week, please phone home and reverse charges and I'll call you back. It's been far too long since we spoke. Will give Morse a hug from you tomorrow - can't believe he's nearly 2! Tell David he still behaves like a chav!

Huge love and hugs and missing you too.

Mum xxxxooooooooxxxxx

=========

I was glad how easy I found it to cover up the truth in an email. It made me realise just how impersonal a method of communication it is.

The next day I phoned the vet and was thrilled to be told that I could collect Einstein in a couple of hours. We were all at home as Nick's case had been adjourned and John's tutor was off sick. Nick fixed the baby gate across the coats section of the kitchen where Einstein could rest. It brought back memories of thirteen months ago when Morse had to be shut behind the same gate to recuperate from his leg operation. I shuddered at the thought.

The three of us drove into Wells. We stopped off at the pet shop en route as I needed to buy lots of warm comfy bedding for Einstein. When we arrived he looked so much better and wagged his tail non-stop!

Whilst I received instructions on food, medication and general care, the boys helped him to the car and lifted him into the back. When we got home he was very shaky from the journey, so I put down all but one of the blankets I'd bought into his temporary bed, led him in, settled him and covered him with the remaining one.

Tallinn and Riga quickly discovered they could fit through the baby gate bars and snuggled up next to him. Morse sat the other side and whined but was obviously delighted to have his pal back. The next morning, Einstein seemed stronger and was fine, until after he'd had his lunch when he was dreadfully sick in the garden. Afterwards, he went completely motionless with head down and tail between his legs. Something was obviously very wrong. I raced into the house and called the surgery. I was told that Ian was operating but would be free in half an hour. I asked if anyone else was available for an emergency home visit but the answer was no. I said I'd bring him down.

I needed help. There was no way on earth I could lift Einstein into the car by myself. I called Ian and told him the problem. He said he'd be with me directly. He was marvellous. Einstein couldn't walk so between us we carried him to the car and lifted him into the back. Ian offered to accompany me but I was pretty sure Einstein would have to stay in. As I drove slowly out of the driveway, I could hear Morse's pitiful whines. If I could whine, I would have done so too.

Luckily, I arrived at the surgery just as Ian became free. He and Tricia (who is the nicest and kindest receptionist in the world) carried Einstein inside. Ian said he needed to stay in overnight for observation. He would give him something to ease the sickness and settle him down. I asked Ian to call me if Einstein's condition deteriorated. 'Of course' he replied. 'But let's hope not, especially as he's come this far.' When I returned home, Morse craved my attention and whined almost continuously.

To cap it all, that afternoon John failed his driving theory test – by one mark. What an utterly shitty week, I thought. Tomorrow would be 1 February. I hoped that a new month would bring in better luck all round.

Chapter Nineteen

Bites

1 February 2007

Hi!

Tell John I'm really sorry about his test. Better luck next time. I can't believe those pics are of his old room!! It looks SO different! I couldn't work out where they were taken to start with! I've sent you an Oz day postcard and attach some pics of the day. I'll give you a call either tonight or tomorrow morning. I'm just getting over a 4 day migraine which isn't very nice. No work yesterday - I had to take Stu to A&E because he had kidney stones. He's much better now and I needed the day off anyway because I felt like rubbish.

Glad to here everything at home is great. Thinking of you all lots. I can't believe it's only 6 months till I come home, the trip has gone so quickly! I love it out here; it will be strange coming back to Wells. We *might* (depending on how our trip up the coast goes) be home for Glastonbury but it is a very big might because that cuts our trip short by 2 months. Watch this space! When do the tickets go on sale? Thank you very much for the Glasto DVD! It's great, have watched it quite a few times and it reminds me of home and all the great times we had!

I think that's about all I have to say, send my love to everyone and thinking of you all lots. Will speak to you soon, lol xox

ps. thought the pic named 'toilets' (sorry 'loo'!) will remind John of Glasto!

=========

I was worried. There was something about the tone in her email which was not quite right. Lottie had never had a migraine before and rarely got a headache. Why now? I wondered. Plus, she had to take Stu to hospital. As for the possibility of her coming home earlier than planned, that would be just incredible. I hardly dared think about it. I tried to phone her but had to leave a message.

I saw Einstein who was a little better and I was told he could go home on Saturday. The next day he was heaps stronger and had even put on a little weight. I was absolutely thrilled. When I got home, as soon as I saw Morse I knew he had been up to something naughty. There was no exuberant welcome for me this time. He met me at the back door with a decidedly guilty look on his face and scuttled past me to his bed. As I walked into the kitchen all was revealed. The flagstone floor was completely littered with chewed up pieces of cardboard and polythene.

Just before I'd left to visit Einstein, Roger, my butcher, had delivered a fresh supply of bacon to me. There were three large packets, vacuum packed in thick polythene, all contained inside a cardboard box. As I didn't have time to freeze the bacon, I had placed the box on top of the chest of drawers and pushed it to the back, out of harm's way. Or so I thought. Whilst I was out, Morse had somehow managed to pull the box down, rip it open, chew his way through the polythene and devour much of the bacon inside. The little devil had scoffed over a kilo of raw British best back!

'Oh, Morse!' I shouted. 'You naughty dog!'

I got down on my hands and knees to pick up (or rather scrape up) the debris. The pack he'd mostly feasted on was in his bed and only a few sorry looking rashers remained. Those went straight in the bin. Luckily, the other two packs were still intact – under the kitchen table.

Morse's belly was badly distended. I didn't want to run the risk of another pet emergency and so I phoned the vet and told them what Morse had done. I think they had difficulty not to laugh. The advice was simple. He'll be thirsty so ensure there is plenty of fresh water... hopefully he'll be sick and get rid of the damage... keep him on a light diet for a couple of days... phone back if you are worried.

As soon as I put the phone down Morse's tummy started to make the most extraordinary noises – and loud. Oh Lord! I thought, better get him outside quick! I was too late. He gave a huge burp and then spewed up a large pile of half-chewed bacon at my feet, plus several bits of polythene and cardboard. That's all I needed, but at least most of it was out.

I rushed him into the garden where he was sick again. The vet was absolutely right about the thirst - over the next hour he drained his water bowl at least four times.

With all evidence of the mess cleared up and the two rescued bacon packs in the safety of my freezer, I gratefully escaped to the study to reply to Lottie's email.

I knew she'd love to hear about the bacon episode but I didn't mention it. She would have wondered why Einstein hadn't tucked in also.

2 February, 2007

Hi Darling!

Do hope your migraine's gone – absolutely wretched for you - and poor Stu, kidney stones are very painful.

Would be utterly *fantastic* if you were home for Glasto! But I quite understand you can't decide yet. Tickets go on sale 1 April and this year, everyone has to pre-register. Pre-registration opened yesterday so I've registered you and David, and John. Didn't cost anything so don't worry about that. Just let me know by end March. Tickets are £145 which is a great price.

There are lots of rumours of bands but The Who are now confirmed (for Sunday) and possibly Eric Clapton. Have attached latest list. I've got EMI people booked in already. Hope we get the Kasabian manager again!

Fab pictures - loved the mooning! I miss the chants of 'toilet, toilet...serviette'!!! I feel very pale compared to your tans!

Lizzie came for supper last night. All very emotional as Guy flew to India and it was her birthday. John is really pissed off about his theory test disaster. Couldn't rebook it until 7 March. Colin's taking him to Weston for his next lesson to 'learn the route'. Bet you remember that!

John and Phil off to London tonight to see England v Scotland tomorrow, so that will cheer him up. Naturally, I shall shout for

Scotland! Have you heard from Emily? Morse had a great birthday and got a new tennis ball.

So pleased DVD arrived and you like it. It's a favourite late-nite watch for John. Can't wait to get your pc. Missing you loads and loads! And sending all love from us all - and big hugs too!

Mum xxxxxxxxxxxxooooooooxxxxxxxxxx

=========

Nick gave John a lift to the bus stop where he was due to meet Phil. Thank God he asked him if he'd got tickets, bus pass, etc. You know - the usual parental last minute check that kids so hate. Fortunately there was just time to turn around and collect his wallet. With the boys safely on their way to London, Nick and I went to the horse race evening.

It was great fun! The opening race was the one we had sponsored. 'Lottie's Choice' came in third but the tote only paid out for first and second. Luckily I'd bought a ticket for 'Inspector Morse' who won so, although I was over £50 down, at least I got £6 back! By the end of the evening a whopping £950 had been raised for a local good cause.

The following day we collected Einstein and he was obviously glad to be home again. He was as good as gold. John returned from his rugby weekend which he talked about non stop.

I sent Lottie a text: '*Hi Lot! Your horse came 3rd! Inspector Morse won. Hope u had great w/end. All well here. John had brill time in London + sends lol, so do I! Mxoxxxx*'

First thing Monday morning, I got this email:

4 February, 2007

Hi!

Horse race sounded great! Shame my horse didn't win. Worked all weekend, not much fun - was going to ring but I was so tired when I finished at just past midnight that I fell asleep on the sofa. They certainly get their moneys worth from you for less than 5 pounds an hr but only a few weeks to go now - then up the East coast!

Glad John enjoyed the match. I've told the guys in the hostel about the competition he won and they are all deadly jealous! I showed them a pic of him so everyone will look out for him in the crowds. Tell him he'll be famous!

I think that's about it, better get ready for work. Been bitten really badly all up my legs by mossies! When I scratch the bites they grow to the size of saucers and then bruise, not nice! Nine of them are really nasty.

Missing you all lots and lots and speak to you soon! Hopefully tomorrow! Xox

=========

Bites the size of *saucers*?! Something was terribly wrong. I sent a text straight away: '*Bites sound awful. See doctor asap for cortisone injection & claim on insurance. I had one in Greece + it worked a treat. Lol mxxx*'

I received no response and tried to call several times but, again, couldn't get a signal. I emailed early the following day:

6 February, 2007

Hi Lot!

How are your bites? If they're not any better, PLEASE go and see a doctor. Have left messages on your phone - do call me!

All fine here. Heavy frost so Mr. T needed much de-icing before John drove me into Wells. Incredible change from Saturday when we had drinks outside in lovely sunshine. John thrilled to bits he could be famous in Sydney! I hope someone spots him!

Your working hours are long indeed - and not brilliantly paid - but as you say, not long to wait before the big trip. Bet you can't wait.

Is the van fixed? Please let me know if you need anything as I could post to Mark before he leaves for Sydney and he can bring it over.

Nicola's birthday on 19 Feb - do send her a card. She often phones to find out how you are. Ganda & Ann send lol - they're exhausted after Beth, Paul & Imogen stayed for 6 nights but had lovely time. Daddy had final tutorial last night which is great.

I've bought scented climbers to replace ivy over garden gate so should smell gorgeous by the summer! Roll on. Boys off to Lundy a week on Friday, then Daddy & I to Palma a month today!

Sending huge amounts of love as usual and do hope to speak soon!

Mum xxxxxxxxoooooooooxxxxxxxxx

=========

Einstein's recovery continued, so much so that he chased Morse up the garden. He could run again! I was terrified he might do some internal damage and kept a watchful eye on him, and after a few minutes I took them both back inside. It was now three days since I'd heard anything from Lottie and I was very worried about her bites. It was therefore a great relief to get this email:

7 February, 2007

Hi!

Sorry about not being in contact - I ran out of credit again. I sent an email yesterday but perhaps it didn't come through. I was going to ring last night but had a whole Piriton and it knocked me out. I went to the pharmacy and they said my bites are infected and that's the reason I've been getting bad headaches and not been feeling well. They told me to take a Piriton and get an early night and if they were no better in the morning to see a doctor but luckily they are a bit better today!

New injury! - I went surfing and a jelly fish got stuck up my board shorts! It's stung me all up one leg and on my bum! It then continued to sting me on my belly and arm! The stings feel like a stinging nettle sting but worse. I had to take my shorts off whilst I was bobbing around in the water to get it out and then swim into shore in my pants! I got some funny looks but it was a good job I was wearing something underneath. I finish work at about 11pm tonight so I'll give you a ring then.

I've been thinking about what I want to do when I get home. I've got a few ideas. One is to come back out here and work in Sydney. There are good job opportunities for me with my A'levels where I could quickly work my way up. Don't panic though, it's only an idea and it wouldn't be permanent! Maybe for 6 months or so to see how it goes! Because I'm a backpacker I can't get a real job and I don't want to be a waitress all my life! Another is to come home and get on the job ladder in England. I'm still really interested in I.T. I was thinking of trying to get a job maybe in Bristol or another bigger city (bigger than Wells!) and seeing how that works out. If I need a degree/qualification etc I can get one. I'm still not sure about the Uni idea - I can't decide on a course and if I do go I'd want it to be for a purpose and marketable. I've met so many people out here that have degrees and can't get a half decent job because what they studied was worthless.

Another idea is to do a bit more travelling. Nothing as long as a year though. I would love to travel round Europe for a couple of months or even South America. I've been looking into the TEFL courses (English as foreign language) which could open the door on becoming a teacher.

Anyway, just some things I've been thinking of, what do you think?

Really, really sorry for worrying you again. I love you lots and lots and speak to you later xox

=========

Oh God! *More* bites! This time from a bloody jellyfish! I was very concerned; Lottie had obviously felt poorly for a while and definitely required professional medical attention, not just a pharmacist and Piriton tablets.

I waited anxiously for her call. Lottie's comments on the job situation saddened me. She was obviously fed up with menial jobs and poor pay, particularly when she's capable of much more. I was somewhat surprised that she had already given some thought to her future and written at length about her ideas. The thought of her returning home only to jet back to Sydney horrified me. How I wished she could come home for a few days so we could all sit round the kitchen table and discuss her future together. She obviously wanted our input but it wasn't going to be easy, even with today's international communication facilities.

Our plumber, Dave, arrived to fix new kitchen taps. Nick was at home and helped him. I was also in the kitchen as it would soon be breakfast time. The phone rang. I answered it with my usual 'Good morning, Manor Farm!' A quiet voice replied 'Hi Mum!' It was Lottie! She hadn't reversed the charges so I phoned her back and actually got through. Boy was it good to hear her voice!

As we spoke, my fears grew. She'd seen another pharmacist who informed her that the bites were not caused by mosquitoes but by bed bugs! Lottie said they must be in the camper van's mattress, which would be dumped. Thank God for that!

David had also been bitten but his bites had cleared up. Lottie's were still very red and sore and oozed puss. So much for the first pharmacist's diagnosis, I thought, and added him to my 'should be shot' list. Piriton indeed. Why the hell hadn't he referred her to a doctor? The poor girl had been poisoned! And on top of all this, she now had jelly fish bites to contend with.

Her encounter with the beast sounded frightful. She said it was 'very painful and a bit scary', but we laughed about how awful it would have been if she hadn't worn pants.

What was even funnier was when I told Lottie the recommended treatment I had found for jellyfish bites via Google - a liberal squirt of fresh male urine!

'You'll have to get David to pee on you!' I said. She roared with laughter, as did I, and Nick and Dave from under the sink. I told her to go and see a doctor. In fact, I said 'go now!'

'Mum,' she replied, 'I can't! It's after eleven at night!'

Bugger the time difference, I thought, but I had to settle with her promise to see one tomorrow and text or call me afterwards.

I decided to send her an emailed:

7 February 2007

Hi Darling!

FANTASTIC speaking to you - and lovely that Daddy did too. GOOD LUCK at the doctors tomorrow. Bloody mattress! Glad you're throwing it away. Don't forget to fumigate bed board, cushions, corners etc. Look out for little black spots anywhere!

Life Without Lottie: How I Coped (or didn't) During my Daughter's Gap Year

Missing you terribly - I hate it when my offspring suffer! But so look forward to speaking to you tomorrow.

All love and more

Mum xxxxxxxxooooooooxxxxxxxx

=========

I hoped and prayed that both sets of bites did not deteriorate overnight. I tried to call Lottie first thing but couldn't get a signal so I sent her a text to say I'd be at home all day. Her call came through at lunch time. She sounded a bit low, but had seen a doctor, who had prescribed hydro-cortisone (at last, I thought!). He was very kind, she told me and the cream had already helped. As for the jellyfish encounter, the doctor said she'd been stung by the 'Blue Bottle' variety, which wasn't dangerous and the rash should clear up in about a week. That was a relief!

As we chatted on, Lottie's voice gained strength and she sounded more like the confident and fun-loving girl I knew and loved so much. I was delighted to learn that she had two days off work so she could rest.

I told her about Einstein. As his recovery continued in leaps and bounds, I thought the time was right. Naturally, she was shocked but glad to learn that he was on the mend. We agreed to speak again in a few days time, but she'd call me sooner if she was worried.

When I put the phone down, the distance in miles between us seemed greater than ever. It is one thing for a mother to be so far apart from her daughter when she is well and happy, but quite a different matter altogether when she is unwell and sad.

I emailed her:

8 February, 2007

Hi Darling!

SO relieved you've at last got proper cream and it's already helped. Get lots of R&R in over the next couple of days and watch out for jellyfish - little buggers!!!

Am posting a parcel to you tomorrow - a few little somethings for the van. Though they'd cheer you up.

Enormous amounts of love and hugs. Get rid of those bites very soon. Miss you heaps.

Mum xxooooooooooxxxxxxxxx

=========

Einstein had his stitches removed and gradually returned to his normal diet. Much to everyone's complete joy and relief, the 'Miracle Dog' would be with us for a lot longer.

Chapter Twenty

Sleep Walking

Text from Lottie:
'Great news about Einstein! Give him a big hug. The hostel owner is getting the van sprayed 2moz because her flat has bugs as well! She's also getting our bedroom done which is great and we don't have 2 pay 4 it! Off to rugby club now for cheap drinks! Lol x'

Bed bugs must be rife in Australia! Bloody good thing the kids' dorm was also being treated. I replied:

'So pleased about free bug sprays! Stay cool! Lol mxx'

I had contacted Oxfam in the UK and told them of the horror Lottie had experienced in Sydney. One of their Australian 'bureaucracy' phoned me. She told me that Lottie's trainer had been 'severely reprimanded'. Furthermore, she not only offered her profuse apologies but also compensation for Lottie. I texted Lottie with the news and her reply showed obvious delight:

'Wow! How much do they want to give me? Thanks 4 doing that 4 me. Lol x'

I had no idea how much Oxfam would pay and I certainly wasn't prepared to ask. I replied:

'My pleasure. Don't know amount. Let me know when it arrives. John's got a new bird – out on 1st date tonite! Have great week, will email 2moz and speak soon. Lol mxxoxx'

An email came through overnight:

13 February, 2007

Hi!

Gt news about the Oxfam pay out! What did you say to them? Thank you so much for helping. If I get a lot of money I will send you some.

Didn't go to the rugby club in the end. It was closed so we went to the sailing club and had drinks overlooking the bay - only problem was there was another tropical storm but it was good fun!

Let me know how John's date went! I'm working on Wednesday - 4pm till close and on same shift all week which isn't much fun. I've got Thursday off so I think David and I will go out for a valentine's supper then. Only two weeks of work left. I can't wait!

Van has been fumigated, kept the mattress but got rid of all the old pillows, curtains and covers that the bed bugs could have got into. No more bites so fingers crossed that's got rid of them for good.

Nothing else exciting to report. I will watch out for Oxfam's cheque. Missing you all lots and lots. I'll call one night this week. I can't reverse charges from my mobile because for some reason it still charges me which seems stupid! Xox

==========

13 February, 2007

Hi Lot!

I was so outraged that I sent Oxfam HQ a copy of your email to me ('...*sign this and I'll make it worth your while*') and asked them to contact me urgently to explain why they blatantly encouraged innocent young girls to become prostitutes in order to benefit Oxfam's income. I obviously ruffled more than a few feathers as since then I've received several emails and calls, lastly by a woman in Oz. You keep whatever you get darling - you deserve it. If you don't receive cheque within a week I'll chase up. Do also check for your 'van' parcel (John posted it last Fri). I had such fun choosing stuff!

Please DITCH THE MATTRESS!!! Don't rely on fumigation to have killed all the beasties and their millions of eggs - which I've learnt are mighty resilient. DO buy new one (you mentioned 2nd hand shop which sold cheap new ones). Please, please!!!

Another tropical storm - at least you were in the right place! Sorry you're working so late on Valentine's Day. Enjoy supper out Thurs. John's date went well and has arranged another one. Hils sends love. She left her deep freeze slightly open overnight so had to bin half the contents - discovered at 4.30 in the morning as she was about to leave for London. She's lived off smoked salmon for two days!

Well, breakfast to clear away, beds to strip - the usual.

Missing you loads as ever and sending huge hugs and love. Take great care.

Mum xxxxxxxxooooooooxxxxxxxxx

=========

16 February, 2007

Hi!

Thanks so much again for help with Oxfam. I'll check post shop today. I had to go into work yesterday but off today - the roster got changed at the last minute but it works better for me because I get Friday night off...except I've to be at work for 8am on Saturday so I think it's going to be a quiet, cheap night in!

Valentines evening at work was absolute hell. It was so so busy and the manager hadn't put nearly enough staff on. I got many complaints about cold food and food that took over an hour to arrive - not fun. Only a week to go now and I'm handing in my notice tomorrow.

Went out for drinks after work on Valentines Day with some hostel friends. The strangest thing happened...I sleep walked that night!! I had this really strange dream that John had flown over from home to see us and we were at the airport, but I couldn't find him anywhere so I was running around searching for him. In the morning I found out that I had woken up Will, one of the boys in our room, and kept saying 'John, John' and then gibbered on, not making any sense. Will is about the same size as John. He told me go to back to bed, I said 'OK John' and started getting into bed with him! Will showed me back to my bed but I ran out of the room so he followed me. I did a circuit of the bathrooms and then climbed into MY bed and went to sleep! How embarrassing! David thinks it's hilarious and is winding me up non-stop so I keep reminding him of the B&B incident and that shuts him up! Ha ha! It's strange and I don't know what made it happen!

Apart from that I had a nice Valentines Day. David got back from work early so we spent the afternoon together before I went to work. He bought me a big bunch of roses and a bottle of nice fizzy wine.

How did Johns 2nd date go? Hope it went well. Anything exciting been happening at home?

Not much else to report here. Mark arrives in six days and now counting down till we leave for the coast!

Missing you all lots and lots and speak to you soon! xox
==========

I had lunch with Hils and told her about the sleepwalking. She was convinced it was due to Lottie feeling homesick. After some careful thought, I emailed Lottie:

17 February, 2007

Hi Darling!

How weird about the sleepwalking! Still, you're obviously amongst friends who care - well done Will. And naughty D for winding you up - most unnecessary.

Wish I was there to give you a big hug. I really wouldn't worry about it though - put it down to over-work and over-stress.

The café work sounds hard and it's soon all change for you having to leave mates behind and wonder what lies ahead up the coast.

With David's bro coming over you probably feel a bit on the vulnerable side. At least you had yesterday off work which will have helped recharge your batteries. We need to speak soon!

The helicopter couldn't fly to Lundy yesterday - bad weather. Such a disappointment but the boys stayed overnight in Bideford (at hotel run by ex Lundy barman & his wife) and hope to get across later today. I'll let you know by text.

Einstein marvellous and has gained some more weight. Cats crazy as ever. Their latest trick is to dive under the dogs' blankets and play 'catch the tail'! Riga had a shock yesterday when Morse sat on him by mistake!

Life Without Lottie: How I Coped (or didn't) During my Daughter's Gap Year

Missing you so much, darling. Wish you weren't so bloody far away! It's hard but the time does seem to be going quicker now. Have a great weekend, hope work isn't too busy and you find time to relax and enjoy.

Loads of love and loads more.

Mum xxxxxxxxoooooooooxxxxxxxxx

=========

Nick called me from Lundy – they had arrived and, he told me, were enjoying their first (of many) drinks in the Marisco tavern.

I texted Lottie and she phoned me on Monday morning. I was devastated to learn she had been stung by another jellyfish! This time one got stuck on the Velcro ankle strap of her surf board and had stung her several times before she managed to pull the blasted thing off.

Lottie said it was punishment for having bunked off work because she was so tired. At least she could show her boss the marks tomorrow.

She said she couldn't wait to finish there on Saturday. Mark and Hannah arrived safely and are staying at the 'posh' hostel down the road.

We talked about their trip. The van was almost ready and I asked how the curtains had turned out.

'Oh Mum! They were a disaster!'

'Oh, what a shame!' I replied. 'But at least you tried.'

Oxfam's payment hadn't arrived, nor had my goodies for the van. I had included a bag of mini Easter eggs. Maybe they had been snaffled by customs and thus delayed delivery? Lottie said she would check again on Tuesday.

We agreed to keep in touch via text and occasional phone calls. The internet café was a fair distance from the hostel, was expensive to use and Lottie was busy preparing for the trip.

I would very much miss her emails. It always gave me such pleasure when I pressed the 'send and receive' button on Outlook Express and up popped a message from her. I would also miss composing emails to her. I could say so much more in an email compared with a text message but at least we still had that.

Fiona Fridd

After the call, I felt elated for two reasons. First, I had spoken to Lottie and, second, Nick and John would be back in the afternoon. It was a very happy moment for me when they arrived. Two days later, Lottie received Oxfam's payment.

'Cheque arrived this morn. for $200, so about 80 pounds! Thanks so much again, it'll really help with trip costs. Going to bank then off 2 work. Envelope on cheque said 'next day delivery' but it was posted 4 days ago – slow Australians! No parcel yet. Lol x'

We continued to text one another for a while. I emailed Oxfam and thanked them on Lottie's behalf. A satisfactory conclusion.

Later that week, I was terribly disappointed to get this text:

'Tried callin u a few times, no answer. Guess u were doin the shoppin or rooms. Will try again in a bit or 2moro morn. Nothing exciting 2 report, just callin 4 a chat. Speak soon. Lol xxx'

I replied immediately:

'Really sorry missed yr calls. You were right – I was shopping, then had pedicure. Dad gone to God camp. Roll on Palma! When do u leave Manly? Lol mxxx'

It was Friday evening. John had gone into town, Nick would have arrived at God camp and was probably in his first of many lectures about the importance of family life – ironically the theme for the weekend. I felt deserted. I had B&B guests in but didn't count them as company. Hils was on holiday in Gran Canaria with Joe & Anita and the boys. As for tomorrow, Janine already had a lunch appointment and everyone else I had spoken to was busy. To cap it all, I'd caught John's cold. At least my pedicure was a treat. I could only describe it as luscious. If you have never had one, make an appointment now. Just do it!

The phrase 'just do it' was often used by my favourite uncle, David. He was my father's only brother who died a few years ago, just before his eightieth birthday, from bone cancer. He didn't deserve that, no one does. In addition to my father, David was also my hero. I adored him. I feel tearful as I write about him now, for I still miss him very much. He was a great character, always life and soul of the party, and had the most canny business sense you could ever imagine. He had his fingers in many pies and never failed to come up trumps.

Life Without Lottie: How I Coped (or didn't) During my Daughter's Gap Year

David was tall, dark, handsome and forceful. When he spoke it was difficult to get a word in edgeways. Like my father, he always had a funny story to tell, which he did with great aplomb. He made stonkingly good wine from a variety of garden produce which ranged from white birch (my absolute favourite) to raspberry, nettle and rhubarb. All of it rendered you completely senseless within a very short space of time. It was dangerous stuff! His best advice to me, and it has paid dividends for which I shall forever be in his debt, was not to think too long about a business venture but 'just do it'.

We all stayed with David and his second wife, Hilda, a lovely lady, a few months before he died. I was so pleased that the children met him and I hoped they took notice of at least some of his words of wisdom. I have a lovely photograph of us all taken outside the front of his house just before we left – my last picture of David. I treasure it.

I didn't feel lonely for all of Friday evening as, just after ten o'clock, Lottie phoned! She told me they had finished work which was a huge relief as they were both knackered!

Stu would now only accompany them for the first two days of the trip as his father was poorly and he was going home. Mark and Hannah had bought a second hand Shogun and would drive up the coast with them.

But what she told me next made my day, my week, and my entire year. She said there was now a *much* stronger possibility that she and David would be home for Glastonbury! I shrieked with glee but back-peddled slightly, as I knew the reason behind this was lack of money. I had previously thought this *may* happen, but hadn't dwelt on it in case they continued to work and thus could finance their travels a while longer. But now Lottie had told me they'd given up work for good!

I said how fantastic it would be to have her home sooner than expected, but I also told her how sorry I was that she simply couldn't afford to backpack for much longer. She said with all sincerity how wonderful it would be to come home. When I put the phone down, I could hardly wait to text Nick and John with the news.

Morse excelled himself this week. Or rather his nose did. Not only did he sniff out a rabbit in the garden but also a rat – inside the house! The rabbit was discovered whilst the dogs were out for a final pee before bedtime. When I called them back in, Einstein quickly appeared and had his usual biscuit, but there was no sign of Morse. I found him round the side of the house by the wall, nose down and tail wagging furiously. I called him but he took no notice whatsoever.

As I approached I saw something move but it was dark so I couldn't make out what it was. I ran inside to get the torch, returned, flicked the switch on to full beam and there it was - a big fat grey rabbit. I took Morse by the collar and with some difficulty pulled him away in order to inspect his find. To my horror the rabbit was covered in sores and its eyes bulged and oozed yellow stuff. I dragged Morse back inside, grabbed a cardboard box to put the rabbit in and called Nick to come and help me. As soon as he saw it, he said:

'It's got Myxy.' That shocked me!

'Oh God, no. The poor thing!' I replied. I knew the rabbit was in a bad way, but I had never seen one with myxymotosis before. 'What can we do? We must do something!'

'Absolutely nothing. That's a very sick rabbit. Doesn't look as if it'll survive the night.'

'Oh Nick, that's awful. It must be suffering dreadfully. Can't you bash it on the head or something?'

'I'll see what I can do. You go back inside.'

It seemed an eternity before Nick returned. This gave me more than enough time for my imagination to run riot. I pictured the rabbit as it was hit by a spade, a log of wood, an iron bar – anything I could think of that would be to hand. The visions were horrid, particularly the bloody mess which resulted from the iron bar. Had Nick killed it with one blow or had it taken two? Those pictures were even worse.

However, whilst Nick searched for a suitable implement, the rabbit had hopped down the drive, under the gate, across the road and disappeared from sight. I was thankful in two ways - that the rabbit had escaped (well, it *might* recover, I thought) and that Nick had been spared from killing it. The next morning, soon after Nick had left for work, he phoned me to say he'd passed the rabbit on his way up the hill. It had been run over and was very dead. Its suffering was over.

As for the rat episode, I should have known that things would not be 'normal' that day. From the very start it seemed jinxed. First of all I broke a ramekin dish when I washed up. Next, the bin liner burst as I emptied the soiled cat litter into it. Not nice.

Then, at breakfast time, Tallinn knocked over my mug and coffee spilled all over the worktop and dowsed the bacon I'd just got out of the fridge. Much to Einstein's delight I also dropped a raw egg in front of the Aga and he flatly refused to move until he'd licked the floor to death, shell included This didn't help at all as I needed to put plates into the bottom oven to warm. If you've ever tried to shift a basset away from food, you'll know how impossible a task that is.

At the other end of the kitchen, Tallinn was busy again. He had knocked over the old enamel jug where we keep our used corks. Of course it was full. There followed a dreadful crash as it fell to the floor and corks rolled everywhere. Did I have a broom handy? No! At least the noise made Einstein run to his bed and I grabbed the opportunity to put the plates into the oven.

I then smelt burning, swore at the toaster and chucked the blackened offerings into the bin. My guests had to wait longer than usual for their cooked breakfasts, but they told me it was the best they had had for ages! They made no mention of the strange sounds which they must have heard.

I cleared away and handed out leftover toast to the dogs. Einstein wolfed down his slice. Morse, on the other hand, seemed far more interested in what was under the long case clock. I peered underneath. The gap was small but I could just make out a round grey thing. Ah! I thought, it must be one of his tennis balls. But the gap wasn't big enough so how the hell had it got there? I used an old knife to ease it forward. Out popped a face – of a large dead mouse! I squealed, dropped the knife, shoved the dogs into the kitchen and flew into the study to get Nick.

'That's not a mouse, it's a rat!' he told me.

'Shit!' I replied and quickly grabbed the kitchen roll and thrust it towards him.

'Here! Pick it up with this!'

'No, I need gloves,' Nick said.

As he went into the kitchen, I shouted after him, 'Well, be quick! B&Bs will be down any minute.'

The last thing I wanted was for my guests to see a dead rat in the room where they had just eaten breakfast. And where the hell had Nick got to? How, in an emergency situation, can it take a man such a long time to find a pair of gloves? Eventually he returned with the biggest, toughest pair on his hands and pulled the rat out by its head. It was disgusting. Its tail was twice as long as it's body. Nick tried to pick it up by the tail. This took several attempts because his gloves were so thick. Just as he had carried the creature into the kitchen and I'd closed the door behind him, in walked my guests, ready to settle their account. If they'd turned up seconds earlier…

Chapter Twenty-One

Palma

Shortly after Nick returned from God camp, I received a text from Lottie. Her East Coast trip had begun.

'We're on the road! On way 2 Newcastle. Van still going! Surprise surprise its rainin as it does every time we use it. Oh well, camping will be fun! Have a great time on hols, you deserve it with all the b+b work! Speak 2 u soon. Lol x'

I replied: *'Bon voyage! Have fab time! Will track you on map! Am sure weather will improve soon. Will txt when we get to Palma. Lol + happy drivin! Mxxx'*

The night before we left I woke up every hour, partly due to my cold which had developed into a real stinker and partly due to the excitement of the holiday.

We were booked on Easyjet's 7.45am flight from Bristol. At 5am I gave up all attempts to sleep, got up and took two cold control pills. Although I felt terrible, I was determined not to let this spoil our holiday. I had looked forward to it for months. I was, however, worried about the effect the flight may have on my ears.

Ian was in the kitchen. He had moved in last night to housesit and to look after John. He was far too perky for the early hour but his cheerfulness helped me concentrate on Palma and not how feverish I felt, despite the pills.

I made myself coffee and went into the study to do a final check on emails and pack my B&B diary. Ian had a replica diary in the kitchen so between us we could continue to take bookings whilst I was away, and phone each other as and when they came in – essential to avoid any danger of rooms being double-booked, which would be a disaster.

Emails done and computer shut down, I went through to the Snug. It was a mess. I found a piece of paper and scribbled a note to John.

'Hi Johnny! Have a great week! Good luck with theory test and AS results! Will miss you! lol M xxx PS Tidy snug!'

I left the note on top of his college bag, tucked under the flap.

It was time to leave. I glugged down a final swig of coffee, hugged the animals and apologised to Ian that I didn't have time to empty the dishwasher. He laughed and told me to get in the car. I sniffed and coughed in the back whilst Nick and Ian exchanged pleasantries in the front.

We arrived at Bristol airport and joined the check-in queue. When our turn came, the hostess said we had to pay the newly introduced flight tax before she could check us in. She pointed to the 'tax desk'. The queue was horrendous – it snaked back to the main entrance. When I asked if there was any danger of us missing check-in, I was told we had plenty of time as our flight had been delayed over an hour. Ha!

We queued for a good forty minutes and were finally attended to, only to be told that it was too late to pay the tax because check-in for our flight had closed. In addition, one of our seats had already been reallocated! I exploded with anger. Nick told me to calm down. Calm down? No way! Particularly when it was clearly the check-in hostess who was at fault. I made sure I got this point across, several times over. We were offered a taxi to Gatwick to take an afternoon flight to Palma. I looked at Nick – a look that told him this was not an option. The next flight out of Bristol to Palma wasn't until two days later. I made it known to the now two hostesses who hovered over us *that* wasn't an option either.

One of the hostesses, Julie, who seemed genuinely sorry about our predicament, came up with another solution. She would label us as 'stand-by' passengers on our originally booked flight. Bloody cheek, I thought, but we calmed down when she explained that five stand-by seats had been booked but, from her experience, it was most unlikely that all of them would be taken up. It only required one 'no show' for us to fly. She crossed her fingers. So did we!

We went upstairs to the bar and awaited her call. The bar was packed out and quite filthy but we didn't care. Fags and alcohol were definitely required even if it was a tad early in the day for the latter. I downed a large vodka and tonic and took more cold pills.

Life Without Lottie: How I Coped (or didn't) During my Daughter's Gap Year

Nick hit the gin. We had to stand for over an hour before any seats became available. I was so grateful to sit down, for the cocktail of vodka and cold pills had made me feel as weak as a kitten.

Nick went downstairs to buy a newspaper, a converter plug for his laptop (we'd left ours at home) and a Sudoku puzzle book for me (also left at home). When he returned, he bought more drinks. What the hell, I thought as I sipped my way through another vodka. At last we heard Julie call our names out over the tannoy and we made our way to passport control where she whisked us to the front of the queue, waved our passports at the guard and he nodded us straight through.

Then on to security where we were similarly treated. I liked that! At speed we followed Julie to our departure gate where she asked us to wait to one side. We watched streams of successfully checked in passengers pass through the doors and out towards the plane. Surely there couldn't be many more, I thought. It seemed an eternity until Julie turned towards us, grinned and beckoned us to join her. One stand-by seat had remained untaken. We could fly!

We didn't sit together on the plane. Nick boarded first and was pointed to a seat at the back, while I was shown to the last free seat near the front. Nick managed to sleep. I didn't. I was too full of pills and thus grateful for my Sudoku book. I must have completed at least twenty puzzles. I turned around to try and catch Nick's eye but couldn't, although I did have a brief chat with him en route to the loo. My ears were fine during take off. During our descent it was a different matter. I was in such agony that all I could do was press my hands tightly against them and pray it would end soon. Never have I been so grateful to land.

As we drove through Palma I was enthralled by the magnificent architecture the city had to offer. And the shops were to die for! Palma would be fab – damn my cold. Within fifteen minutes we arrived at the apartment and met the owner, Alan. It was quite something - huge and light and decorated throughout with an Egyptian theme. The main bathroom was fit for Cleopatra and I wouldn't have been the least bit surprised had milk come out of the bath taps! Alan wished us a happy holiday, we thanked him and he left us to it.

We made a beeline for the terrace, where we sat in the sunshine and enjoyed the bottle of champagne which Alan had kindly left in the fridge. I sent a text to the children, and to Ian, to say we had arrived safely, the apartment was fabulous and all was well. At last we could relax! Only Lottie replied:

'Sounds great! Sittin on cliffs lookin at the sea outside Coffs harbour. V green - bit like lookin out over the cliffs on Lundy wen its sunny. Wot u up 2? Lol x'

I replied: *'Absolutely nothing! Sheer heaven! Mxxx'*

It was a delight to explore Palma and we found several first-class tapas bars and restaurants to more than satisfy our thirst and hunger. Also, only a three minute walk from the apartment was an excellent department store complete with an impressive and reasonably priced supermarket in the basement. It reminded us of Peter Jones in Sloane Square where, over twenty years ago, we had compiled our wedding list. From then on the supermarket was always known as 'PJ's'.

The cathedral was breathtaking. What I liked the most was the immense round stained glass window behind the altar. The colours were jettisoned in by the sunshine and landed on pillars down either side of the main aisle. I sat down for a while and watched the colours change and move.

The old castle stood next to the cathedral. The queue was long so we decided to give it a miss. We had great news from John. He phoned to say he had passed his theory test! I texted Lottie and received this reply:

'Well done to John! In Byron bay, very hippy, just like Glasto but on the beach! Did Coffs harbour, Taree, Woolgoolga yesterday. In great hostel, has everythin, plus splashed out on our own room. Happy hour soon! Stayin 2 nights then on to Brisbane. Van running fine, fingers crossed! Speak soon. Lol x'

Wow! They had certainly travelled at speed. If only Glastonbury *was* on the beach, I thought!

One morning, Nick attended the early communion service in the cathedral. My cold was much better but I stayed behind and texted Lottie:

'Love sound of Byron bay! Peace man...! Havin gt time. Done cathedal+amazing shops-v chic. Got another scarf! Torrential rain all nite so

Life Without Lottie: How I Coped (or didn't) During my Daughter's Gap Year

will go up mountains tmoz. Dad at communion service. I'm lazing in 10ft wide Egyptian bed – must do camel dance!! lol mxxx'

A reply came through almost immediately:

'Sounds fab. Enjoy mountain trip, hope rain holds off. Off for happy hr now and Simpsons on tv. David in heaven! Goin 2 find a little hippy restaurant for supper. Lol x'

Did they ever stop drinking?! I stayed in bed a while longer and happily flipped through some glossy magazines, until one article about moles and skin cancer terrified me. It included full colour pictures of suspicious lumps and bumps and in the half light I managed to convince myself that a mole on my chest matched one of the images almost to a tee. Heck! I vowed to make an appointment with Chris, our GP, as soon as I got home.

Nick returned from the cathedral. His description of the service was a hoot! Both the words and the music were pre-recorded and no less than eight priests had mimed their way through! At the appropriate times chants would blare out from deftly hidden speakers and fill the cathedral. Nick was so astounded by the peculiar goings on that he missed communion altogether.

We never made the train journey up to the mountains, partly due to the wet weather but mostly due to an earlier than planned return home. John was in trouble again. Ian phoned me to say that John had taken out Mr T late at night and crashed it.

Physically, he was fine, but mentally in a dreadful state of remorse for what he had done. I told Ian we'd get a flight home tomorrow. He said there was no need but my mind was made up. When I spoke to John, I could feel his pain. Ian was a brick and the whole sorry mess was sorted out before we returned.

Reunited with John, it was blatantly obvious that he knew full well how utterly thoughtless and irresponsible he had been. There was no point being angry with him; he needed our support and love. And he got it.

The incident, albeit unpleasant for us all, helped John to mature a great deal. On a lighter note, the snug had been tidied!

A text came in from Lottie. It was just what I needed: *'Hello from Queensland! In Surfers Paradise. So so expensive here, v touristy, pretty tacky. Surfers is Oz version of Florida, but an experience! Goin 2 biggest water park in s. hemisphere 2day. Went 2 hard rock café, chilled out by the pool yest. Hope 2 speak soon. Lol x'*

I replied: *'Wow! You've certainly covered some miles! Have splashin' gud time at water pk... Will call in few minutes. mxxx'*

Could I get a line? No! Over the next couple of days I tried repeatedly but without success. I couldn't even get a text through. Lottie sent me this text:

'Hi! Hope all fine at home. Now in Brisbane, pretty city. So so so hot and humid, its been 39 today! Give me Somerset cold! Its still 25 at 10pm. Hostel a bit shitty but movin in2 nicer 1 2moz. Stayin here 4 a week or so. Must speak soon! Lol x'

Hooray! Contact was resumed!

Then I received the *most* tremendous news. Lottie phoned me and said that she and David would *definitely* be home in time for Glastonbury! Wow! I could hardly believe it! It felt as if the most excruciatingly heavy weight had been lifted from my shoulders, no, from my entire body. I hadn't realised quite how heavy it was. After a very long seven months without her, and another five expected, I now only had three to go! I could have jumped Mount Everest.

There was more good news. Lottie told me she had decided upon a career. She wanted to study IT and had been in touch with her college tutor to discuss appropriate degree courses. When Lottie has made her mind up about something, she puts it into action without delay. I thought of Uncle David and 'Just do it'. I whooped with joy, called Nick and John and sent her a text:

'Fantastic news! Wow and super wow!!! And fantastic to speak! John and Dad over the moon! Champers tonite! lol mxx'

In the afternoon, I went to the surgery and saw Chris. He examined my mole, said he was sure I had nothing to worry about and made an appointment for it to be removed, two weeks later. That evening, we celebrated.

Chapter Twenty-Two

Lottie's Coming Home!

The next morning I opened the bedroom curtains to see thick fog outside. This came as rather a shock after the clear skies of the past few days. Thank goodness Ian had cut the grass yesterday – the first cut of the year.

I was in for a much bigger shock when I came downstairs and checked my mobile for messages.

'Got a coming home date – 23rd may 5am! Will call later, lol x'

I had to read Lottie's text several times before it sunk in. When it registered that she would be home in two months time, not three, I screamed, 'Yes! Yes!' in delight and danced around the kitchen. The bassets shot out of bed and Morse did a little pee on the floor. I had obviously frightened him! I shook with excitement as I punched in a quick reply:

'Wow! Date in all diaries! Will meet u at Heathrow. Am so happy! Speak later. Lol. Hooray! M xxx'

Morse did another little pee. The poor dogs, such was my excitement I had forgotten to let them out. I opened the back door and they charged down the drive. Nick had already left for court so I called his mobile. Damn it, it was switched off so I left a message. John was still asleep but not for much longer. I raced upstairs to his room, knocked on the door and burst in. I didn't wait for an answer today!

'John! John!' I cried, 'Lottie's coming home – on 23rd of May! At 5 o'clock in the morning!'

He gave a groan and appeared from under the bedclothes.

'Wow-yeah-wow-awesome!' he stammered out.

'And we're all going to Heathrow!'

'Wow! That's unreal!' He paused. 'What's the time, Mum?' He sounded worried.

'Twenty to nine,' I replied. 'And don't be too late getting up – your room could do with a tidy before college,' I added, as I viewed the piles of discarded clothes and books all over the floor. '…and please bring your washing down!'

'Yeah, OK, Mum. I'll be down soon.'

'Great,' I replied. 'I'll make you a bacon sarnie,' and I sang all the way downstairs.

John wasn't 'down soon'. There was the usual last minute panic before I stuffed the sarnie into his hands and raced him into Wells. He left me with the crusts to dispose of and I did some shopping, quickly, for I wanted to get home as soon as possible. No way would I miss Lottie's call.

When we spoke we were both so excited that our conversation was rather garbled. However, we calmed down (just a little!) and Lottie gave me the flight details. They land at Heathrow at 5.25 in the morning – at Terminal 4. When I told her that we'd all be there to meet them, she was overjoyed. I said we wouldn't miss it for the world.

I left it for her to discuss with David whether they wanted to come straight home or stay in London for the night. She thought they'd prefer to come home but would let me know when we spoke again next week.

She also told me that they had sold the van to two girls in their hostel and from now on will travel in Mark's car. No profit was made but they did get their money back. She got food-poisoning last week from an overpriced dish of fried squid and spent the entire night being ill in the van whilst a tropical storm raged outside. I felt dreadful for her!

Their next stop was Fraser Island – the world's largest sand island – for a few days to include an eight hour excursion in a 4x4. That sounded fun! Lottie warned me there would be emergency phone signals only but she would text me as soon as she could. Then up to the Great Barrier Reef and four nights on a yacht (with food, booze and snorkelling trips included) before going on to their final stop, Cairns. They had booked the 4x4 trip and the yacht at the same time and saved over 30 per cent of the cost. Well done! I told her.

Life Without Lottie: How I Coped (or didn't) During my Daughter's Gap Year

They would fly back to Sydney for a week or so, and then on to Perth for their final time in Australia. They would then spend a month in a hotel in Bali before they return to Heathrow via Singapore. Lottie was thrilled about Bali because she said it would be *very* cheap!

I asked where they were now. On the Sunshine Coast in a town called Noosa, she told me, a stunningly beautiful place and very French. They were sharing their hostel bedroom with four Frenchmen! For the umpteenth time I thanked God that David was with her.

Yesterday they went to Australia Zoo, which she said was fantastic. She cuddled a koala and hugged a kangaroo and a camel! Within the zoo compound was Steve Irwin's 'Crocoseum', where they saw a live show and the crocs hurled themselves out of the water for lumps of food.

She told me that money was very tight. Could I please send them some? They'd pay me back when they got home. I said I'd jot down her bank details next time we spoke and wire transfer the money to her. The last thing she said to me was how she couldn't wait to come home, see the dogs, meet the cats and sit round the kitchen table. With great delight, I started to make a list of things to do in preparation for her return. Parties were very much at the top.

The rest of that day was equally as amazing. I bought an old Land Rover for John (to which he would contribute). It was in great condition and I negotiated a great price. Later that afternoon, I went through to the Snug for a rest. I switched on the TV. The programme about to end was a phone-in quiz show. You had to guess the word in front of the one on the screen. I didn't pay much attention to it until I heard the presenter say 'I'll give you all a clue'. The clue was so obvious that I had to phone in. I won £500! Nick had some good fortune too. He was in London for the day and was successful in the Court of Appeal. He also ordered his first cassock.

I didn't have to wait long for Lottie to phone again – she called the following morning to say she wanted to head straight home rather than stay overnight in London. That was fine by me. Also, she said it may be some time before they could afford to rent somewhere to live. Would it be okay for them to stay at home for a while? I felt my motherly instincts swell to bursting. I told her they could stay as long as they liked. I texted her after the call:

'Thx for phoning! Will stock up on champers! I look forward to bangin tunes, buying pasta + more washing! Have gt time in sand + on Onassis yacht! Don't forget your shades! Lolmxxx'

I thought about the early start we would have to make in order to arrive at Heathrow in time. Also, how tiring it would be for Nick to drive there and back in a day. This, added to the emotion and excitement of our reunion, would not be conducive to safe motoring! I knew that Mervyn had just bought a 6-seater. I called him. He gave me a most reasonable quote for the return journey and I arranged for him to collect us at 3.30am. Perfect.

That evening, John, Ian and Adam went to Cardiff for the final RBS Six Nations match. They all agreed it was the best weekend they'd had for ages.

On Sunday, which was Mothers Day, I was thrilled to bits when John returned home with a lovely bunch of flowers for me. I knew I wouldn't hear from Lottie as she was on Fraser Island, but I thought of her often. Two days later, I was so touched to receive this email from her. It made me glow inside! She is a truly special person.

20 March, 2007

Hi hi!

Back from Fraser. Had a great time, just a quick email to say I'm ok. We're in the middle of nowhere with no mobile signal. Internet expensive and about to close - will call tomorrow when we get to Airlie beach and chat about Fraser experience etc. A very very happy mothers day! I didn't forget i just didn't realise that i would be on fraser and not be able to contact you. I've sent a postcard/mothers day card but it will be late. Anyway got to go - will talk soon. Lots of love xoxox
=========

'Fantastic to get email! Thx so much 4 m. day wishes. Can't wait to get card + hear all about fraser! Lol mxxx'

Life Without Lottie: How I Coped (or didn't) During my Daughter's Gap Year

I looked up Airlie Beach on Google. I read that it is '...*on the Whitsundays, 74 islands floating like jewels in the tropical warm waters of the Coral Sea.*'

It sounded idyllic. However, the journey up there wasn't:

'Hi! Goin 2 sleep now even tho its only 8.30, so tired. Sat in the car 4 over 11hrs 2 get 2 Airlie 4 Whitsundays 2moz. Got 2 get up early 4 yacht trip so will try and call if have time or if not will call when we get back on Saturday. Belated happy mothers day again! Lol xx'

I replied: *'Boy u must be glad 2 get out of car! Sleep well darling. Lets speak on sat. thx 4 more mothers day wishes! Have truly amazing time. Lol mxxx'*

With the best of intentions, Nick plugged my mobile in to recharge but switched it off in the process. As a result, I didn't pick up Lottie's next two texts until Saturday evening when I realised what had happened:

'Hi! Not got enough credit to call but ready to chat whenever u r. Lol x'

Her second text read:

'V tired, trip was amazing but up 4 sunrise both mornings. Got 2 be up at 6 to get to Cairns for a reasonable time 2moz, another long drive- 8/10 hrs or so. Will speak 2moz! Lol x'

I hoped she wasn't disappointed by my late reply:

'Just got yr txts! Glad trip woz fab despite early starts! Will be wonderful 2 speak tmoz! I'll txt before phoning u. lol mxxx'

I didn't bother to text first. I phoned and, after a long wait Lottie picked it up! Fraser Island was even better than the brochures made out, she said. Ten of them had travelled in a safari truck each day and camped under the stars at night. The Milky Way was as clear as it could be. The island was not without its dangers, however, for wild dingoes were about and everyone was warned *never* to go near them or go anywhere alone. Lottie said she even had to wake David up to accompany her to the loo during the night - in case her bum got bitten!

On the yacht, there was a major screw up with the cabins. David was allocated a single berth and Lottie a 3-berth with two strangers who obviously didn't want her around for they kept locking her out! She spent the first night in David's cabin but the air-conditioning didn't work and the bed was so narrow neither of them got much sleep. Thereafter, they took their bedclothes up on deck and slept outside. She said that was magic.

They visited Whitehaven Beach – one of the top five beaches in the world – and did lots of snorkelling. On their last 'go', one of the crew threw some bread into the water. Within seconds they were completely surrounded by thousands of the most beautiful tropical fish she had ever seen. Reef sharks were about but were not a problem, as they don't attack humans. On the other hand, Thrasher sharks do and a large group of them came fairly near. Fortunately they seemed much more interested in reducing the squid population!

They woke up one morning to a school of dolphins right next to the yacht. She said it was the most wonderful sight and got some great photos. I asked if she had used the underwater camera which Jennie had given them at their farewell party. She told me that was being saved for snorkelling off Cairns where the coral and the varieties of tropical fish were meant to be even better. Without any warning the phone went dead and we got cut off. B&B guests were ready to check out, so I dealt with them whilst Nick called Lottie back and he noted down her bank details.

After a period of seven months, Nick and I finally cleared the dining room of Lottie and David's boxes and bits and returned it to normality. However, it looked shabby and we decided to redecorate and replace the carpet. Nick transferred the money and I let Lottie know by text.

She replied:

'Sent Daddy a text but do thank him very very very much. Did they say wen it wud go in2 my account? Cairns is great, doin lots of sittin by the pool! Bookin reef trip. Goin 2 the nightmarkets 2nite, shud b gud. Lol x x x'

They were obviously short of cash… I hoped to put her mind at rest:

'Dad says 2-3 days. Pc came today! thx so much and love u loads too! Emailing Easter pics 2u. Have fun at markets. Lol mxxx'

The photographs were in lieu of an Easter card. I took two of Snoopy and Blue Bunny inside Nick's top hat next to a vase of daffodils from the garden, one of the bassets and one of the newly arrived Landy.

Life Without Lottie: How I Coped (or didn't) During my Daughter's Gap Year

26 March, 2007

Hi Guys!

Welcome back to Sydney! Absolutely thrilled East coast was so wonderful. To see dolphins up close and all those tropical fish must have been out of this world. Hope you pick this email up before jetting off to Perth... Photos attached for Easter! Enjoy your last few days in Sydney. Make sure you have a HUGE send off party!!

Am keeping everything crossed for success when I apply for Glasto tickets on Sunday. Will text you! John and I will both be on line. Probably the only Sunday he'll ever get out of bed early! If I get tickets, we'll have to buy (yet) another tent when you get back!

Am SO excited about your coming home date! Have booked Mervyn to drive us as he's just bought a 6 seater.

Huge amounts of love and cuddles and have A GREAT EASTER!

Will speak soon.

Mum xxxxxxxxoooooxxxxxxxx

==========

Two days later:

'Got the email - thanks for the pics! David likes the landy! Still in Cairns, doin a rainforest tour where u see platypus in the wild and slide down waterfalls, shud b fun! Money arrived today, thanks again! Goin 2 the bank tomor plus sendin some pics home of NY + coast trip! Lol x'

I was impressed with the speed of the wire transfer system. Nick also received a text:

'Thank u so much daddy that's so kind of u, and for the extra, it will really help. We will pay u back as soon as we can. Thank u! Lots and lots of love xxx ps, good texting!'

Nick much appreciated Lottie's comment about his texting skills as they are basic, for he doesn't use the facility often. Her messages came through as I was on my way to the surgery – it was mole removal time. As luck would have it, Nick wasn't in court so he drove me there, waited, and brought me home. It was far from pleasant when the needle was shoved into my chest, but afterwards I didn't feel a thing. The worst part of it was the horrific stench of burning flesh as my wound was cauterized! I was glad when the process was over. I replied to Lottie:

'Brill that money arrived so fast! Rainforest tour will be fab! Look forward to getting pics. Saw Les today about new carpet for dining room. He highly recommends you go a bit further north to Port Douglas. He says the drive is magic... Lol m xxx'

Les has fitted every carpet in the house since we moved in. He is a brilliant carpet-fitter, and has become a good friend to us all.

I decided to research holiday villas in Majorca for John's half term week in October. I Googled my way through dozens until I found the perfect one, close to a little sandy beach and to the centre of town. It had a separate annexe – perfect for the kids – and I thought how fantastic it would be if Lottie and David could join us. I texted her:

'Hi! Goin back 2 Majorca Oct. half term. Do u + d want 2 join us? Have fun! Lol mxxx'

She replied:

'Just been on a great tour, saw platypus + hiked through rainforest. Oct sounds great but bit early 4 us 2 say, depends on wen I've got my i.t. exams, money etc. But dus sound v cool so don't count us out! Lol x'

Lottie's reply gave me hope. I thought money was the big issue, tried not to get my hopes up and replied:

'Glad tour fab. Lovely pc arrived fm Fraser-thanks v much! Ganda+Ann say thx 4 theirs 2. Oct villa on me. Hedge cut y'day + spuds planted. Have gt w.end+safe flight on Monday. Lol + miss you! Mxxx'

I must have hit the right note for the following morning, this email came in:

31 March, 2007

Hi!

Holiday in October sounds great! I checked my exam dates and they don't clash so count us in! Thank you so much for paying for us, should be v cool!

Had a great time on the rainforest trip! We swam under some amazing waterfalls - one was where the Peter Andre music video 'Mysterious Girl' and the Herbal Essence shampoo ads were filmed.

Life Without Lottie: How I Coped (or didn't) During my Daughter's Gap Year

The water was absolutely freezing! We saw some platypus and our tour guide told us lots about the rainforest which was really interesting, oh and we got to swim in a volcanic crater, also freezing!

Glasto tickets come out tomorrow, very excited! David got an email from Smiler who really wants to go. I said I'd email you to find out if you could get one for him, but I don't think he's been organised enough to even register yet.

Might check emails tomorrow but probably not till we get to Sydney, so plse text me with Glasto news! Hope everything is great at home, send my love to everyone and speak soon! lots of love xox
=========

Yes! They could come to Majorca! In no time at all I had completed the on line reservation form and paid a deposit. John asked if Will could join us again. I said that would be great. I texted Lottie:

'Over moon you can make holiday! Booked villa with separate annex 4 u young uns! Can't wait! Can David drive us 2 villa from airport? Fingers x'd 4 Glasto tkts tmoz. Beautiful day-lunch in gdn. Barbie time is here. Hooray! Lol mxxx'

'Villa sounds great! David says drivin no prob. Bbq at home-wow, weather must b hottin up! Cant wait 2 hear about Glasto. Last day in cairns, takin lots of pics + packin 4 the flight. Lol x'

There were now only 24 hours left before the tickets went on sale and I became increasingly nervous about my chances of success. I knew the kids were desperate to go – the pressure was on, on me. The sale date just happened to be Diesel's birthday. That was a good omen, I thought.

The day dawned. This was it! Nick started breakfasts for me and, just before nine, I signed on to the ticket site several times over, as did John on his laptop. The countdown was nerve-wracking to say the least. Alas, when nine o'clock came, the site froze due to demand. *Refresh, refresh,* went our browsers. Nothing. At 9.30 I left John on his laptop and returned to the kitchen. I needed a break from the frustration and helped Nick with the cooked breakfasts.

That done, Nick said he'd make the toast and I beetled back to the study. By the time that tickets had been on sale for over an hour and a half, I realised the odds of getting any were against me.

'Come on, come on, come on!' I muttered, but the site was still frozen. I decided to close down all but one of my ticket links and clicked *Refresh*. Suddenly, a booking form popped up. It was unbelievable! I kept quiet for I feared the link would crash at any moment. It didn't, and a few minutes later I had bought tickets. In total amazement and delight, I screamed:

'I've got them!'

'What?!' said John from the Snug.

'I've got them!' I repeated. He raced through.

'All of them?' he asked in amazement.

'Yes.' For you and Lottie and David – and one for me,' I replied. 'And a parking ticket so you can take the Landy!'

We hugged and whooped with joy. I charged back to the kitchen to tell Nick and whooped some more as I passed my guests, now on toast and marmalade. They looked astounded. If I caused them chronic indigestion, what the hell! Whilst I made them more coffee and tea, Nick phoned Lottie. It was a pity she didn't answer but he left her a message with the good news. Within the hour she texted me:

'Great news about tickets!!! We r both v v excited! And thank u so much! Havin a few drinks to celebrate whilst it pisses it down outside – bloody tropical weather! Glasto - Yay! Bring it on! The old team, me, david and john! Speak soon. Lol x x x x x'

That said it all.

Now it was April, I realised that I could say 'Lottie's coming home **next** month!' Sadly, my 'high spirits' were dampened for I had to say goodbye to Nick. It was God camp time again – this time for six days. However, I was so busy with guests all week that I hardly had the time to miss him, although I did. I spoke to him twice each day and we exchanged a few short texts. Nick's funniest one, received late one night, was:

'This is awful. Lost glasses. Getting pissed in car. Love N xxx'

Lottie was absolutely right. His texting *had* improved!

Chapter Twenty-Three

Farewell to Oz

'Just got back into Sydney, waitin 4 luggage, its bloody freezing! Well, its 19c but been used to 35 most days. Will call later, check in2 hostel and then 2 Manly 4 afternoon surf. Lol x'

The East Coast trip was over. Lottie was now truly on her way home! I texted her back:

'Gt 2 hear fm u! Still can't believe I got tickets! 15 here, wish it woz 19! Cats left present in dogs bed during nite - a half chewed very dead mouse! Excellent! That's more like it. Lol mxxx'

The newly painted dining room was a transformation of the very best kind. I could hardly wait for Les to fit the carpet. There was only one mishap along the way – messy but funny. Early one morning, Morse got into the room and padded across the upturned lid of the biggest paint pot. I chased him out. That was the worst thing I could have done, for he ran back into the kitchen and left perfect white paw prints all along the way. How he hated having his feet (and his nose and right ear) washed! With Morse *almost* free of paint, I put him into the garden whilst I scrubbed the floor.

Lottie texted to say they had touched down in Perth and asked when would be a good time to phone. I replied:

'Glad you've arrived safely. I'll call u after b'fast-just about to start 10! Heck! Mx'

Over two hours later, after three sittings, breakfast was finally over, or so I thought. But my last sitting, two American guests, demanded more coffee. When I took it through, there were maps spread all over the table. The woman complained to me that one of them had got 'buttered' from her half-eaten piece of toast underneath. I offered to clear away.

'No, no,' the man said, and waved me away with his hand. 'There's no hurry.' Not for them, maybe!

I asked if they would like to move through to the drawing room but was ignored, and they continued to pour over the maps. I had no option but to leave them to it. However, that gave me the chance to call Lottie and I started to dial her number.

Half way through I had to swiftly abandon that idea for the Americans shouted for me. 'Fiooooona!' Shit! I had to answer endless questions about roads and routes and journey times and the 'we just have to see' archaeological sites along the way – all the way down to deepest ****ing Cornwall.

My brain completely addled, I had to make yet more coffee and another hour passed by. It would soon be too late to call Lottie so, despite their protests, I cleared the table, noisily, and hoped they would get the hint. Not a chance! I let the dogs through and they begged for leftovers. That didn't work either, not even when Einstein slobbered copiously on the woman's trousers.

She got her camera out! I could have screamed. Both dogs let me down – they posed beautifully. When the Americans eventually got up I couldn't resist but say 'Have a nice day!' in my poshest of English accents.

'Theeenk yew, dahhhhling,' the woman replied.

I could have hit her. I gave them the 'V' sign once they'd turned their backs to walk away. I didn't feel in the least bit guilty. In fact, I hoped they fell down the very first archaeological hole they visited.

It was way too late to phone Lottie, so I sent her a brief text. I hoped her mobile was turned off so the beeps wouldn't wake her:

'So sorry didn't call. Ghastly guests. Promise talk tmoz. Mxxx'

The postman knocked on the door; I had a parcel to sign for. This done, he handed it over together with a bundle of post. I recognised David's writing on a white jiffy bag. Great! It was their photos! I left B&B rooms until later and spent the most wonderful time viewing them – all 768!

The photos of the 'Crocoseum' fascinated me. One in particular caught my eye. It was of a tea towel, especially printed as a tribute to Steve Irwin. The poem, 'The Crocodiles are Crying' is by Australia's Rupert McCall, who is a critically acclaimed poet. I was so pleased when Rupert's manager gave permission from Rupert to include the poem in this book.

Life Without Lottie: How I Coped (or didn't) During my Daughter's Gap Year

'The Crocodiles are Crying'

Endless visions fill my head – this man – as large as life
And instantly my heart mourns for his angels and his wife
Because the way I see Steve Irwin – just put everything aside
It comes back to his family – it comes back to his pride

His animals inclusive – Crikey – light the place with love!
Shine his star with everything he fought to rise above
The crazy-man of Khaki from the day he left the pouch
Living out his dream and in that classic 'Stevo' crouch

Exploding forth with character and redefining cheek
It's one thing to be honoured as a champion unique
It's one thing to have microphones and spotlight cameras shoved
It's another to be taken in and genuinely loved

But that was where he had it right – I guess he always knew
From his father's modest reptile park and then Australia Zoo
We cringed at times and shook our heads – but true to nature's call
There was something very Irwin in the make up of us all

Yes the more I care to think of it – the more he had it right
If you're going to make a difference – make it big and make it bright!
Yes - he was a lunatic! Yes - he went head first!
But he made the world feel happy with his energetic burst

A world so large and loyal that it's hard to comprehend
I doubt we truly count the warmth until life meets an end
To count it now I say a prayer with words of inspiration
May the spotlight shine forever on his dream for conservation

…My daughter broke the news to me – my six year old in tears
It was like she'd just turned old enough to show her honest fears
I tried to make some sense of it but whilst her Dad was trying
His little girl explained it best…she said 'The crocodiles are crying'

Their best mate's up in heaven now – the crocs up there are smiling!
And as sure as flowers, poems and cards and memories are piling
As sure as we'll continue with the trademarks of his spiel
Of all the tributes worthy – he was rough…but he was real

As sure as 'Crikey!' fills the sky
I think we'll miss ya Steve…goodbye

© RUPERT McCALL 2006
www.rupertmccall.com.au

There were also some comments made by Steve's admirers. One read:

'I think this poem made me think more about Steve Irwin - What he tried to do and what he did and especially his innocence. I hadn't thought about him one way or the other before he died so suddenly. I hope he is remembered as a person who tried to do his best and I hope that more Australians become like him instead of continuing with the 'me me me' attitude which seems to be eating at our sense of sharing and eroding our children's future.'

Sadly, I had to agree. Lottie had previously told me that unless the Australians are actually involved in an event – sporting or otherwise – they show no interest whatsoever and give it zero media coverage. This was particularly evident throughout the RBS 2007 Six Nations tournament. None of the games were televised or even reported on. I had to text Lottie the results and John did not become famous.

There were lots of photos of the kids' camper van. It had *'Sparticus'* written across the bonnet in thick black paint. When I mentioned the spelling to Lottie, she told me that she and David were both 'five drinks down' when they painted it!

There were some other amusing shots too, many at parties and one, which I'm sure David hadn't meant to include, of him and some lads in the front of the van. They all looked completely pissed and clutched tinnies and opened porn magazines!

The pictures of Fraser Island were stunning. The beaches were simply to die for with the whitest, cleanest sand. Some had dingoes on them which looked deceivingly laid-back and contented. The final pictures were of the yacht. It was beautiful and had far too many sails for me to count. The little coves they had sailed into looked almost too perfect. And that was it, I'd seen them all. I had hoped to see pictures of dolphins and the kids snorkelling but there weren't any. No doubt they were still on the camera.

The next morning, I spoke to Lottie. We chatted about the photos and, yes, she did have more pictures on her memory card. They'd both received a tax rebate of around $400! The money couldn't have come at a better time as, surprise, surprise, they were broke, so much so that David may have to do a couple of days labouring next week. I didn't envy him - not in that heat.

Lottie told me she will definitely sell her mobile before they leave Perth and hopes to get $30 for it. She'll use David's to keep in touch with me. The hostel they were currently staying in had free internet access – hooray, we could exchange emails again! We laughed about David's growing desperation for oxtail soup and I said I'd get some in.

Surf boards were not being sold as originally planned – both were coming home with them. I sensed a definite feeling of their sentimental value.

Could I insure David to drive the Landy for a month or so when they get back – just to give him enough time to buy his own car? No problem, I said.

Lottie texted me shortly after we had spoken:

'Great talking 2u. Just a thought – will Mervyn's car take the surfboards? Or does it have roof racks? Lol x

I spoke to Mervyn and texted Lottie again:

'Merv needs u 2 measure boards. No roof rack but he says they shd fit thro centre of car! Lol Mxxx'

That evening I emailed her and attached a recent photo of Einstein:

5 April, 2007

Hi Lot!

Fantastic as ever to speak this morning! Great to hear all about your travels etc. Photos David posted are wonderful although you guys look smashed in most of them! Ha! Good on you. You only live once. Before you get to Bali, do let me have David's mobile number. And tell him I shall clear Tesco's shelves of their best Oxtail soup!!!

Haven't bought any Easter eggs yet - must do that tomorrow. Will be fab to have Daddy home on Saturday! John's gone to a birthday bash in Tor Woods so he's camping out - very brave as the nights are still a bit nippy. At least he's taken a sleeping bag... Driving test on 20th. Keep everything crossed - and more.

Huge amounts of love, have a ball in Perth and make the most of it. Will call on Sunday to wish you both happy chocie time and will keep in touch via text/email. Love you loads! Mum xxx

PS It's wonderful to be emailing again - I've really missed it!
=========

A reply came through overnight:

6 April, 2007

Hi!

Great talking yesterday, I didn't think we looked too drunk in the pictures! I can't remember which ones David sent but I know we look a bit blurry eyed on New Years Eve!

The boards are approx 6ft 10 long and 2ft wide. Hope they'll fit!

Could we please have Smiler etc and maybe a couple of my friends (Emily & Laura) to come over the night before Glasto? That would be great! Ezetie has left for her trip around the world with Trev so we've missed her. I've kept in contact with her a lot.

David is very happy about soup! And Landy insurance. He says thanks v much. I've texted you his mobile no. Good Friday today and Perth is like a ghost town. We forgot to buy anything for dinner tonight (oops!) but I'm sure some little corner shop will be open. Still sticking to v. small budget. Buying each other Easter eggs on Monday because they will be half price! Trying to save more money for nice trips and a big last night out!

Life Without Lottie: How I Coped (or didn't) During my Daughter's Gap Year

Picture of Einstein is v cute! Glad everything is great at home. Send my love to everyone and will speak on Sunday! lots of love xoxoxoxoxox

=========

I spoke to Mervyn about the boards and sent Lottie this text:
'Gd news – Merv says boards will fit! Lol mxx'
I didn't speak to Lottie on Sunday. Desperate for cash, they had both sold their mobiles only hours before I tried to call. This was her final text to me before I saw her again:
'Selling fones at 3pm so wont be able 2 use from then. We put sum money on the b.card. Was real emergency-we ran out of $$$! Bad luck with visas, food etc meant we had 2 spend more than we had. We've taken about £65-that will cover us 4 everything including meal and a few drinks. Hope that's ok. Will email later with details. Lol x'
I wondered what on earth the bad luck with visas was all about. I texted back, told her not to worry and asked if it was a good time to call. Lottie didn't reply but I received this text from the new mobile owner: *'Sorry, lotte has sold her phone!'*
I replied: *'Thanx 4 letting me know!'*
Nick was with me when the message came through.
'Ah,' he said, 'I'd better take her number of my mobile.' He picked it up, pressed several buttons and then said, 'That's it. All gone.'
'Oh, that's sad, isn't it?' I said.
'Yes, but not really, it means we're now a bit closer to her coming home.'
'Hmm, I suppose so,' I replied.
I hated it when I deleted Lottie's number from my mobile. It felt as if I had severed such an important part of me from her, and vice versa. When my mobile asked me to confirm the deletion, I paused before I hit the 'yes' button. By early evening I hadn't received an email from Lottie so I sent one to her:

22 April, 2007

Hi Lot!

Thanks for text re phones. Do hope you got a decent price. Sorry we didn't get to talk beforehand. Give me a quick call or email when you arrive in Bali to let me know what hotel is like! Safe journey!

Please don't worry about using card - that's what it's there for. Do use it to pay for your farewell supper and drinks. Pity about probs with visa etc. What happened?! Have you got enough money to see you thro Bali?

Went to HAMRA 'Bard's Supper' last night. Met Janine & Lavinia there. Had great time. We won the Shakespeare quiz!!! I made some mini pavlovas - stuffed with cream and first Cheddar strawberries - delicious! They're ready so early this year. John played his first of season match for Horrington yesterday. They won and he got 4 wickets but was out for a duck!

Weather continues to astound. We haven't had rain for over 3 weeks. Hosepipes and watering cans flat out. Tallinn keeps getting stuck on the bakehouse roof. We know because he yowls for help! Daddy rescued him yesterday and got his face scratched! Looking forward to your email and news. And stop worrying about money - you have a whole month's hols to look forward to. And then we'll see you again! WOW!

Loads of love as ever. Mum xxx

=========

23 April, 2007

Hi!

Thanks again for letting us use the b.card! Things all went a bit wrong. First, we went to change our money into Balinese and to sort out visas which had to be paid in US dollars. We went back a couple of days later and were seen by this VERY useless girl who didn't have a clue what she was doing. She had forgotten the money for our visas and transferred everything into Balinese and then said she couldn't change any into US without changing it all back into Australian, which would incur $10 fee! So we had to use some of our money we'd put aside for our last week to pay for the visas.

Life Without Lottie: How I Coped (or didn't) During my Daughter's Gap Year

Next, we decided to go for a really big lunch so it would fill us up for the day. We tried a Chinese which looked like it served massive portions, but the food was absolutely disgusting. I had beef & rice stir fry and it tasted of oil and David had a spicy pork dish with hardly any meat, just battered bones! He complained and the boss came over, who was also the head chef, a horrible fat Chinese man who stank and had long greasy hair and a beard. We didn't want to re-order and asked for our money back. The boss shouted at David and refused, so we left very hungry and very out of pocket! Then we had to buy another lunch which meant that we had to use the money we'd put aside for our airport transfers. Oh dear!

We used b.card to go for a really nice meal last night. We had chilli mussels in a pretty little restaurant and watched the storm out of the window. The food was amazing and it was the best we've had in Oz! David even put on a proper shirt for the occasion!

Off to Bali tomorrow! Lots to do today - really excited. We sold the phones for so little money but otherwise we wouldn't have got rid of them. The lucky person who bought them only paid ten pounds for the two! We arrive in Bali early tomorrow evening so I will scout out some way to get in contact to let you know I'm OK.

This is my last email from Australia, wow! Speak to you soon from Bali and lots of love xoxoxoxox

=========

What a dreadful cock up over visas and money! On top of that, the kids had paid over the odds for shocking food. I was appalled that they had sold their mobiles for so little. I got the distinct impression that Lottie was glad her time in Australia was nearly over.

At lunch time, Nick's father phoned. He told me that Pet was in hospital following an accident with a quad bike. It sounded pretty bad as her right leg required a skin graft. She was due to be operated on that afternoon. I then received a phone call from Pet. I was surprised, as I thought she would either be in theatre or the recovery room.

She sounded pretty low – an emergency case had come in and her op. had been put off until tomorrow. I said how sorry I was, tried my best to cheer her up and wished her good luck. I ordered her a big bunch of flowers to be delivered tomorrow.

She phoned again the next morning to say that at midnight she had been woken up and moved into the main ward to make way for another emergency.

The nurse who helped her to move had said 'Welcome to the NHS!' We laughed about that. Ten minutes later, she called again. A theatre space had just become available for her. That evening, I was delighted when Peter phoned to say the operation had been a great success.

I was concerned that I hadn't heard from Lottie since she'd left Perth and so I emailed her again. I didn't mention Pet's operation. I would tell her next time we spoke:

25 April, 2007

Hi Lot!

So sorry final days in Perth were fraught with crazy problems. Ah well, all behind you now you're relaxing in beautiful Bali! Hope flight was good. Must be fun exploring a new country. What's hotel like? Can't wait to hear news. If you are still broke, do use card for essentials and decent food. I have visions of you returning like stick insects!

My final text to you was replied to by the new owner! Awful you got so little but better than nothing. Maybe you could pick up some hotel/bar/cleaning work in Bali to help out. Watch out for those demons in the hills!! Take great care, missing you loads but not long to go now - only 28 days!!!

Loads of love, hugs and everything!

Mum xxxxxxxxoooooooooxxxxxxxxx

=========

The next morning I still hadn't heard from Lottie so I emailed her hotel and requested confirmation that she and David had checked in. The reply, which came in twenty minutes later, horrified me:

Thanks for your email do you have another name we no have the guest

Life Without Lottie: How I Coped (or didn't) During my Daughter's Gap Year

check in yesterday under the name Carlotta'

I was distraught. Where the hell was Lottie? And why hadn't they mentioned David? Where was *he*?! Had they missed their flight? Were they still in Perth? Or had they arrived safely in Bali? If so, why hadn't they checked in?

All I could do was hope the hotel staff hadn't had the imagination to check under their surnames.

I emailed back and asked them to do just that – in as simple words as I could. Time ticked by and no reply came in. The phone rang. As if by telepathy, it was Lottie! She was at the hotel, was fine but the call was costing £5 per minute so I jotted down her number and phoned her back. The connection was bad and sometimes it crackled so much that we couldn't hear each other at all, but we persevered and managed to talk for about twenty minutes.

She said the hotel was great - it had two bars, one in the middle of the pool. Lottie loved that facility! Their bedroom was 'basic' but clean and they were glad to be away from the noisy Irish and their didgery-dos! It was incredibly hot and they'd both got sunburnt – after only twenty minutes in the sun! I told her to stay in the shade and keep a hat on. Bali was much cheaper than Australia but not for wine. That costs £5 per glass. Fortunately the local beer was great and only sets them back 80p per pint. The local liquor, made from rice, was dirt cheap and 'pretty strong'. She was going to bring a bottle home for us all to try.

The night they arrived, they'd had a cheap Thai meal but it had given them both upset tummies. The next day they played it safe and stuck to soup and spaghetti bolognaise. I asked if they had enough money to see them through Bali. Yes, she told me, which was just as well for the jobs they could get only paid the equivalent of a pint per hour.

I told Lottie about Auntie Pet's accident and she said she was really sorry. She wished me a happy birthday for Monday. I told her it was on Tuesday! We laughed when I suggested she cut down her intake of rice liquor! She said she had posted me a card in a bright blue envelope and hoped it arrived in time.

I was sorry to learn that internet access was not readily available in Bali and it would be difficult for her email me. As a result, we agreed to speak weekly and fixed a time for me to phone her next Thursday. I looked forward to that. I realised how lucky I had been so far to have had four means of contact – text, mobile phone, email and land line. Now, I only had the latter to rely upon. I hoped that next week's connection would be better than today's.

When I went to collect the post, amongst a wad of letters held together with the usual red rubber band, was a bright blue envelope. That made my day!

The following day, Nick and I went to Appledore. Much to my relief, the cottage was a huge improvement on the last one and the entire weekend was perfect. When we got home, Keir and Ann stayed for a few days over my birthday. I had a simply lovely day. In the morning, Norman and Beryl came over for coffee and they gave me a pink hydrangea for the garden. In the evening, we had dinner at The Fountain Inn. Janine and Will joined us. It was such a happy gathering and Lottie and David were often mentioned.

I so wished they could have been there too but, with the greatest of delight, I could now say 'They're coming home THIS month!' I did so, several times over.

Chapter Twenty-Four

Bali and Home

2 May, 2007

Hi!

Happy Birthday to you, happy birthday to you! Hope you had great time. Sorry my card was rubbish. Australia doesn't have any card shops and the only ones on sale were for mother's day on the 14th May. Strange!

Not had much luck over the past week. We had to put approx fifty pounds on the card. We went to the pharmacy because David had terrible earache and he got ear drops and cold tablets. He felt a bit better but then got a really sore jaw. We both went to the doctors as David's earache got worse (and he was deaf in one ear) and I had a chesty cough and temperature. We read in the travel book that if you start to feel ill in Bali its best to see a doctor sooner rather than later in case something bad is wrong.

Anyway, turns out that I have a bit of a flu-y cold and was given flu tablets. I now feel much better but poor David is on new drops and antibiotics as he has a perforated ear drum which is infected! The reason he got a sore jaw was because the first ear drops went straight through the ear drum and down his throat. Yuk! Now he can't drink, swim or get his ear wet for at least three days. Not much fun. The doctor told David that his ear drum must have burst when we landed in Bali.

All in all the treatment etc was more expensive than we thought but the doctor charged us one consultation only, so we got that half price. We might be able to claim on our insurance but not til we return. David is doing lots of resting! We've rented a DVD player - DVDs here are good copies and really cheap (approx 40p) so he has those to keep him occupied. We haven't done much but once David is better we'll check out tours, although they are quite expensive. Our hotel does free volcano trips so hopefully we'll manage that later this week.

Got to go now - time for David's medicines. Will speak to you tomorrow, hope using card was OK. I miss texting you too! Lots and lots of love xoxoxoxoxox

=========

2 May, 2007

Hi Darling!

Oh you poor, poor things! David's ear must be agony but glad you're both on the mend. I strongly advise getting ear re-checked after a week and no swimming until doctor gives the okay. Only going on what John used to have to do. For heaven's sake, don't worry about card - needs must! Enjoy volcano trip - that should be fascinating.

Your card was fabulous – the best! Had a great birthday. Sat outside most of the day in glorious sunshine. Head not good this morning and have early breakfasts… Daddy gave me a pair of pink 'Crocs' - the new shoes all the rage this season. I love them! And a huge box of chocolates from John which we hit last night after supper at Fountain. Yummy! Pub was excellent.

GET WELL SOON! Glad you can watch DVDs. Will be fab to speak tomorrow.

Loads of love, hugs etc as ever. Snoopy enjoying the sunshine!

Mum xxxxxxooooooooxxxxxx

=========

I got through to Lottie but the line was absolutely shocking. However, before we hung up I managed to make her understand that I'd call again at the same time tomorrow.

4 May, 2007

Hi mum

Phone call yesterday didn't go too well - hopefully it will be better tonight. On the sick front – I'm fine. As for David, we went back to the doctors to get more antibios and a free check up. Bad news - he probably won't fully regain his hearing for another two months and mustn't get his ear wet for the rest of our trip! David's not a very happy bunny! He still feels groggy and is really congested which the doctor said could last the rest of the trip too! He's taking Osmycin 500mg, three times a day. We wondered if Ganda knew if they were any good. The doctor seems really capable but it's always good to check with someone we trust.

Apart from that we've watched lots of films. Saw Da Vinci Code last night which was ok, not as good as the book though. When David's better we'll start exploring - at the moment he doesn't feel like doing much and is quite down in the dumps. He misses doing 'bombs' into the pool!

Glad you had a lovely birthday! Crocs were very big in Australia. I never tried them but was told they were very comfy. I'll keep you updated on the David situation. Hopefully he'll feel better soon. Lots and lots of love xoxoxoxoxox

=========

Lottie was obviously very concerned about David, and rightly so. I replied without delay:

4 May, 2007

Hi Lot!

Oh, poor David - I do feel so sorry for him. Send him lots of love from us all and wish him a speedy recovery. I've looked up Osmycin - not used in UK but amongst other things is prescribed for ear infections so sounds as if he's on the right stuff. It's a big dose so no wonder he feels crap but persevere - don't miss any tablets. I'll make an appt. for him to see GP when you get home.

I'll call you later this morning (it's now 7.30, I'm not dressed and have b'fast at 8!!). Hope we can hear each other better this time. I don't think much of Bali phone lines! All fine here. Having lunch with Jennie C today.

Loads of love and everything
Mum xxxxxxxxoooooooooooxx

=========

I *did* get a decent connection and we spoke for ages. Lottie sounded rather down but, thankfully, she told me that David felt slightly better. I cheered her up with a couple of funny stories about my current guests and the cats' antics.

8 May, 2007

Hi Lot!

Hope David's ear is much improved and you had a great weekend! Hectic one here. We painted the snug and put up the Guinness posters I've *at last* had framed! Looks super. Have ordered flat screen TV - should be here Sat. We'll move snug one into drawing room.

Hils will be at Heathrow too! Sorry Jill can't join us but I know you're staying with her for a few days soon after you get back. Only 15 days to go! Enjoy the last of your hols - am sure you will. I hope Morse has dug his last hole in the lawn. Had to fill in and re-seed a large one four times last week! John played cricket on Sat. He got bowled out as Daddy watched him so you can imagine how cross he was. At least he got some wickets.

Loads of love and hugs from us all and from Snoopy (who's *very* excited too!)

Mum xxxxxxxxoooooo

=========

I didn't know it at the time but the next email I received was Lottie's final one to me before she returned home:

10 May, 2007

Hi!

Sounds like everything is great! Nothing too exciting to report here, the weather has been lovely if a bit hot! High 30's every day, certainly building up a good tan. David is much better – his hearing has improved but he's still keeping his head above water. Pills finished and doctor said swelling has gone down. He still has a slight cold which he's given back to me, bloody boy! So now I'm sniffly again, but had left over flu tablets from first time round so back on those. Hopefully should be ok in a couple of days!

I hope you don't mind but I had to buy a new bikini and put it on the card. It was 30 pounds and I couldn't afford to take it out of my budget. It would cost double that at home. The bikini you got me 3 years ago in Jersey is now see through in private places! And the one I bought in Oz got destroyed in the washing machine.

We're exploring this weekend! On Saturday we'll visit a temple on the cliffs with the best sunset in Bali and we'll see Balinese dancing. On Sunday we are going to Ubud where all the rice fields are. We'll also see the 'monkey forest' where lots of monkeys come and jump on your shoulders. Should be fun! Also doing the volcano tour but we have to wait until enough people sign up before the hotel will run the mini bus.

Been into Kuta which is the main party and shopping area. Saw a couple of nice sarongs etc. and got a floaty top from a market stall which was only two pounds but it's already starting to fall apart! David bought a bongo drum. Been looking around for pressies to bring home but not got anything yet.

Look forward to hearing from you tonight! Lots and lots of love and say hi to everyone! Xoxoxoxox
=========

I phoned the hotel and got a pre-recorded message which said (in Balinese, then in English, fortunately!) that there was currently no telephone service and to try later. I did, several times, but had to give up once it was too late, Bali time, to call. I sent Lottie a short email to explain what had happened although I doubted she would pick it up before tomorrow. I phoned again in the morning, got through but the line was diabolical so we didn't speak for long. At least I managed to establish that apart from her cold, all was well and we agreed I would call again on Monday. I hoped that communications would have improved by then.

They had. I learnt that Lottie's cold had gone, David's ear was heaps better and, much to his delight, he was back on the booze! They hadn't done the trips she'd previously mentioned - the minibus wasn't air-conditioned so they didn't fancy being stuck on it for over four hours. Wise decision, I told her. Also, they'd heard that the monkeys could be dangerously vicious!

When Lottie told me that all they could think about was coming home, I became quite emotional. We talked about how hard it was to believe that they would be back in just nine days' time. I asked if the local food was good and was surprised when she said it wasn't up to much. All dishes contain vast quantities of MSG which often upsets them. They really look forward to simple food; she mentioned bangers and mash! I made a mental note for my shopping list. We agreed to speak again on the day before they flew to Singapore.

On Friday, Nick went to God camp for the weekend. He phoned me to say that this time he had a decent bedroom *and* it was en suite! However, he'd forgotten to take a bath towel. I said I was sure someone would lend him one.

'Oh, no need to worry about that,' he said. 'I can use the old throw in the back of the car – you know, the one you washed after Tallinn had dumped on it!'

'Christ, Nick! That's disgusting!' I replied

'It's quite clean,' he said, obviously not put off at all, 'and nice and thick so it will dry me quickly.'

On that note, I changed the subject!

My final conversation with Lottie in Bali was brief and rather stilted. I think we were overcome by the fact that within 48 hours we would be reunited. I wished her safe flights and we both said we could hardly wait to see each other again.

By Tuesday, I was a complete bundle of nerves, had constant butterflies in my stomach and shook with excitement. I bought a 'Welcome Home' banner to put up above the back door and two lime green helium filled balloons with smiley faces and sunglasses on them. These I would take to Heathrow.

I meant to go to bed early but didn't. When I did, I woke up just after midnight, raring to go. I willed myself back to sleep and the alarm woke me up at three. This was it! My hands trembled, my heart pounded and the butterflies were worse than ever. My application of mascara was an utter disaster and I got through many cotton buds. I quickly put on the clothes I had laid out the night before, sprayed some perfume on (most of which scented the air rather than me), woke Nick up and went downstairs.

The dogs didn't stir and I left them to it. I took champagne and fresh orange juice out of the fridge and put them into a cool bag together with ice packs and some plastic cups. I grabbed a packet of chocolate biscuits too, in case the kids were hungry. Nick came down and, much to the dogs' dismay, booted them out for a wee. I wrote a quick note to John and left it in the middle of the kitchen table so he would be sure to see it:

'Morning J! Will call from H'row! Don't forget the banner and good luck with revision! Lol MXXX'

Within minutes Mervyn arrived and without further ado we left for Heathrow. It seemed hardly feasible that after all the months I had spent without Lottie, very soon I would see her again. I almost had to pinch myself in case Mervyn and his car were just a dream.

We sat in the back. The balloons bobbed up to the roof of the car and Nick had to tie them down to one of the seat legs so that Mervyn could actually see behind him. We tipped our seats back in the hope of some more sleep but that was impossible. A few miles into the journey I felt sick with nerves and had to open my side window. I reached for Nick's hand and breathed in the air deeply until the sickness eased. Never has a journey seemed to take so long and I lost track, very early on, of the number of times I checked my watch.

At last we neared the airport. There were several planes in the sky and I counted them, which helped the minutes tick by. I wondered if Lottie was on one of them for her flight was due to land - in about 20 minutes! Then I had a text from Hils:

'At airport. Plane landed 505. H'

Shit! If Mervyn hadn't put his foot down, and hard, he knew without a shadow of a doubt that I would have pushed him out of the driver's seat and taken over. I got another text from Hils for which I couldn't have been more grateful:

'Head 2wards wh smith on ground floor'

Mervyn stopped directly outside 'Arrivals' and told us to phone him when we were ready. Nick grabbed the cool box, I grabbed my handbag and the balloons and we ran inside. I was terrified that we wouldn't be able to find W.H. Smith, but that was easy and then we saw Hils, only a few yards away, in front of a huge metal barrier. We joined her and I laughed nervously as we hugged one another. In a blind panic, I asked,

'We haven't missed them have we?'

'No, no,' Hils replied. 'They probably haven't even got their luggage yet.'

I was thankful that at least one of us could think straight.

Nick tied the balloons to my handbag for fear I'd let them go - a wise decision. In no time at all, ahead of us from behind a corner, passengers from Lottie's flight started to trickle through, walked towards us, turned to the right and followed the barrier to the exit.

I stood slap bang in the middle of the barrier, eyes glued to that corner. My emotions got the better of me and I started to cry, which took me by surprise as I hadn't expected the tears to flow until I actually saw Lottie. Not that I wanted them to, quite the opposite.

But that release was necessary for, within a couple of minutes, I felt a little more composed and dabbed my eyes, grateful for waterproof mascara, although I did ask Hils if they looked okay. She said they were fine and we both ooh'ed with anticipation.

Nick took my hand. I squeezed it gratefully. The trickle of passengers turned into a stream which made me panic again. Nick told me not to worry and said we'd easily spot them as they would have huge surf boards with them, something few passengers had so far appeared with. Such was my excitement I hadn't thought of that!

'Can't I go the other side and wait?' I asked.

'No, Fi, you can't,' Hils replied. 'You'll get arrested!'

'Hm,' was all I replied.

I let go of Nick's hand and wiped my palm down my trousers for it was clammy. I now shook so much that every movement I made was a bit like a robot's and my legs felt decidedly wobbly, so I grabbed the barrier. It was wonderfully cool. Then I had a hot flush. Of all the times…!

Life Without Lottie: How I Coped (or didn't) During my Daughter's Gap Year

'Not now! Not now!' I pleaded inwardly. I madly fanned myself with one hand and we all chuckled as my face turned bright red. I took several deep breaths and it passed.

'What if they missed the plane?!' I asked.

'Calm down!' Nick replied. 'Of course they didn't.' From the way he said it, he was obviously terribly nervous too.

More 'Oohs' from Hils followed. I smiled but my lips wobbled. I ruffled my hair and hoped that Lottie wouldn't notice the increased amount of grey. Did I look good, especially after little sleep and in such a state? More important, would *she* think *I* looked good?

Those thoughts were interrupted when another passenger, a young man, appeared and waved at someone in the crowd. I heard a girl behind me squeal with delight. I turned to see her run up to the barrier and they embraced over the top of it, right next to me.

My heart pounded so fast I thought I would faint. Where were Lottie and David? Why hadn't they come through yet? Were they stuck in Customs? Had they really made the flight?

I was desperate. I had stared for so long at that damned corner that my eyes started to play tricks with me. Or so I thought. I screwed up my eyes.

Suddenly my body tingled from top to bottom. Two little people had just appeared, with surfboards. It was Lottie! It really was! And with David right behind her!

Without even a split second of hesitation I flung my bag to the floor, climbed through the barrier and ran towards her.

'Lottie! Lottie!' I shrieked. 'Mum!' she shrieked back. And then, after eight long months apart, we were finally reunited and clung on to each other for dear life. It was absolutely fantastic, spell-binding, sensational and more, much more.

There are not the words to describe that initial embrace. I wished I could have held on to her for longer but I thought of Nick and Hils on the other side of the barrier.

I let go of Lottie and she ran towards them and grabbed Nick whilst I hugged David. Then the three of us climbed through to the other side. I didn't get arrested. I think it was far too early in the day for the security guards to be out in force. Even if some were there, I didn't notice any.

We all embraced and kissed several times and shed tears, this time of utter joy, and I am certain that Lottie's were too. She looked so beautiful but was terribly thin. I could easily feel her ribs and beneath her shorts her legs looked like sticks, but were superbly tanned, as was the rest of her. Her face positively glowed with the deepest tan she had ever had, as did David's.

They looked well, even though they had both lost a fair amount of weight. Lottie's hair was much longer and when I commented on this, she said that she hadn't had it cut since she left. It was the most stunning colour and I told her so. A much lighter blonde and with fabulous natural streaks, some of which were almost white. She told me my hair looked nice. I muttered something about the grey and she told me not to be silly.

We held hands and chatted about the flight and our surprise that it had landed earlier than expected.

David said that Lottie had slept for nearly six hours, but he couldn't sleep at all (he never can on planes) and was left to talk to the most boring man in the world who sat on his other side. We all laughed some more.

Their surf boards were huge! And heavy, as were their rucksacks, particularly Lottie's which David told us was because it contained presents, some of which she'd travelled around with for months.

'Oh, Lottie!' I exclaimed, and hugged her again.

Between us, we carried everything back to the car park and looked for a suitable spot to open the champagne. We ended up in the lifts lobby! It was filthy dirty with rubbish piled up in the corners but it didn't matter. At least we had somewhere to offload the boards and bags away from the line of cars.

Hardly surprisingly, within a very short space of time we all felt quite drunk, apart from Hils. She only had the tiniest sip of fizz for she had to go to work and so left soon afterwards.

Lottie phoned John and woke him up. I shall never forget how her face lit up when she spoke to him. I phoned Mervyn and asked him to collect us and, within ten minutes, the four of us were on our way back home to Manor Farm.

The kids were tired but so relieved to be off the plane and reunited with us. Spirits were high throughout the journey, although at one point they wanted more champagne! I could have kicked myself for only taking one bottle. The biscuits were untouched.

Nick and I listened as Lottie recounted some of their adventures, and David some more – of the scary kind. How he had been bitten twice in Bali by dogs which looked decidedly rabid. How, only because they'd had the sense to be careful, one of their snorkelling jaunts *hadn't* turned into a major disaster, for the men in charge hadn't a clue and didn't give a damn anyway. I told him to stop – I'd heard quite enough for one day! But we heard lots more and countless times I was incredibly grateful that they were back safe and sound.

I gave Lottie my long scarf and she draped it over her knees. The poor kid was cold, hardly a surprise after the high temperatures she had been used to. I had fully intended to take a couple of jumpers with me but such was my panic that morning, I had forgotten. I tried not to stare at her which was difficult. Her face had matured considerably since I had last seen her. She looked more confident, wiser and totally in control, but hadn't lost any of her impetuosity or fun. I could have burst with pride.

A few miles from home, Lottie gazed out of the window, just as she had done when Nick had driven us all to London, only this time there were no tears. She smiled broadly and her eyes sparkled.

At last Mervyn swung the car into the entrance by our main gate. Lottie and I left the boys to sort out the luggage and we walked, arm in arm, down the drive. Lottie made that walk incredibly slowly. She took everything in and commented on it all – the flowers either side of the driveway and the grass which grew along the centre, the view over the stone wall into the garden, the hanging baskets, and so on.

And then she saw the 'Welcome Home' banner which John had put up earlier. She beamed, we both did, and went inside. We were eagerly greeted by the dogs who were glad to be let out, but they went mad with delight when they saw Lottie. They certainly recognised her!

'Wow!' Lottie said, as she looked down the kitchen. 'It's just the same as I remembered it!'

The cats were on the boiler and she cuddled them both and said they were gorgeous. Nick and David came in with the luggage, dumped it down and without further ado champagne was popped open. All of a sudden the kitchen seemed so full - of people, of dogs and cats, surf boards, backpacks and the rest – and of happiness and laughter.

I loved it, and realised just how much I had missed the mayhem that comes with two bubbly youngsters in the house. David couldn't wait to put on some 'Bangin' Tunes'. Blow me, he chose the CD with 'Fix You' on it! 'Lights will guide you home…' wafted around us. This time I wiped away happy tears.

We were in the garden when John got back from college. He charged up to Lottie, lifted her high up into the air and practically squeezed the stuffing out her. To see them reunited was sensational. At long last, my family was back together again. Life without Lottie had finally ended for us all.

That evening, when I went up to bed, Nick's top hat was empty. Both Snoopy and Blue Bunny were gone. I asked Lottie about them the following morning. With a broad grin on her beautiful little face, she said '…they slept with me last night.'

* * *

Postscript

During the summer, Lottie worked as a recruitment consultant, and, in September 2007, commenced her IT degree at Bath Uni. Two weeks' later, she quit in favour of a career in recruitment and returned to her summer job.

John turned 18 (a three day event), continued to party as often as possible but studied harder and was accepted by Kingston Uni to read Business and the Environment. He is planning a Gap Year with Will, part of which will also to be spent in Australia.

Christmas was a joy and a far cry from the previous one. The joy was short-lived. In the New Year, Lottie and David rented a flat in Wells and moved out. That was expected but only the beginning. Shortly afterwards they announced their plan to return to Sydney, not as backpackers this time, but to pursue their respective careers. Visas permitting, they will be gone by October 2008. At least I have a few more months.

Some Other Titles From Mirage Publishing

A Prescription from The Love Doctor: How to find Love in 7 Easy Steps - Dr Joanne 'The Love Doctor' Coyle

Burnt: One Man's Inspiring Story of Survival - Ian Colquhoun

Cosmic Ordering Guide - Stephen Richards

Cosmic Ordering Connection - Stephen Richards

Cosmic Ordering: Chakra Clearing - Stephen Richards

Cosmic Ordering: Oracle Healing Cards – Stephen Richards

Cosmic Ordering: Oracle Wish Cards – Stephen Richards & Karen Whitelaw Smith

Mrs Darley's Pagan Whispers: A Celebration of Pagan Festivals, Sacred Days, Spirituality and Traditions of the Year – Carole Carlton

Past Life Tourism - Barbara Ford-Hammond

The Butterfly Experience: Inspiration For Change - Karen Whitelaw Smith

The Hell of Allegiance: My Living Nightmare of being Gang Raped and Held for Ten days by the British Army – Charmaine Maeer with Stephen Richards

The Real Office: An Uncharacteristic Gesture of Magnanimity by Management Supremo Hilary Wilson-Savage - Hilary Wilson-Savage

The Tumbler: Kassa (Košice) – Auschwitz – Sweden - Israel - Azriel Feuerstein

Internet Dating King's Diaries: Life, Dating and Love – Clive Worth

Mirage Publishing Website:
www.miragepublishing.com

Submissions of Mind, Body & Spirit manuscripts welcomed from new authors.